THIS IS...
CHRISTY DIGNAM

THIS IS... CHRISTY DIGNAM

WITH

NEIL FETHERSTONHAUGH

MERLIN

PUBLISHING

First published in 2004 by
Merlin Publishing
16 Upper Pembroke Street
Dublin 2, Ireland
Tel: + 353 1 6764373
Fax: + 353 1 6764368
publishing@merlin.ie
www.merlin-publishing.com

ISBN 1-903582-56-3

A CIP catalogue record for this book is available
from the British Library.

10 9 8 7 6 5 4 3 2 1

Typeset by Carrigboy Typesetting Services
Cover Design by Faye Keegan Design
Cover Image courtesy of Darren Kinsella
Printed and bound in Denmark, by Nørhaven Paperback A/S

Acknowledgements

I'd like to thank the followin' people for all their help: Kathryn, Kiera, Cián an' Darren. Janice, Jade an' Zoe. Tony, Joe, Alan an' Billy. Me ma an' me da an' the family. Bessie, Seamus an' the family. Aoife an' Chenile at Merlin for all their patience. Gerard Quinn, Gerry Fanning an' Peter Aiken. Neil and Liz for helpin' me through some painful memories an' to Fod.

I want to say a special thanks to Ron Wood who's been a great inspiration to me throughout me life.

This book is dedicated to all the people who supported me in this journey in music an' life. It's been at times a hard, painful an' humorous stroll though me memory that sometimes, ya know, isn't perfect but it's as I remember it.

Contents

Growin' Pains

I was born Christopher Patrick Dignam in Holles Street Hospital, Dublin, on May 23, 1960. Me parents were livin' in Cabra at the time, where me mother was from. I'll just briefly tell you me mother's vibe, right, an' then you'll kinda get where I came from.

She was the eldest of eight kids an' her father was an alcoholic – both me grandfathers were alcoholics an' were dead before I was born. One day me mother's comin' home from school, at 14 years of age, an' she passes her mother in the street. Her mother says, 'Here, will you give the kids their dinner – it's in the oven.' An' that day her mother fucked off to England.

The vibe I got from the whole thing was, like me ma was only 14 or 15, right, an' she went from bein' a teenager to rearin' her own siblings 'til the last one left the house. There were seven under me ma an' she had to bring them up pretty much on her own. She became their mother an' then when each of her brothers an' sisters reached 16 years of age, her mother would send for them to come over to England 'cause they were of workin' age an' could start earnin' a livin'.

Me mother met me da when they were both fairly young. He moved into the house after they were married an' they had me an' me eldest sister. Although his wages were providin' for her family, an' they were gonna' take the house over as their home when all the brothers an' sisters had moved out, it still wasn't me da's house. What would happen was, at any time, one of me mother's brothers or sisters would have a row with their husband or wife an' leave them to come back to Cabra. Me da didn't have a say in the matter 'cause the house was their family home. He never felt that he could make the house his own so when I was about six months old we moved out to Finglas, to a Corporation house that he'd put his name down for.

The weird thing about me old dear was, although she was busy runnin' around after eight kids she still had time for all of us. Me ma really relished bein' the boss of that house. She ran it like a ship. Me aul fella wouldn't touch a plug or anythin' like – me aul one did all that. Anybody that got a puncture on the road, she'd fix it. We used to have these plastic balls when we were kids an' if they burst you'd get a knife an' hold it over the gas 'til it got red hot then melt the hole closed. Anyone that had a ball burst on the road, they'd bring it to me ma.

Just as the last of us, me youngest brother, was leavin' the house about 10 years ago, me grandmother was brought back from England. She had Alzheimer's or whatever the fuck it was an' she was dumped on me mother. It was like me mother was landed with another kid – just as she was startin' to see a chance of gettin' her life back. She had me grandmother for 10 years after that. So, from the age of 14 to whatever she is now, about 60 odd, she was rearin' kids the whole time.

At her mother's funeral me ma just – she just couldn't get over the anger. I remember she was very upset. Me ma couldn't get over the way she was abandoned an' had to look after her family like that.

I often think about it now. I just don't know how the fuck me ma an' da did it, ya know? I really don't know how they coped. I'm the second eldest after me sister an' there are six under me. We were only in a two-bedroom house so the parlour downstairs was made into a bedroom. Then me aul fella built an extension at the back an' there was two more bedrooms put on – but that was only as we got a bit older. When they first moved in there was no wallpaper an' fuck all furniture for years. There was one chair that me aul lad sat in an' me aul wan used one from the kitchen – that was it as far as furnishin's were concerned.

Me aul lad used to work in CIE as a coach trimmer, ya know? He was fixin' all the seats an' stuff on the buses but by trade he was an upholsterer. People round the neighbourhood would give him their furniture to mend an' at night he'd be out the back strippin' settees an' chairs for a few extra bob. I spent me whole childhood volunteerin' to help him but the only reason was 'cause we knew there was money hidden in the chairs. We'd all leg it in 'cause all the old pennies would be after fallin' down the back an' that's how we got our few bob when we were kids. I could strip down a couch since I was a baby.

Thinkin' about it now, we were really, really fuckin' poverty stricken. At the bottom of the hill in Finglas there's a place called the Stew House. People know it as a disco but not many know why it was called the Stew House. When I was a young kid we'd be brought there to be fed. Basically it was a soup kitchen for the homeless an' down an' outs. We used to go down there an' get a bowl of stew an' a sliced batch loaf, for a penny or a shilling or somethin' like that. I'd be in the gaff a couple of times when me aunts'd be there an' I'd say, 'Ma are ya bringin' us down to the Stew House to get our dindin?' She'd glare at me an' say, 'You were never down there – shuddup.' Me mother was ashamed. She didn't want her sisters to know she was goin' to a fuckin' soup kitchen to feed her family but I didn't care – I just thought the food was deadly.

Lookin' back though, ya know, it was real turn of the century stuff – dependin' on a soup kitchen to get fed. For the first four of us kids growin' up it was tough but things got better as I got older an' there was a bigger spread in the family. Some of us were able to work for the second half of the family an' there was a little bit more money to go round.

I remember I started workin' in the Buttercrust bakery when I was about 10 years old. Every Saturday I used to walk to the Jamestown Road, a good distance from my house, at five or six in the morning to help on the bread vans. I used to get a pound for the day. I gave me ma 50 pence out of it an' I'd keep the rest. One of the first things I ever bought for meself was a *Wrangler* jacket, which was the buzz then, in O'Connor's in Abbey Street. It was £7.50 an' I remember it takin' me 15 weeks to save up for it.

That was the only way you'd ever get clothes that ya particularly wanted. Like, if ya didn't do that ya just got what you were given, d'ya know what I mean? I have photos of meself in jumpers where the fuckin' sleeves are half-way up me arm. Me ma bought a knitting machine, ya know, an' she used to knit clothes for all the kids on the street. Her clothes were made to last – you'd be given a jumper an' you'd have it for about 15 years, d'ya know what I mean? You'd wear it to bed in the winter an' you'd wear it to school as well 'cause we didn't have uniforms or anythin' like that.

We'd to make our own entertainment as kids. Like, fuck all people had tellies – I remember one family on the road had a telly an' me mate would go in an' leave the curtain open for a big gang of us to look in the window. There was a picture house near where we lived called The Casino an' we used to go down there as kids an' hang round outside.

The only way we could get to go in was by collectin' tokens off the bottom of a Lyons Tea box an' savin' them up for a special promotional ticket to the cinema. I was the second eldest so I was able to grab enough tokens so I could go into the pictures once every other month.

When I think about it now, though, it's weird. I compare what I got when I was a kid to what kids get now. Like, I was down in a friend's house yesterday an' her young wan came in an' said she'd lost her mobile phone. She was sayin' she'd left it on a table an' her ma was askin' her would she leave €300 on a table like that. But her daughter didn't care about the value – she was just demandin' a new phone. It was as if she couldn't survive without one. I don't know – I mean when we were kids I used to have to walk about half a mile to use a public phone. It was the only phone in the fuckin' area an' you'd be lucky if it was working.

Just gettin' back to the cinema though for a second. One memory I have of it is when we got thrown out for usin' these syringes for water pistols, ya know? We were squirtin' them at people in the audience. I was just thinkin' there 'bout where we got the syringes from an' I remembered that it was after me ma lost a coupla babies at home. I have three kinda family members who never lived. Me younger sister is Deirdre an' I have a brother that came after her called James, an' then the next three babies died before me next sister, Thêrese, was born.

We used to find the syringes out the back after the nurses were finished usin' them. I was very young at the time an' I thought babies came in eggs. I remember standin' in the garden an' tellin' all me mates I'd found eggshells in the sheets. Back then ya didn't buy a coffin for the baby when it died, ya know? It just went to the angel's plot in Glasnevin Cemetary. I don't think me ma even knows where the babies are buried.

At that time there was so much to do just to survive that ya had to get on with life, d'ya know what I mean? I wouldn't have been aware of the traumatic relevance of somethin' like that. It wasn't discussed really – that was just the way it was. All I remember is me ma havin' the babies an' the babies dyin' at home in the bed an' then her bein' up two or three days later, workin' round the house.

To me it was part an' parcel of the way life was. Like, obviously we weren't happy about the fact that the babies died, ya know? It was just an incident an' we all got on with it. But it's only now when I look at it that I kinda realise how traumatic that must have been for me ma.

Man, all this seems so long ago. I still shake me head in wonder when I think how different Dublin was when I was growin' up an' compare it to the way it is now. I mean all these massive housing estates used to be green, farmer's fields. There were no huge estates like Finglas South or anythin' like that when I was a kid. When we first moved to Finglas there was an actual little village, with a shop an' a post office. The city centre was miles away to us. You couldn't have gone in there on your own. We were only brought in for a treat.

I didn't have that much of a relationship with me brothers an' sisters when I was growin' up. I mean, when you're in a big family like that you're involved in the day-to-day stuff but I'd never be hangin' around with them. Anyway, 'cause I was the eldest brother, I was always the one who'd to go out an' sort their shit out if they got into trouble. The rest of the time they were off doin' their own thing while I was off with me mates.

Every single day after school I'd go up the fields with a couple of lads an' look for birds' nests – that was the buzz, back then, ya know? I used to breed Irish native birds, finches an' that, an' bring them to a market on Bride Street where the Jacobs factory used to be. On a Sunday morning I'd go in with all the bird sellers an' I developed a great interest in birds. I've been into ornithology for years.

I was always gettin' into bumps an' scrapes when I was a kid – I was a hardy little bollix. Me ma was constantly stickin' bits of paper on me head where I got a cut or bruise an' I'd be back out the door again. But one day, when I was eleven, I fell into a coma after I cracked me skull. I'll never forget this actually . . .

We had these trolleys that we used years ago. You'd sit on them an' you'd steer them with your feet. They were wooden but they'd these heavy steel wheels that used to come off the trains. One day I was sittin' on the green bit where we played football an' I'm lookin' across the road at me mates. There was one particular friend I had, Fireball Quirny, who used to hate me pushin' him 'cause I used to go too fast an' he couldn't take the corners. So I remember gettin' this thought, 'I'm gonna freak this fucker out' kinda thing. So I started pushin' him across to the other footpath, really fast, when me foot slipped through this shore that had two bars missin' out of it. Me leg went down the hole an' I fractured me skull off the kerb.

If ya can imagine this now, right, it's like I closed me eyes, opened them up again, an' I'm lyin' in a bed. There's a young fella sittin' beside me with no face. He's got two slits for eyes, two holes on both sides of his head an' his face looks all melted. The last thing I could remember thinkin' was I wanted to give Fireball a fright an' then it was like . . . blink . . . an' now this fella is sittin' there starin' at me. I was really freaked out an' I started to cry. Me da came over, hugged me an' told me I was okay.

I'd been out cold in a coma in Temple Street Children's Hospital for two weeks. I found out later that this poor kid that was sittin' beside me had been in a fire. But when I first woke up I thought God had struck me dead for havin' had the evil thought of wantin' to scare me mate. I was convinced I was in hell an' that this burnt kid was the devil. This was the fear of God that I had instilled in me when I was younger, ya know? Church influence in Ireland now is absolutely nil compared to the way it was when I was a kid. We'd all that religious education in school – the Catechism an' all that carry on – but at home we were taught a healthy disrespect for religion 'cause me father hated the clergy.

Me father knew this family that were very religious, right, an' he was tellin' us years later that they used to always give a shillin' to the priest, ya know, the way now people give money to the collection every week. Sometimes they wouldn't even have money for food but the priest always got his shillin'. When the woman of the house died, me da told us her family asked the priest to come up to the house an' give her the Last Rites. But the priest wouldn't do it 'cause the family didn't have a half crown to give him. That just sickened me old fella. He never went to Mass after that. He was always goin' on to us about how much the Church ran the country. He'd say things like: 'Do youse know the clergy own 75 per cent of the fuckin' land in this country?'

I think me ma was actually more religious to try an' balance the fact with the neighbours that me da wasn't. He caused a dilemma for me as well 'cause in school we were told that people like him, who didn't go to mass, were goin' to hell. But then, when I got a bit older, I started readin' 'bout Mafia people in books an' that, who were extremely religious, yet murderin' bastards. I'd be thinkin' here was me father – a good man who did nothin' but work all his life, every hour of every day – an' he'd be goin' to hell for not goin' to Mass while these murderers were all right by God 'cause they said a few prayers? It seemed like a fucked up system to me.

Me da's stance made me very uncomfortable as a kid but as I got older I came around to thinkin' that that aspect of his personality was cool – very cool. It gave me the ability to question what everybody else was tellin' me about religion an' stuff. It taught me to think for meself.

I was very close to me da. When I was three or four years of age, I used to run up to the corner at the top of our road just to meet him on his way home from work. I remember that he had one of them bikes that ya pedal an' then ya start the engine an' he'd give me a lift back down the road. Then he started doin' overtime an' he was gone when I got up for school in the mornin' an' I'd be in bed when he came home.

It was me da who gave me my first love of music. Every Sunday he'd cook the dinner for the family an' we'd all hang out in the kitchen with him. He was mad into John McCormack. At the time John McCormack would have been one of the top five opera singers in the world. He wasn't another Cliff Richards or Elvis Presley. John McCormack was massive in the world in his own right. I think he became a Count in Athlone before he died. Me da loved just walkin' around playin' his records an' singin' along to them when he was makin' the dinner on a Sunday. That's a very vivid memory I have an' I think that ignited somethin' in me – I loved music from that moment.

I started singin' all this classical stuff like *Ave Maria* that I'd picked up from him. I remember there was another song from the radio that for some reason hit a nerve with me. It was an old country an' western song called *Down by the banks of the Old Ohio*. It went:

> *'I asked my love to take a walk, to take a walk down beside where the waters flow, down by the banks of the Old Ohio . . .'*

So I'd be goin' out on the street singin' all these songs an' at the time Gilbert O Sullivan was Ireland's big pop star. All me mates'd be singin' Gilbert O Sullivan songs an' they'd be lookin' at me like I was a mad dickhead looper. But I didn't care – I loved singin' an' from those early days on all I can remember is that's what I wanted to be – a singer. It wasn't 'til I went to school though that I got me first taste of performin' an' that really convinced me that this was somethin' I wanted to do for the rest of me life.

* * *

I started goin' to school at five years of age in St Brigid's on Wellmount Avenue. It was like a pre-school up to first class. Then, from second to sixth class, I went to St Fergal's Primary School up on Cappagh Road. That's where I actually had me first experience with music in public – in the school choir.

I was only in St Fergal's a couple of days when a Mr Hanley, who turned out to be the choir master, came round all the classes an' got us all to sing a 'doh-ray-me scale. He'd pick three or four kids an' they'd join the choir – to replace the sixth class lads that had left. I didn't even know they'd a choir in the school an' I didn't know what to expect if I joined. All I knew was that it was music an' I wanted to be involved in it.

Most of the other kids were messin' up the scales on purpose, so they wouldn't be picked. They didn't want to be in the choir 'cause ya had to stay behind after school for half an hour. To me, that wasn't even an issue. I mean, yeah, if they wanted me to stay in to do fuckin' maths for a half-hour I'd have been appalled. But I just thought, 'what's wrong with these people?' ya know? I mean to me, for the sake of half an hour, ya got a great chance to sing all these songs like *Ave Maria* an' not get slagged for it.

I'd no doubt that I was goin' to get picked 'cause I had a lot of confidence. It wasn't that I was bein' encouraged by anyone sayin' that I had this amazin' gifted talent or anythin' like that. I just believed that 'cause I'd discovered what I wanted to do for the rest of me life then that's the way it would be. For that reason I thought that everybody else would want me to be singin' as much as I wanted to sing. I was convinced that everyone would want me to achieve me dream as much as I wanted to achieve it. I mean, I wanted it so much, why would anyone not want to help me? It's only when ya get a bit older an' wiser that ya realise that people have their own desires an' wants an' your particular needs aren't what they give a shit about. At the time though, I had more confidence than I have now. All the stuff I did later on, where, let's say I was performin' a showcase for a record company or whatever, it was seekin' some sort of approval, ya know? I'd be gettin' up on the stage goin', 'Jaysus, I hope this lot like the song.' But back then I was like sayin', 'Well, wait 'til you hear this,' kinda thing. When I was a kid I absolutely believed people were in for a treat when I opened me mouth an' started to sing. I know that sounds a bit cocky, but believe me I had that confidence battered out of me over the years. Me first setback was that although I was picked straight away for the choir, I never really stood out. That surprised me actually, at the time, ya know? I think it's those little things that start knockin' the confidence out of you.

I was a soprano at that age, ya know, like a girl singer. Me voice was not as good a soprano as it is now 'cause it wasn't trained. Like, Mr Hanley was a choirmaster but he wouldn't have been a great singin' teacher, a vocal coach, let's say. I'm not sayin' he was a bad teacher but he wouldn't have had the knowledge of voice that I picked up later on from professional singin' teachers but I mean, he knew the basics. I learned that if ya wanted any kind of improvement you had to work at it an' rehearse, that sorta thing. I realised that it wasn't all fun an' games – that there was a tight discipline involved. He taught me that there's a kinda work ethic within music, if ya know what I'm sayin'.

I'd go in after school an' he'd have us do these exercises to open up your voice. We'd be practisin' for midnight mass at Christmas or somethin' like that an' we'd be divided into first an' seconds. One group'd be singin' lead an' the others would be singin' harmonies, so by implication then ya learnt that there was a thing called harmonies. We learned how to do them an' about the timin' of harmonies an' how different notes sounded together, ya know? Mr Hanley didn't sit down an' say, 'Now listen this is how it is', ya just realised as he was teachin' ya a particular song or a particular hymn that this was how music works an' stuff, d'ya understand what I'm saying? It wasn't that he kinda said, 'Now listen, this is great, wait 'til ya see how I do this' an' he showed you how somethin' worked – it wasn't like that. I was learnin' meself as I went along an' that woulda given me a desire for improvement.

I took part in some choir performances in school an' we were really good. We even played at Mr Hanley's weddin'. But the first time we went on stage for a public show outside the school was at a Feis Ceol, a sort of traditional music competition, in the Metropolitan Hall, just across from the Peacock Theatre on Abbey Street.

That Feis just blew me away. I think that's when I first felt appreciation for somethin' I'd done. I hate goin' into all this arty bullshit, right, but what I think happens is, people kinda ridicule an' minimize your creativity throughout your life. Ya have this absolute love for a particular art form – in my case it's music – so ya try to do somethin' with it. Ya exhibit it an' ya look for people to appreciate it an' see what you're tryin' to show them. What I want to do is, I want to share this gift with people. I want them to see the beauty of what I'm seein'. An' when ya go out an' do somethin' on a public platform an' people are appreciatin' it an' actually recognisin' what you've been tryin' to tell them all along, it's a fuckin' excellent buzz. It really is. It confirms what ya suspected all along about havin' some talent an' that keeps ya goin' against all the tide of disbelievers an' shit. An' it has to 'cause you get a lot of that. So standin' up on stage at that Feis was amazin'. The applause at the end of our little performance seemed to drown out all the slaggin' that I'd been gettin'. Like, Finglas was a tough place to grow up in an' bein' a singer in a school choir wasn't somethin' that got you kudos. It was considered a bit nansy pansy. Everyone else is outta school at 3 o'clock – 'see ya later' – an' you're hangin' round to sing bleedin' opera songs? Walkin' off the stage that night after the Feis made it all worthwhile.

Leavin' school later than everyone else was a bit dodgy actually 'cause if you'd any problems with anybody, the odds were ya were goin' to get battered when ya stayed behind. Every other day you'd be goin' home with your mates so ya had some support. But on choir practice days ya were fucked. There was always one fella waitin' outside with a gang to batter the bollix outta me. Ya know the way someone is 'after' ya? Well this fella Frankie was one who was 'after' me for years. Frankie fancied this young wan called Tricia, right, who was the first girl I ever got off with. I was only very, very young, around seven or eight or whatever. I remember I kissed her once an' I was goin' out with her about three years, that sort of kids' thing. Anyway, this guy fancied her, ya know, an' he was tryin' to chase me away. He would follow me home to get me to stay away from her. I was avoidin' him for years.

One day I came out of the choir an' I seen him an' a mate hangin' 'round so I jumped up on top of the bicycle shed to hide, right. But he seen me an' told me to get down or he'd come up an' kill me. An' I remember the humiliation of havin' to get down, 'cause I was afraid not to. This guy was a boxer, right, an' he gave me a punch in the face. I'll never forget that punch. I'd been in a few fights, scrappy fights, when I was a kid, but I remember this was the first time I got hit by someone who was trained to hit. It was like a sledgehammer hittin' me in the face.

There was this other guy called Danny with Frankie an' he was takin' the piss outta me, sayin', 'Ah go on, ya singin' fairy, ya . . .', all the way home, 'cause he lived up near my end of Finglas. I'm goin' home, bloody nose, right, an' yer man is tauntin' me all the way. I'm shoutin', 'Shut up ya fucker,' back at him. The next minute I think, 'hang on, you're on yer own now, ye prick'. I turned around an' I'm like, 'Danny, c'mere you. Who're you fuckin' talkin' to. . . . ' an' I battered him. All the anger an' the humiliation I'd suffered . . . yer man got. He was the same age an' the same size as me but he hadn't got Frankie with him then. It was great but I'll never forget the punch I got off Frankie, ya know? It was somethin' else. An' that was it – one dig an' it was over. He wasn't after me any more. I only met Frankie there a while ago. I said it to him 'bout that day when he punched me in the face an' he said he didn't remember it. But I think he was just embarrassed.

I ended up goin' out with another young wan after that. I first saw Kathryn Harris when I was about 9 years of age. She was just up the road from where I lived, 'bout half a mile away. She had these skates on an' she came whizzin' past me house one day on her skates. She made an immediate impression on me, even though I was still just a kid. Me hormones must've kicked in early 'cause I remember me an' a mate of mine fancied her. It must've been somethin' about the way she skated! I think maybe she rejected me advances or somethin' 'cause I didn't see her for years after that. But I never forgot her either.

* * *

When I was 'round the same age, like 10 or 11, there was this young wan in the area who was tryin' to keep the kids off the streets, kinda buzz. An' she had this group called *The Black and White Minstrel Show* that she organised for the kids in the area an' me da an' his mate used to help them out drivin' them 'round to their shows. He told me they were lookin' for male sopranos so me an' me mate, Ray Tyroll, joined them. It's a scene that doesn't exist now. St Anthony's Hall on the quays was one of the places we'd perform in. It was like a little Vaudeville thing that we kinda got in at the tail end of an' it was really popular.

There was about 32 girls in the show an' me an' Ray were the only two fellas. We used to have to wear these white satin trousers, a green an' white stripy kinda top an' a little hat, ya know, like one of those straw hats? We blackened our faces an' painted our lips white to look like a golliwog – that's what I looked like. We used to do this song in choir practice called *Shannon Doagh* from a film, right, an' the song goes *'Oh, Shannon Doagh. . . .'* I only heard another version of it the other day on the radio. I think it was Van Morrison. Anyway, we used to do this song an' me an' Ray were like two little angels, although, at the same time, we used to watch the young wans gettin' changed 'cause we were kinda gettin' to that age. That was fuckin' deadly!

There's a pub called Murray's in Lusk, Co Dublin an' we went into a talent contest there, right, but we were too young to sit in the boozer after performin'. We all had to wait outside 'til it was over. We must have been two or three hours sittin' in the bus outside Murray's in Lusk in the middle of winter. Fuckin' freezin'. Then, I'll never forget it right, one of the bleedin' judges came out to us at the end of the show an' says somethin' like, 'Listen youse're after winnin' but there's another guy singin' – an aul fella, ya know, an' he's only two months to live. Would yis mind if we gave him the prize?' We didn't have much choice in it. We thought he'd only two months to live, so we said, 'No problem.'

About a year later we were playin' in St Anthony's Hall at another talent contest an' there was this same aul fella singin' at it. At the end the judge came out an' says, 'Listen there's a fella out here, he's two months to live. . . .', I swear to God. Fuckin' scumbag – even though I was only 11, if I'd got me hands on him he'd have had less than two months to live.

Me days in the choir came to an end when I reached sixth class an' it was time to move on to secondary school. I was comin' into adolescence an' I was very lucky when me voice broke that I could still sing. Some boys have this dramatic, sudden deepenin' of their voice as they're walkin' down the road but mine wasn't like that. Mine was a very gradual break over a longer period of time. I've known people that were fantastic soprano singers as kids an' then when their voices broke they hadn't a note in their bleedin' head – that can easily happen, so I was lucky that it wasn't like that with me.

The Minstrels had petered out a bit before then. All the young wans were a year or two older than me an' Ray. They started hittin' puberty so they kinda got distracted by boys an' cigarettes an' stopped showin' up for practice. It was probably just as well that *The Minstrels* came to an end when it did 'cause the whole thing became very politically incorrect after a while. Ya know the way it is now – ya couldn't dress up in white an' blacken your face an' dance round. This was the mid-seventies an' it was becomin' uncool to mimic black people like that. I didn't realise it at the time, obviously I was still just a kid. I thought I was puttin' on make-up the way a clown puts on make-up d'ya know what I mean? It was part of that whole Vaudeville, Music Hall kinda tradition. I didn't know that I was dressin' up as a Negro. It was only when I started gettin' older that I realised the implication of the *Black and White Minstrel* thing.

I remember bein' appalled when I thought back about it. Like, for years, I wouldn't even mention the fact that I did that, d'ya know what I mean? Years later, when I started out on me career, I'd be talkin' about me history in interviews an' I woulda never even touched on that subject because it was so politically incorrect. It's only now that I know that it wasn't somethin' that I did on purpose – I didn't consciously go out to take the piss outta black people – that I talk 'bout it. Now, if I went on stage tonight dressed as a golliwog an' started singin', '*Ah How I Love Ya', How I love ya . . .*', ya know, I'd be shot off the fuckin' stage.

I'd a huge confrontation with me da when it was time to leave St Fergal's for secondary school. Basically, there were two schools in Finglas, right – there was the Tech with a gym, metalwork an' woodwork, an' that's where I wanted to go, an' there was the Patrician Brothers where me aul fella wanted me to go. Me da was insistin' that I go to the Brothers 'cause it was a better school, better education an' more academic. But to me, this was the height of hypocrisy. Here was the man who was turnin' me off the clergy all me life, now tellin' me that I'd to fuckin' get into bed with them. I couldn't abide that, right.

I fought him tooth an' nail on it but he didn't see the irony. He wasn't lookin' at it from a religious perspective at all. He wasn't tellin' me to go there for religious reasons. He was tellin' me to go for academic reasons. Obviously, he wanted me to have a better life 'cause he struggled an' he didn't want me to have to as well but I didn't see it that way at the time.

The vibe with me was I was tryin' to fight me own way 'cause since bein' involved in the choir an' *The Minstrels* I was bein' looked at as a fuckin' namby, pamby boy. So, I used to have to compensate for that by bein' a little bit tougher. I wanted to go to the Tech 'cause, like, all the lads went to the vocational school while all the faggots went to Patrician. Everybody, everybody, that I knew – all me mates on the road, all the Fireball Quirneys, all the kids I grew up with – were goin' to the Tech. But me da put his foot down an' I was the only one of the whole lot who was goin' to the Patrician.

Now, up to then, in primary school an' all, I'd never been inta messin' round. I was always a bit of a bleedin' joker, but not in a bad way. At the same time, I wasn't a lick arse or anything. I just found it fairly easy to breeze through school shit. But the way I felt about Patrician was completely different, ya know?

I got into 1A, which was the top class in the school. For the first coupla years I did all right an' if I'd committed meself, I probably would've done well, but I started mitchin' from the start of third year. I used to fuck off from my school an' go up an' hang around outside the Tech where all me mates were. I'd be handin' cigarettes in the window to them.

One day, I'm handin' one to me mate an' he says, 'I can't reach it.' So, I'm stretchin' further in until he grabs me arm. 'He's tryin' to get out the window,' me mate shouts. Next thing the teacher runs down, grabs me in, an' says, 'You sit down there an' shut up or I'll get the headmaster after ye.' He musta thought I was part of the class.

So after that I used to go on the bounce almost every day an' bunk into the Tech. Officially I wasn't there. I wasn't even on the register an' it wasn't of benefit to me in anyway 'cause I wouldn't be able to do me exams or anythin'. But I was with me mates. The only thing was though I used to have to get up every mornin' an' wait for the postman. If he dropped a letter in the door from the school I'd whip it before me ma could see it. The start of every day was spent interceptin' the bleedin' postman.

I got away with it for fuckin' months. I sat me Inter in Patrician at the end of that third year an' at the start of the summer I used to have to get up at fuckin' 8 o'clock every morning, an' be sittin' there for the post to come. I didn't want me aul dear gettin' the report that would come before I got me results. Then one day I slept it out an' I woke up with her screamin' 'CHRISTOPHER' from the bottom of the stairs. Out of 190 school days, I was in for

31 days. As far as me ma knew, she'd kept me out for maybe two days in the whole year but the rest, the other 160 odd days . . .

I'll never forget it – it was the worst hidin' I ever got. I got a hidin' off me aul one – she hit me with a stick – an' then me aul fella came home an' he battered me as well. It was the first time ever I got two hidings for one fuckin' incident. There was no hesitation about dishin' out the punishment in the Dignam house. But I would've preferred to get it all off me aul lad than off me ma 'cause she was stuck with us for most of the day an' we drove her mental half the time. She'd no qualms about givin' us all a few slaps. Like, we'd be in bed an' we'd be messin' 'round, makin' noise. Then you'd hear, 'Quiet now', but you'd keep messin''. Ya can imagine, we'd the two bedrooms in the house at the time – me ma an' da had one bedroom an' the rest of us were in the other. So we'd all be messin' 'til we heard one of them comin' up the stairs. Me ma's knee used to crack when she got up an' we'd be listenin' for the crack. If it was me da' then that wasn't too bad 'cause he wouldn't even really hit us but if there was a crack, that was it – we were dead.

Me parents went up to the school an' came to a deal with me teachers that they'd decide me fate in September – whether I'd be allowed to go back an' do me Leavin' Cert. In the meantime me aul lad said I was gonna have to get a job for the summer to help me ma out with a few bob. I started workin' in a bakery doin' a bread round. It was a right pain in the bollix gettin' up at the crack of dawn but I met this one lad there who was bit older than me an' he was mad into music, ya know? He'd long hair an' used to wear these cowboy boots under his work clothes. He was always playin' air guitar, pretendin' he was the guitarist outta Slade. He told me that Slade were five mates from a place in England called Wolverhampton, which was just like Finglas. That to me was a big revelation. I'd always thought that bands were born in a box, ya know, pre-packaged. I'd no idea that you could be an ordinary Joe Soap an' become a musician in a band.

I think I'd always actually wanted to be in a band but I didn't think that option was available to me 'til then. When this bloke told me about Slade I suddenly realised that if they were from a place like Finglas an' had become a band, then I could do it too.

Up 'til then I thought people had a divine right to be in a band, let's say. Now it occurred to me that an angel didn't just appear to Mick Jagger or fuckin' Noddy Holder out of Slade an' say, 'Ya have the divine right to be a rock star.' I just thought 'fuck me' – it had a huge effect on me. I'd look at Slade an' say to meself, 'Jaysus, I'd love to do that. Wouldn't it be great if I was born to be able to do all that?' An' all of a sudden this bloke made me realise that it was possible – it was a huge fuckin' moment of enlightenment for me.

I got so into the idea I started workin' out what songs I'd put on me album. Like *Angie* was released by *The Rolling Stones* an' I remember sayin' to meself, 'Right, when I'm a singer I'm goin' to put that on me record.' I thought there was just this well of songs that existed in the world an' ya picked the ones that ya liked an' put them on your record. I didn't know that new songs were written or anythin' like that . . . I hadn't even established that fact.

But now at least I knew I wanted to be in a band. To be honest I hadn't a clue about the ins an' outs of what a band was all about but fuck it – that wasn't important. I just knew I wanted to be in one.

The Dreamer

When I was still a kid I thought that just 'cause I had dreams of bein' a singer in a band then it was goin' to be. When you're that age ya don't be thinkin' of the reasons why ya can't have what ya want. I woulda thought that if I wanted to be a fuckin' brain-surgeon, then I was goin' to become a brain surgeon. But by the time I got to 15 or 16 I realised that this wasn't necessarily the case. I was brought up in an environment where ya were told if ya broke your bollix an' got 28 Honours in your Leaving Cert ya might get a job in the Civil Service. Otherwise you'd have to try an' go for a mechanic or a carpenter. That's the best ya were to aspire to. Bein' a musician or an artist didn't even come into it. I didn't see that society is designed for ya never to achieve things like that. Nothin' is ever said to ya directly, it was just the general vibe I got that I should know me place. Dreamers were treated like they were mad. I see a dreamer as somethin' positive but back then I was dismissed as, 'You're only a fuckin' dreamer.' It was like, 'Snap out of it – yer only a scumbag from Finglas. There's no way you'll ever be a singer, that's not for the likes of us', kinda thing, ya know? That was the message I got all through me life. Even back in school workin'-class people were geared towards manual work, d'ya know what I mean? Ya were told ya could be a driver or a bus conductor or somethin' in the Corporation. If ya really worked hard ya could get a job in the P&T or something.

If it weren't for music there is every chance that I woulda just accepted me place an' ended up doin' the workin' man's job. There's nothin' wrong with that at all –

me aul man was a workin' man – I'm just sayin' that I saw a way out. It all started with a guy called Bob Dylan.

I was about 14 years of age when I heard Dylan singin' *Like a Rolling Stone* on the radio. The first chance I got I saved up a few quid an' bought a Dylan album, *The Times, They Are A Changing*. Dylan wasn't a great melody head an' a terrible singer but 'cause he wasn't great on melody, the importance of the lyrics caught me attention. I thought, 'hold on, like he's not even tryin' for a great melody in this. It's the fuckin' words that make it brilliant'.

As I listened to it I realised that this guy was writin' songs that meant somethin' – it wasn't Mary loves John kinda thing. That day I realised lyrics mattered an' that to me was as a big a deal as findin' out that Slade were from the same kinda background as me. Up 'til then I didn't actually think about what songs were about. To me a song was just a song. The words were incidental to the music. I thought the only reason someone sang, *'Are ye hangin' up yer stocking on the wall?'* or any other lyric was 'cause it fit the melody. I just flipped off the album at that last song an' played it again an' again. I probably know every single note on that record. I wore it out an' had to get another one.

I was at that age where you're smokin' out the back of the church, early teens an' talkin' to your mates. I started to see the shit around me. Even then, at that young age, I was aware of the prejudice that existed in society an' I thought it was outrageous. When I listened to Dylan singin' about the stuff that was goin' on in the wider world it kicked in me own sense of social awareness. I started to understand what me aul fella was talkin' about – the clergy an' their money an' the whole thing about the eye of a needle, ya know, that it's easier for a camel to walk through the eye of a needle than for a rich man to enter heaven. I remember thinkin' about Karl Marx sayin' that religion was the opium of the masses. That one statement summed up how the Church allowed people like me mother to think, 'I'll get me reward in heaven', while she was forced to live in squalor an' feed her children in soup kitchens. Meanwhile, them rich fuckers in their Mercs were laughin' at us, ya know? All that kinda shit was goin' on in my head.

Listenin' to Dylan singin' 'bout these great social changes started me thinkin'. He gave me a reason to dedicate me life to music. I started sayin' to meself, 'Let's say, if I write great words with great melodies, I mean, how good is that goin' to be?' I wanted to sing 'bout where I was brought up an' the way I lived.

Finglas was already buildin' up a reputation as bein' a very rough area. I was growin' up in a place where people had to lie an' say they were from somewhere else if they wanted to get a job. Like the education system was absolutely geared for workin'-class people not to get to university. It's financially impractical for a workin'-class person to get to college. I mean me sister was brilliant at art, ya know, an' she ended up becomin' an art teacher, but she was probably close to the age of 30 by the time she achieved that. It was simply 'cause she'd to work to get money, then do a year in college an' work another year. Like she couldn't just go to college an' have me parents pay her tuition fees. All that really started to fuckin' piss me off.

I seen then that wantin' to sing an' write songs an' be in a band had given me a dual interest. One was this awareness of social injustices 'cause of where I was from an' the other was music. All of a sudden, I seen that I could combine them both an' that was a fuckin' massive deal. I can't even emphasise the hugeness of that concept. I wasn't aware of how it was affectin' me at the time but it would form the basis for much of me early attempts at song-writin'.

* * *

The troubles in the North were really kickin' off around the same time an' even though we didn't live there it'd still affected me. I remember one afternoon I was sittin' in me garden when I heard – badom, badom, badom – three huge explosions. I was wonderin' what the fuck had happened. It was 1974 an' I found out after that it was the three bombs planted in Dublin that I heard goin' off. A bomb went off in Monaghan as well. I knew some of those people that were killed in those bombin's: a mother, father an' two kids I knew were all killed in the Parnell Street bombin'. About six months after the bombs went off we heard that a baby was found on the roof of the Shakespeare Inn on Talbot Street.

Even though I didn't have a clue what those bombin's were really about I knew they were connected to a history of oppression in this country. I was aware of what was goin' on in the North 'cause we used to be taught about the history of it in school. Like, we were told that when the British first came over to Ireland hundreds of years ago one of the things they used to do was make people wear a special board if they spoke an Irish word. They'd put a mark on it an' you'd get that many lashes for how many Irish words ya spoke. That was a massive injustice. This is a country separate to ours – how the fuck can they be over here tellin' us what do?

Hundreds of years later an' they were still here doin' stuff. Like some nights on the TV we used to watch the riots on the streets in the North. They struck a huge chord with me. I identified with the oppression 'cause I felt I was growin' up in an oppressed environment where there was loads of discrimination. It was like the way the black Civil Rights' marches in America inspired the people in Northern Ireland to follow Martin Luther King's example. When ya see someone who's downtrodden an' you're downtrodden, of course you're going to identify with it. It's not Republicanism. It's just that throughout me life I've been aware of injustice an' it remains with me to this day.

A lot of kids I was hangin' around with didn't give a fuck about that sort of thing but I was takin' it more seriously. I couldn't disregard it. I got wound up 'bout shit like that. Even now I still get kinda get wound up about it. I mean, right, why do we sit an' let people starve to death all over the world when we're burning food? Some people can just say, 'That's the way it is . . .', ya know, 'shit happens' but I never had that attitude 'cause I could always relate to what was goin' on around me. If I had a 'shit happens' attitude then that would've worn me down – to accept me place. I couldn't do that. I would never have achieved anythin' with music if I'd done that. I mean if I didn't acknowledge an' empathise with other injustices, I couldn't have justifiably screamed about me own, ya know? Any beliefs I had woulda been eroded over time an' then the apathy that would've set in would've extinguished me urge to say what I felt about the injustices I could see around me.

Every time I listened to Dylan singin' 'bout changin' times it made me aware of the massive social changes Ireland was startin' to go through at the time. The music was tyin' in with what was happenin' around me an' seemed more relevant to me now than ever before.

The rate that music was takin' over me life kept acceleratin'. I had very little interest in anythin' outside of wonderin' how I could get in a band. I was buyin' magazines like *NME* or whatever an' readin' about music. I'd pick up *The Evening Herald* an' *The Irish Press*, lookin' for any ads that said 'vocalist wanted'. I did this all the time. That's all that occupied me mind – all else fell by the wayside. I didn't care about goin' back to school to do me Leavin' or anythin' like that. I remember thinkin', 'everythin' I do from here on in is bidin' me time – it's only a stop gap 'til I get a chance to go full-time with music'.

The only other thing that distracted me from the bands was the birds. I used to drink flagons of cider down the fields with me mates an' we'd all be talkin' about gettin' our hole. I was a young teenager an' the determination to lose me virginity was as heavy as wantin' to be a singer.

There was this one young wan hangin' round Finglas at the time – I won't say her name 'cause it wouldn't be fair – an' the rumour was that she was ridin'. Now, she was a fuckin' reptile, ya know? God forgive me for sayin' it but she was like a Rottweiler but I didn't give a bollix. I just wanted to lose me cherry. I remember I went off down the field with her but I'd to bring me mate 'cause I didn't have the courage to go off with her on me own. So, he was with her first an' then she called me over. I remember pullin' her bra off an' there was love-bites all over her tits an' all. It was bleedin' terrible – it put me right off. I didn't manage to sow me oats that night.

Then this lovely lookin' girl came back on me scene. I remembered her from seein' her on these skates when I was a kid. We were hangin' round with a gang of young wans that were goin' to a school called the Mater Christie in Finglas an' Kathryn Harris was in the class with them. I was out playin' the field a bit when I met Kathryn again. I made sure to get her attention any chance I got. We'd all be hangin' round down the village an' then walkin' home later. There was a big gang of us but eventually after a few weeks it was just me an' Kathryn left sittin' at the end of the road on the wall talkin'. We got to be mates before we were boyfriend an' girlfriend but I remember the first time I kissed her was different than anyone else I'd ever kissed before. It's not what attracted me to her in the first place but it was one of the hooks that kept me there.

At the start we were just kids goin' out with each other but it got more serious as we got a bit older. We became really good friends an' we did everythin' together – if I wasn't at her house she was over at mine.

When I wasn't thinkin' about Kathryn I was thinkin' about how I could get a band together. Her vibe was she wanted to be a hairdresser an' she was off busy startin' to do that. That left me a bit of time on me own which was great 'cause any spare moment I had was spent on hasslin' a guy I knew, called Joe Jewell, to be in me band. Since I'd finished with the choir I knew I didn't want to be a piano player or a guitarist. But I also knew I couldn't be a singer unless I'd some kind of an accompanist.

I'd vaguely known Joe Jewell from the choir in St Fergal's. He went into Patrician the same year as me but he was in a different class. He wasn't a mate of mine or anythin' like that I just knew of him 'cause he got this folky type of band together with one or two other folkies while he was still there. I remember they were called Electron an' they were goin' for a while 'til Joe left school after the Inter Cert.

I heard that the band split up an' I remember thinkin' this was me chance. Joe had played guitar in Electron so I thought that he could be me gateway into the whole band thing – he was the only one in the world I knew that could play an instrument. Another reason why I think I tuned into Joe as a musician was 'cause he was into the same type of music as me. I bought a single about this time called *Life On Mars* by David Bowie. It would've been very early Bowie, ya know? All the others I was listenin' to were great musicians but Bowie was the daddy for me, an' he was for Joe as well. Bowie introduced me to another way of playin' music. While Dylan was a poet, who used music to get his message across, Bowie was an artist who used lyrics to get his art across. The fact that they were each deliverin' a different flavour of music added to the reasons why I believed I could make me own, unique, impression on music. I could put a flavour in which wasn't Bowie or Dylan – it was me.

I knocked down to Joe one Friday night an' told him I wanted to get a band together. I asked was he interested. He said, 'Yeah, knock down to me next Friday.' An' I did. I knocked down again an' asked him, 'So c'mon d'ya wanna do this?', an' he says, 'Yeah, but not now, knock down to me next Friday.' So I knocked down to him every Friday night, after I was finished for the day on the bread round, for weeks. sayin', 'Are we goin to this?' an' he'd say, 'No, try next week.' He kept palmin' me off. He wasn't that enthusiastic about gettin' it together. Havin' already been in a band he obviously knew that it was a bit of work. He was aware of that, I wasn't. I didn't realise what was involved –I just thought ya get a few blokes together, toss a coin to see who's on drums, who's on guitar, who's the singer, d'ya know what I mean? I musta givin' him a pain in the bollix but I didn't let up.

And then, one of the guys who'd been a guitarist in Electron, a guy called Martin Marr, came up to Joe an' asked him would he do a benefit gig in the Towers in Ballymun for whatever it was at the time, youth foundation or somethin' like that. They decided to get Electron back together to do the gig. They got some guy they knew from the Patrician, a drummer called Terry McParland, who'd later go on to play with Rocky De Valera an' The Gravediggers, an' Joe asked me did I want to sing. After months of chasin' the bastard I'd finally been given me chance.

We started our first rehearsals in this community hall near Joe's house up on Wellmount Road. We were doin' versions of songs like *Honky Tonk Woman* an' *Brown Sugar* – all that sort of stuff. We were absolutely dreadful, I mean we thought we were great of course, but Jesus. I remember the first time we heard a tape that was recorded at a rehearsal an' I thought somebody was after messin' with it. There was no way we were that bad, I thought. When you're rehearsin' an' singin' for the first time ya think ya sound like Mick Jagger, ya don't realise that you're shite.

The big night came an' we headed to Ballymun. We were playin' a fuckin' Sinn Féin fundraisin' gig but we didn't realise what the buzz was 'til we got down there. So we got up an' did the gig, ya know? We did four or five songs for the first half an hour or whatever. It was me first time on a stage, apart from the stuff I did as a kid. I remember gettin' up there in front of this crowd an' grabbin' the mike stand in fear an' I did not let go.

Me knuckles were white an' me hands were cramped by the end of the night. When we finished the last song, we got what I'd call a diplomatic applause. Then someone asked us to play the National Anthem but we didn't know it. We were lookin' at all theses guys wearin' James Connolly badges, standin' to attention, waitin' for us to start up the Anthem. Man, that was a heavy vibe. We'd been playin' all these English songs an' the crowd started shoutin', 'Youse are singin' fuckin' Brit songs an' ya don't know the National

Anthem? Go on, get the fuck outta here.' We just legged it outta the place.

We survived but the fear I felt gettin' up in front of an audience that first time shaped the stage persona I have now. I realised that night that when I'd stopped to look at the crowd I'd started shakin' with nerves. From that moment on, every time I got up on stage I'd take the mike outta the stand an' not look at the audience. I'd move round the stage an' not stay in one spot. But then I'd be trippin' over the wires an' the guitar leads so I started to take me shoes off to feel me way round the floor – all 'cause of that first night at the fundraiser.

We decided to keep the band goin' after the Towers gig. I'd faced that white-knuckle fear an' learned that when ya get through it an' live, the buzz is unbelievable. We played a few other gigs for this guy who ran shows in Portmarnock. Only lookin' back on it now do I realise what a scumbag yer man was. He was involved in a load of talent competitions an' he'd let us do a half-hour slot in some of the shows on condition that we sold somethin' like 200 tickets for him. So off we went an' sold all these tickets between us an' we did four or five gigs durin' the competition heats. Yer man was completely takin' the piss outta us but it was all part of the learnin' process.

We were still very rough though an' Jesus, that's puttin' it mildly. Those rehearsals up on Wellmount Road were absolutely fuckin' dreadful. When ya start off in a band, everybody wants to show how good he is. The drummer's throwin' everythin' he can into the song, the guitarist is tryin' to get louder than the bass-player an' I was screamin' me lungs out to be heard over them. It was just a cacophony of bleedin' noise. I almost destroyed me voice 'cause I was tryin' to sing over all that shit.

When I was singin' at some of our first gigs I'd sometimes wonder why somebody like Mick Jagger, with all his money an' success, why he'd put himself through it. An' I figured out that when ya sing, ya have this ideal version of the song in your head an' ya have to get it from your head into your voice an' from there recorded onto a tape. But through these journeys ya lose somethin' each time. By the time ya get to listen to yer voice, it barely resembles what ya had in your head. I remember thinkin' that's why someone like Jagger keeps doin' it over an' over again – to get that ideal version. Like, I thought it was great the way I sang a Rolling Stones' song at the time but when I heard meself on tape with Electron I realised that what I sounded like in me head was not at all what I sounded like on tape. There were fuck-ups there that I hadn't even realised. But that determination to get it right just makes ya want to keep goin' even more.

Plus there's the thing I spoke about earlier when ya get the chance to express yourself. Ya have a whole stage to show people what you're tryin' to do. Like I remember when I was doin' the bread round that summer right, an' we used to deliver to this aul one in Tallaght. Let's say she was in her forties an' I was only 16. We were out doin' one of these competitions one Saturday night an' I saw this aul one was at the gig. I couldn't wait for the followin' Saturday to come. Like me heart was thumpin' 'cause of the hope that she was gonna run down the road the minute the van came round the corner sayin', 'Christy, I couldn't believe how good ya were last week.' It didn't happen, of course. I was nowhere near fame but it was one of the first instances I'd had of somebody I knew from day-to-day life havin' seen me up on stage. An' I knew I was on the right track.

* * *

When school started back that year there was a bit of a showdown an' the teachers told me parents that I'd have to go back an' sit me Inter Cert for the second time before I could go on to do me Leavin'. I was good at maths, history an' science an' I'd got three passes in these subjects but had failed the exam. They said I'd have to do third year again but there was no fuckin' way I was goin' to go back to a class of kids that were a year younger than me. So me da gave me an ultimatum – I could only leave school if I got a job. I mean they didn't see the band as any kinda job. The whole vibe in me house was that the band was a grand little hobby thing but now, 'cause I was leavin' school, I'd to get it outta of me system. It was time to grow up a bit an' get me shit together, ya know? People settled down a lot younger in those days. I'd just bein' dossin' around so I was told, 'You've had your fun – time to cop on or go back to school.'

Goin' back to school wasn't an option so I was determined to find a job, an' fast. I don't know why but the idea of runnin' away to sea always appealed to me. In fact I'd nearly joined the Navy earlier that summer when me an' me mate walked past a recruitment drive in the village. There was a truck parked on the footpath an' these sailors were handin' out leaflets tellin' ya what a great life it was. Me mate said, 'C'mon, fuck it, let's do it!', an' the fuckin' idiot got up into the truck. I went after him but just as I stepped into the back I changed me mind. I just bottled it. I was goin', 'Nah, fuck this.' But me mate was already sittin' down, signin' somethin'. The sergeant or whoever it was came over an' was tryin' to get me to get back in the truck but there was no way I was listenin' to him. Me mate saw all this goin' on an' he tried to get back out but the sergeant was kinda holdin' him back goin', 'Don't mind him. The Navy's great, you'll see the world.' Then the truck drove off. I was left standin' there lookin' at me mate's face, as the truck went around the corner. For three years he tried to get himself outta the Navy an' he didn't speak to me for years after that.

The sea musta been in me blood somehow 'cause the first job I got was on a car ferry, which sailed from Rosslare to Le Harve. It was fuckin' deadly. It suited me down to the ground. I liked bein' away from home. To this day, I think that there are nomadic people an' there are people who are settled. Years later, I'd get pissed off stayin' in hotels while we were giggin' all around the country. Then we'd get two weeks holidays an' I'd go home but I'd get itchy feet an' be thinkin', 'ah, I've a pain in me bollix with this gaff – I want to get back on the road again.'

So, I was a young kid, 16 or so years of age, startin' work on this boat. There was this big rough, docker guy who worked on the car deck with the chains to tie up the cars an' trucks. He took me under his wing, as it were, 'cause I was the new kid. On me first day I was one of the boys in the galley like, helpin' out the chef in the kitchen. This chef saw I was new an' he says to me, 'Listen, if ya don't do your job here we don't report ya to the pursers', which was the official thing to do. He says, 'We just take ya up to the car deck an' give ya a few slaps. That's how we do it here.' I thought, 'fair enough', an' tried to stay out of his way.

So I'm on the boat about two weeks an' I'm in the mess when this guy who'd taken me under his wing, this big docker fucker, asked me what I thought of the job. So, I said to him, 'Ah, it's great an' all but there's one thing. Say if I ask ya to do somethin' an' ya won't do it, I can hardly take ya up to the car deck an' give ya a few slaps, can I?'

He said, 'What do ya mean?' So I told him what the chef had said to me on me first day.

That night, I'm in me bunk an' there's a knock on me cabin door. I open the door an' the chef is standin' there, soakin' wet, blue with the cold. They'd him tied to the top deck in the pissin' rain for 'bout two hours – bollock naked. He'd been gettin' me to do shit that I wasn't even supposed to do – all his fuckin' work an' I was afraid to say anythin' in case I got the bollix knocked out of me. That story about bringin' me up to the car deck an' givin' me a few slaps was all shit he'd made up. He'd just said that to get me to run 'round like a blue-arsed fly after him. So, he got battered over that.

It was a cool job. I'd no problem with workin'. Once ya did your work, everythin' was grand. Ya know how it is in any work situation – if ya don't do your job then somebody else has to do more. They've to do their own work plus your job. It's the same everywhere – if you're playin' fair an' doin' your job, everythin' ticks over. I was never work-shy from me first job when I was 10. I was on the labour a couple of months here an' there over the years but never for any long period of time. I have mates who've never worked a day in their lives, to this day. They're at my age now an' they've been on the Labour for nearly 30 years. That sickens me. I couldn't do that. I couldn't.

Bein' on the boats was great but ya had to go to sea every couple a days an' I wanted to hang out with Joe an' rehearse an' see Kathryn. So after a bit I jacked the boats in an' got a job in the Player Wills cigarette factory on the South Circular Road. I was only there a coupla weeks when it really started wreckin' me head.

There was one particular thing ya had to do when ya started at Player Wills. For the first six months ya were put in a pool in the mornin' an' whoever was out that day ya took their job, right? A good few days I was put on car park security which meant I'd to sit in a box watchin' the other employees' cars. I used to know what percentage of the cars were fuckin' Minis, what percentage were Fords, ya know, just from sittin' there all day.

Then I was moved to do a job inside the factory. I was put on a thing called a slitter. Basically what they used to do was shove cigarettes that weren't sold by a certain date into this big bin an' turn the machine on. The cigarettes came out mangled up on a conveyer belt an' I'd have to run round an' pick all the white paper out an' let just the pure tobacco go back in. The old tobacco would be re-mixed with fresh tobacco to make new cigarettes. I'd be sittin' there for eight hours a day pickin' out all these white bits of paper. I remember goin' home on the bus in the evenin' an' I'd be snapping at imaginary bits of paper – honest to God me nerves'd be shot, ya know? If ye can imagine, you're goin' along this conveyer belt an' tobacco is pourin' out an' there's butts an' paper mixed in. If ya miss a bit an' ya run to go after it, more an' more start to build up behind ya. It was a fuckin' nightmare. I used to get nuts an' bolts an' throw them into where the cigarettes went so they'd hit the blades an' fuck them up. Then the maintenance head'd have to come in an' the machine'd cut down for a half an hour.

I saw me life slippin' away in that place. There was one guy on the job, right, an' he was there for 30 years. He had this kinda handy number 'cause he was one of the longest workin' there. Him an' another bloke used to bring these stalks of tobacco leaves down from one floor to another an' get them crushed up into snuff. One day I was put onto his job with his mate 'cause he'd died at 11 that morning'.

I remember people sayin' at lunchtime that yer man had dropped dead of a heart attack an' nobody was even that bothered. Here was a bloke, who'd given 30 years of his life to this gig, died on the job, an' now he was like a fuckin' cog in a wheel that was bein' replaced by me. I just thought, 'man, this is fuckin' outrageous'.

We were on a six-month trial period an' at the end of it a manager came along shakin' all our hands an' sayin', 'We'll be in touch with you if we have any more work.' Everybody hated this fella. He was a scumbag. Like he kept me on the car park an' the slitter – two of the poxiest jobs – 'cause I didn't like him an' he knew it. When he came to shake me hand I said, 'Look, I'd be a fuckin' hypocrite to shake yer hand. I hate yer bleedin' guts.' I says, 'All these lot are two-faced bastards shakin' your hand 'cause we used to sit in the canteen an' call ya a fucker.' All the others that wanted their jobs back were goin', 'Thanks, hope to see ya again,' ya know? I didn't want the job back, d'ya know what I mean? I was ensurin' that they weren't gonna take me back – an' they didn't.

The way I was lookin' at it was that every shitty job I had was only bidin' time 'til I became a singer. an' I always knew that. So to me, the whole work thing was like school – purely academic.

* * *

In the meantime, Electron had kinda petered out. We were still rehearsin' in the hall near Joe's gaff on Thursdays an' Sundays with various different lads but mainly me an' Joe hung out up in my gaff. We'd be sittin' on the bunk beds I shared with me brother, just actin' the bollix – Joe playin' chords on his guitar an' me tryin' to come up with lyrics to go with them.

Around this time we met this guy Mick McKenna who'd come over from England. Meself an' Joe were really impressed by him 'cause he said he was friends with Depeche Mode, who were huge at the time. Mick was also a good songwriter an' we formed a new band with him called Meelah XVIII. We got the idea for the name from a Leon Uris book that Mick had read about a Jewish ghetto the Nazis made in Warsaw durin' World War II. It was called *Mila 18* but we used a different spelling an' Roman numerals 'cause we thought we were bein' arty.

Meelah XVIII marked an important departure in our musical ambitions. Even durin' the lifetime of Electron I'd realised there was two kinds of bands in this country. There was the cabaret type like Dickie Rock, ya know, the Red Hurley buzz, which was what we were kinda gettin' involved in by playin' covers of Rolling Stones' songs at the talent competitions. But if ya wanted any kinda respect or credibility ya had to be like the bands that were writin' their own stuff an' playin' certain 'cool' venues around Dublin. When we realised that, that's when we finally moved away from Electron an' got really into Meelah XVIII. It was the first time that we were writin' our own material an' tryin' to be credible an' cool as well. It's a natural progression of bein' in a band. Ya realise that to take it to the next level ya have to accomplish this, this an' this, ya know?

So, we were all havin' a go at songwritin'. What would happen is we'd be in rehearsals jammin' an' everyone was throwin' in ideas. It was kind of like a communal effort but they were fuckin' brutal songs. They were dreadful. They really were. One of the lines was, '*The bombs dropped on Warsaw, they light up the sky* . . .', all that sort of bollix.

Everyone tried to outdo each other an' show off how good they were. We tried to get as much as we possibly could into the song to prove how clever we were, right? So if me best note is a high note I wanted to have 20 high notes. As ya go on an' learn your craft ya realise that the less ya put into the song the better – sometimes it's what ya don't hear, the empty spaces, that ya think are great about a song. But at the start we threw everythin' but the kitchen sink into Meelah XVIII an' like eatin' too much chocolate cake or somethin', it started to sicken us. There's only so much ya can put into a song before it's ruined by enthusiasm. As a result I think the quality of craftsmanship within Meelah XVIII became as shambolic as Electron was when we were coverin' the Rolling Stones.

I was stoned outta me head when I was writin' a lot of those lyrics. This was the late 1970s an' a lot of the music that I was listenin' to round this time was inspired by drugs. One of the albums I was playin' a lot was Pink Floyd's *The Dark Side of the Moon*, which was widely known to have been written under the influence of LSD an' magic mushrooms. I think the album was, an' still is, a fuckin' tribute to drugs an' it'd an immediate impact on me. I completely bought into that whole rock'n'roll drugs myth. I thought drugs were what ya did – that they were what made ya creative.

The first time I'd smoked cannabis was when I was on holidays. I'd gone down to Courtown in Wexford with a couple of mates, when I was 15. We'd met a couple of these hippy dudes down on the beach one day an' they'd started talkin' about hash. They were tellin' us what it was an' what it was like – that ya smoke it an' it was like sittin' on a cloud. They said ya could taste sounds an' all the rest of it. Ya know, to me, this just sounded fascinatin' an' it whetted me appetite for those kinda experiences. So we'd got a bit a hash off them, I think we bought some, an' we smoked a joint, walkin' through this forest. I remember waitin' for somethin' to happen but not really gettin' anythin'.

I didn't think much of it at the time but I got into it more when I was about 17 an' 18 an' I started smokin' it all the time. The whole seventies hash scene was only startin' to kick off in Dublin. At that time I could count on one hand, outta a population of thousands of people in Finglas, the number of hippies that had hash. It wasn't like the way it would be now – with all the massive dealers importin' tons of the stuff. There were no dealers hangin' round street corners, ya know? One of us would get a bit of hash off one of the hippies an' we'd all share it out. Then they started sellin' these long, skinny ten spots of hash in tin foil. They were called strip deals an' were a bit of a rip-off. So we started buyin' quarter ounces or a half-ounce an' we'd split that up with our mates. There was none of this rippin' people off. If ya bought a quarter ounce for 30 quid, you'd sell three ten spots – ya wouldn't think of cuttin' four ten spots an' makin' a profit, d'ya know what I'm sayin? It wasn't 'bout that.

I was still a little bit wary of the whole drugs thing 'cause it was so taboo an' it wasn't what ya were supposed to be doin'. But that was part of the buzz of it. It was livin' through the experience intact after doin' what your parents told you was goin' to kill ya. Somebody said this to me 'bout drugs one time an' I think it's very profound, right. People come on an' talk 'bout drugs, that they kill an' so on. It's true that they do kill an' I accept that. But when a kid goes out an' takes drugs an' he's not lyin' in the gutter the next day with a fuckin' heroin needle stickin' outta his arm, he thinks all the rest he's ever heard about drugs is bullshit. So ya have to establish with kids that initially there are good points to takin' drugs. Ya have to explain that there're good buzzes an' great experiences but that it doesn't last long an' it progressively deteriorates. Of course, at the time, there was no distinction between hard drugs an' soft drugs. It was all just drugs an' it was against the law. I liked the fact that hash was illegal, ya know? It was counter-culture. I wasn't even into drinkin' that much 'cause I was at that age when I'd already seen people's fathers an' grandfathers turn into alcoholics an' the damage that alcohol did in this country. The same way I rejected the clergy I rejected the establishment an' drink was part of the establishment. To me, hash was part of an alternative subculture that I'd kinda gotten into.

Smokin' hash was a kinda cooler thing to be doin' as well. It made me feel more relaxed on stage when we started gettin' our first gigs in town. We knew a few lads that were playin' in bands around Dublin, in places like The Magnet on Pearse Street, where The Widow Scanlan's is now, an' in the Baggot Inn. Now an' again we'd back up the likes of The Zen Alligators an' Les Enfants in The Ivy Rooms at the top of O'Connell Street. It wasn't much different to what Fibbers, which is there now, is like. Ya know it was always cramped an' stuffy an' packed to the gills with people. There was also McGonagle's on South Anne Street, just off Grafton Street an' Toner's on Baggot Street. Dublin had a great live music scene for local bands then that has kinda fallen by the wayside now, ya know?

At the time it was a very vibrant scene an' we knew most of the people who were comin' to see those first gigs 'cause they were all our bleedin' mates from Finglas. They were comin' into town, gettin' out of their heads on hash an' LSD. I started doin' a bit of acid an' it had a big impact on me. What acid does is, it changes yer perception an' 'cause it changes it ya get a different insight into your way of lookin' at things. I was readin' all that stuff, Aldous Huxley, *The Doors of Perception*, *Brave New World*, but I was more into gettin' into the experience of it. I started droppin' acid so I'd be off me head on stage an' I was wasted – I'd be outta me gee on acid at some of those early shows. I've no idea how I went out there an' sang at some of those gigs. I really don't.

A lot of the audience were identifyin' with what we were doin' 'cause they were on the same planet that we were on. We were gettin' into theatre an' there was a lot of performance art involved in each show. Like, what we used to do, right, is we'd have these slides playin' in the background with all these trippy pictures projected onto a screen. It created a big vibe with the crowd. We also used to have this dummy on stage, like a mannequin, an' we'd a cymbal stickin' out of his head. It was like an extra instrument that we'd use at certain parts of the gig. Some of it was really far out stuff.

But as for all that about drugs addin' to your creativity, I think this story says it all. I remember years later we were in the Plunkett Hotel in London an' we met Noddy Holder out of Slade, one of me heroes who'd inspired me to get into music in the first place. I went over an' was handin' him this joint but he just looked at it. There an' then he crystallised the whole thing for me. 'Ya know,' he said, 'you're livin' the life, you're goin' into rehearsal on hash an' acid or whatever an' you're writin' this fuckin' great stuff – another *Dark Side of the Moo*n. You're buzzin'. Then you're comin' in the next day an' it's a pile of cack on the tape.' An' he's right – that's what happens.

We didn't know what we were doin' when we were Meelah XVIII. We were inexperienced an' we didn't know what was a good song, what was a bad song, what made a song sell. Ya know ya write songs an' ya think that because ya like it, that other people will like it as well. Then ya see that that's not the case an' ya start realisin' that there are formulas an' criteria, compromises ya have to make.

Meelah XVIII was a fuckin' terrible attempt at a band but lookin' back on it I suppose we were servin' an apprenticeship in the craft of being songwriters. I was anyway – I was startin' to learn me trade.

Aslan

The noise musta been fuckin' awful. We were all jammed into me bedroom – Joe was playin' his guitar through a little amp propped up on the bed. Mick McKenna was wedged in the corner strummin' his bass an' I was sittin' on the top bunk tryin' to make meself heard over the racket. 'Hold on Joe, hold on,' I was shoutin' at him 'cause I'd thought I heard me ma callin'. Even though he was two feet away he still couldn't hear me. 'JOE, SHUT THE FUCK UP', I screamed. He finally stopped pullin' the bollix outta his guitar an' I listened again, me ears ringin'. 'Christy, there's a lad at the door wants to see ya,' me ma shouted up the stairs. 'Let him up ma,' I shouted out the door. 'That must be Joe,' I told the others.

Joe Byrne was a neighbour of Joe Jewell's who'd played bass in Electron before I joined. Since Mick McKenna had come over from England an' started on bass Joe'd decided he was gonna buy a new keyboard an' play that instead. It was the start of the 1980s an' keyboards were very fashionable. It seemed like every band on *Top of the Pops* had a bloke playin' keyboards. Now, there're two types of keyboards right – monophonic an' polyphonic. A polyphonic keyboard is like a piano but a monophonic plays just one note at a time. Joe stuck his excited face in the door shoutin', 'All right the lads. Check this out!' He'd a brand new monophonic keyboard strapped 'round his neck an' he pushed his way into the room. He was standin' there goin', 'I got this great sound, check it out,' an' he let rip on his one note keyboard. 'BERRRRRREMMM! BERRRRRREMMM! – 'Man, isn't that fuckin' deadly'. I looked over at the other two an' went, 'Joe, what the fuck was that?'

Joe was a mechanic, right, he had no musical ability at all an' I just couldn't see him progressin'. As bad as meself, Mick an' Joe Jewell were at least I could see that we were kinda growin' as musicians. There were a few other lads hangin' around at the time, more 'cause they'd nothin' else to do but me, Joe an' Mick took this band thing seriously an' we decided we'd have to start weedin' out the hangers-on.

Another thing was we still didn't have a proper place to rehearse in. We could only go down to the community hall near Joe's gaff a coupla nights a week an' then it was only one night 'cause we were gettin' in the way of their bingo or whatever the fuck they were doin'. So we were more or less hangin' 'round in my gaff, eatin' biscuits an' askin' me ma to make us tea. She was cool about havin' a load of noisy teenagers upstairs 'cause she was used to a house full of kids.

We were also tryin' to find enough time to get together to jam. Me an' Joe both knew that the only way we were ever goin' to straighten out our sound was by rehearsin' more. It wasn't that we were busy doin' loads of gigs or anythin' like that – ya have to understand there were times in Meelah XVIII that we might have a gig today an' the next one wouldn't be until next fuckin' August. But the excitement of that gig in August would keep us rehearsin' for six months.

I was still doin' the odd job here an' there while Joe was workin' in a window factory. We were always workin' at different times an' we didn't have fuck all time off to get any practice in. So, I went up to Joe in the factory one day an' asked him could he get me a job. He put in a good word for me with his boss an' I started workin' there.

I was only in the windows place a little while when I had to train in another guy who'd just got out of prison. I was curious about this bloke 'cause he was fairly well-to-do an' he didn't strike me as a scumbag, criminal-type head. So one day I asked him how he'd first got into trouble. He said it'd started when him an' his brother had a paintin' an' decoratin' company a good few years ago. This farmer died an' his widow asked them to come in an' do a quote to do the place up – paint it, fix the barn doors an' all that shit –'cause she wanted to sell it. So they gave her a quote of two grand an' they started to do the job. It took them two weeks an' he said they spent around £1,200 on materials. But when they went to get paid they fell out over the amount.

Two days later there's a knock on the widow's door an' when she opens it she sees her dead husband hangin' from the porch. The two lads had gone out an' found her husband's grave, dug him up an' he was hangin' from the rafters. I'd thought yer man was goin' to say somethin' like they'd gone back an' broke her windows but this is what he told me an' it was true. I remembered seein' somethin' about it in the papers around the time.

I was stunned 'cause he'd struck me as a bit of a posh lad. I thought he was in jail 'cause his mate was after robbin' a car an' he got blamed or somethin' like that. I thought he looked innocent an' had just been in the wrong place at the wrong time – but he'd dug up a corpse. He was done for desecratin' a grave an' got two years an' that initiated him into crime. Not long after, he got six years for robbin' a post office with his brother when he got caught with all the cash under his bed.

He started askin' me did I know any banks or jewellers or that but I didn't. I kinda knew one place where there was a lot of money but it wasn't a bank or anythin' like that. So anyway, I started goin' on about how I thought the whole money situation operated an' so on. I was only actin' the bollix, kinda showin' off to this guy but the next thing I knew somebody went an' robbed the gaff.

I remember the day of the robbery yer man wasn't in work an' when I went home Charles Mitchell was on the Six o'clock News sayin', 'There was an armed robbery in such an' such a place.' I remember the fear runnin' through me when I heard it on the news – I'd only been messin' round but now I was terrified this fucker might have been takin' it all in the whole time. I was thinkin', 'oh bollix, if he gets lagged, I'm fucked'.

I went into work the next day an' there he was as if nothin' had happened. I just kept me head down an' tried to avoid him. I didn't want to have anythin' to do with him. I just thought he was a fuckin' nutter.

Around the same time I'd got a tax return back of a good few hundred from the ferries. I was in me early twenties at the time an' Kathryn an' me had kinda been thinkin' of gettin' married. We were sayin' we could spend the money on the weddin' an' maybe put a deposit down on a house but then we decided fuck it, we'd blow it all an' get married again some other time. I wanted to get away from yer man as well just in case.

We told our parents we were jackin' in our jobs an' goin' off to see the world. They thought we were mad, that we should be settlin' down an' savin' up to get married but fuck that. Joe an' Mick were cool about it. Apart from hangin' 'round in my gaff we were doin' fuck all with the band at the time. I told them I was only goin' away for a couple a months anyway an' that we'd really get it together when I got back.

Man, they were excitin' times. I'd never been outside Ireland before, I didn't even have a passport an' here I was – 20 odd years of age, a ticket in me sky rocket for an around the world trip. From Dublin we traveled to Amsterdam an' stayed there for a while. Then we went from Amsterdam to Vancouver in Canada. I remember we nearly got mugged in Vancouver. I was carryin' the money 'round on me 'cause I was afraid to leave it in the hotel in case it was whipped. We were walkin' 'round this kinda, say the Phoenix Park of Vancouver, an' these two fuckers were circlin' us on their bikes. Me an' Kathryn were down in this valley an' there was one of them on each hill, just cyclin' round watchin' us. As we walked along I could see we were gonna have to walk by them to get outta the place. Then we seen this couple, an elderly man an' woman walkin' along in front of us, just stoppin' an' kinda feedin' the ducks. I ran over an' asked them to take a photograph of us an' then we walked out with them. We got out of it by the skin of our teeth 'cause these other fuckers were gonna mug us, no doubt about it, ya know the way ya just know? I was reared among muggers, so I fuckin' knew a mugger when I seen one.

After a few days we flew to Honolulu where I got sunstroke an' ended up in bed for three days. From Hawaii we flew to the Fiji islands an' then went to Sydney in Australia an' stayed there for a month or two. Kathryn had her own money saved up for the trip so we were just happily splashin' out. Both of us fell in love with Australia an' we wanted to make a new life for ourselves over there. But first we'd to go home an' I'd to decide on me future with the band. So I made a deal with Kathryn – I told her I'd give the band a year an' if things didn't happen we'd come back an' live in Australia.

* * *

When we got back home I'd to go an' look for a job sharpish 'cause I'd blown all me cash on the trip. Joe had left the windows factory an' got a job in Telecom Eireann, P & T that was. So I joined P & T as well. I'll tell ya one thing I used to do fuck all there. I don't know how I used to get away with it. We used to go out to the pigeon house, ya know the ESB place in Dublin Bay, an' just sit there watchin' the seagulls all day, honest to God. We'd go in every mornin' an' get the van from the base in Sandwich Street there off Pearse Street. You'd be given a certain amount of faults that ya had to find on a phone line, right? Ya could go out an' find them immediately or ya could spend two days lookin' for them an' nobody was any the wiser.

I remember one time I was down in Sydney Parade I think it was, yeah, Sydney Parade where the DART goes across the street. I was sittin' on the wall of this garden when I heard a police siren an' it was gettin' nearer an' nearer. Next minute a fuckin' cop car skids up onto the path. The cops jump out an' grab me an' pin me against the car. Some judge who was livin' in this gaff had looked out his window an' thought I was tryin' to tunnel into his house or some bollix like that an' rang the police. The cops questioned me for about 10 minutes an' then let me go when they realised what I was doin'. As they were goin' I turned 'round an' saw yer man lookin' out his window so I gave him the finger.

Most of it was borin' work but at the time, at the start of the 1980s, it woulda been considered a very fuckin' sought after job where I grew up. P & T was a state-owned company, it was like the ESB, an' I'd a good, pensionable job which were few an' far between at that time.

I'd a few bob comin' in from the job so meself an' Kathryn finally decided to forget about goin' back to

Australia an' get married. We'd a massive ceremony in The Church of the Annunciation in Finglas on November 23, 1983. It was a great day. All of me parents' brothers an' sisters came over for the weddin'. Most of them had been livin' in England since the 1950s 'cause there was no work here. I think for workin'-class people funerals an' weddin's are big fuckin' events in their lives 'cause they're the only times they ever get into a limousine. Joe Jewell was me best man an' we even got up an' did a few songs at the reception.

Me brother didn't waste any time after I was married out of the house. After the weddin' ceremony I'd to go back down to me mother's house 'cause I'd forgotten an envelope to pay the photographer or somethin', ya know? When I got there, there's me brother, who I'd shared a room with for years, fuckin' me bed out the bleedin' back window.

We went over to London for a week an' stayed with relations over there for a honeymoon kinda thing. We'd already forked out for a big weddin' an' that so it was either get a house or have a big fancy honeymoon. We'd put a deposit on a small cottage up in Ratoath in County Meath but it wasn't ready when we came back from our honeymoon so meself an' Kathryn had to stay in me mother's house for a few nights. I remember me da comin' down with breakfast that first mornin' an' when he walked in the room I kinda jumped. We'd spent years jumpin' whenever me parents walked into the room 'cause we'd be up to somethin' an' even now that we were married it was still the same.

I loved it in Meath when we finally moved out there. The cottage was on a quarter acre an' it was real old. Before the weddin' I'd gone out an' fuckin' gutted it. I remember pullin' up all the carpets an' sandin' all the floors, these beautiful wooden floors an' I painted this big Rasta head in the middle of the floor an' I varnished over it. Kathryn was delighted there as well. We'd a bit of land an' we'd all these great ideas of growin' our own vegetables an' shit like that. We were really picturin' ourselves bein' like the couple outta *The Good Life*, ya know? Kathryn even wanted to build a swimmin' pool in the back garden. We spent months diggin' a big hole but we never got it finished an' we just stuck a shed or somethin' there instead. It was a fuckin' deadly house but one thing about it was it was haunted.

I remember one time we'd friends stayin' with us, ya know, an' the next day one of them came in all freaked out. We'd a kitchen at the back of the cottage an' he'd woken up in the middle of the night an' thought he heard us talkin' in there, at three or four in the morning. But the minute he opened the kitchen door it just all stopped. He stuck 'round long enough to tell us what happened then he fuckin' legged it out of the gaff. Another time Kathryn woke me up in the middle of the night 'cause she thought there was this fuckin' aul fella bendin' over her in the room. Loads of weird shit happened but Kathryn was also a bit psychic so she probably picked up on the vibes in the house more than the average person, ya know? Like in 1983 there was an Air India plane goin' from Canada to Pakistan an' it crashed off the Cork coast. I was in bed one night, I think we were in the cottage at the time, when Kathryn woke me up. She said she was after havin' this mad dream. She was in a plane an' there was all these people with turbans on their heads an' she's sayin' a prayer at each seat an' tryin' to get to all of them. She told me this story at three or four in the mornin' right an' when I woke up that fuckin' crash had happened durin' the night. She could come in now an' start tellin' ya shit about yerself – it's freaky. Like, she's told me people have died before we were told. Loads of stuff like that has happened over the years.

That hauntin' an' shit was just somethin' that we got used to over the years. I've good memories of that cottage. We spent a lot of happy times there.

* * *

I was settlin' into havin' a nice life for meself. I'd just married me childhood sweetheart, I'd a beautiful gaff out in the country an' a job that was bollix but paid well. Maybe loads of blokes in me position woulda said fair enough an' got on an' enjoyed it. But there was no way I could let the band thing go. Since I'd come back from Australia the band had kinda fallen by the wayside but I was determined to give it at least one more serious shot. Lookin' back I was always the drivin' force behind the band from day one, ya know? I was always the one runnin' 'round, gettin' shit together, callin' into the others to get them down to rehearse. But if there was one other person who wanted to make it in music as much as me it was Joe Jewell. Within a few weeks of startin' out together in Electron meself an' Joe had become fuckin' inseparable. Joe had basically grown up with me since an' we were real close. Joe's a cool bloke but what was even more important was that he shared the same belief as me that we could do it.

Whenever Joe an' me talked about the band we always got back to the same thing – we needed to tighten up the rest of them if we were ever gonna improve. Initially we were all crap musicians but I could see who had some talent an' who hadn't. Mick McKenna was grand on bass an' Joe was really becomin' a fuckin' excellent lead guitarist. We decided we'd have to tell Joe Byrne that he was off keyboards. But Joe was a mate, ya know? We didn't just wanna fuck him out so we took him on as a roadie an' he was our roadie for years. We got another guy in called Gerry Conlon who'd a bit more experience on keyboards. I wanted to replace the rest of the blokes that were half-hearted, an' half-arsed or were still just hangin' round hopin' they could get chicks by bein' associated with a band. I spent a lot of me spare time just lookin' around at all the other interestin' musicians that were playin' in bands at the time.

There was a young kid who was a fuckin' excellent drummer that I'd me eye on for a couple of years. All our drummers were always blokes that were playin' drums 'cause they weren't really that good on guitar – but Alan Downey was a real drummer. His father was also a drummer an' he'd been playin' for years. I'd asked Alan to play with us a few years before but he was too young to be able to play in pubs at the time. I was goin' around soundin' out all these people again, an' I remember, like even lookin' back at it now, the absolute conviction I had.

Alan was already in a band called Alien Comfort but I said to him: 'Ok, ya know, yer a good band. Youse will probably do it, but I'm tellin' ya now, if you wanna go all the fuckin' way, this is your chance.' He was a cheeky fucker an' he kept sayin' he was holdin' out for better offers, but eventually I talked him into it.

There was another advantage to gettin' Alan in the band. I sussed out that he'd a garage on the side of his gaff an' I was eyeballin' that as a place where we could rehearse. As soon as we got him in the band we moved all our gear up there an' made ourselves at home. I don't think his ma minded us bein' there 'cause she never tried to kick us out.

So we had our drummer. I'd already found a good rhythm guitarist. I'd spotted Tony McGuiness at gigs 'round town an' I remembered him 'cause he was real cool lookin', ya know? He looked like a rock star, in all the right gear an' all. I asked him did he want to join 'cause I'd found out he could play an acoustic guitar, right, but he wasn't really into it at the start. I remember knockin' down to Tony one day, when we were to do a gig, an' he was still in fuckin' bed. I was like, 'What the fuck are ye doin' in bed? We're doin' a gig.' But Tony was sayin', 'I'm not playin' with that guitar – it's a heap of shite innit?' So we had to go out an' buy him a bleedin' new guitar that day, just so he'd play the gig.

Tony was a bit of a prima donna but he was more committed once he went from guitar to bass. What happened was durin' rehearsals he'd pick up Mick McKenna's bass when we'd stop for a break. I could see that Tony was bleedin' great on the bass an' I made the decision to replace Mick. But it was a tough one 'cause Mick was a good mate. I told Mick that he could switch with Tony an' go on acoustic guitar but Mick wasn't havin' any of it. He said it was bass or nothin' – an' he left the band.

That just left me on vocals, Tony on bass, Joe on guitar, Alan on drums an' Gerry Conlon on keyboards. Me new band was almost complete.

We started rehearsin' as often as we were able down in Alan's gaff. We were startin' to get a better sound together an' I knew that the band I wanted was startin' to take shape. But I still thought we lacked somethin'. We decided we needed a better name. We wanted somethin' distinct an' simple 'cause at the time there was all these bands with pretentious names like Orchestral Maneuvers in the Dark, Light a Big Fire, Cactus World News, ya know, being arty for art's sake an' Meelah XVIII fell into all that bollix. Now ya have all these bands that are called 'The' somethin' – The Strokes, The Thrills – that's what's trendy now, but at the time it was grand titles an' impressive words. I've since discovered that all those bands that had this big arty buzz were tryin' to make up for a lack of talent by blindin' ya with science – usin' all these smokin' mirrors.

We picked the name Aslan to go against all that 'cause it went against the grain. I can't remember who came up with the idea but I liked CS Lewis as an author, ya know? I'd read *Shadowlands* an' the Narnia books an' we decided to call ourselves after the lion in *The Lion, The Witch and The Wardrobe*. It was the good an' evil thing, ya know? Like in Narnia there was the two great forces – the White Witch was the evil force an' Aslan was the good. Also, it fit that Aslan had five letters an' there was five members in the band. It just clicked with us – it sounded right.

Whoever came up with the idea I know it was decided on democratically. While I was the kinda drivin' force in the band we all had our say on how we'd do things. Now, how democracy works in our band is ya go up to one of the lads, Joe say, an' ya say, 'This is the way I think we should do it, Joe.' Me an' Joe would agree on it an' then I'd go to Tony say, an' tell him me plan. Now I've got three people on me side – I've got the majority vote. I suppose it's what politicians might call lobbyin'.

An' it worked. Me attitude was that any decision I made was always for the betterment of the band. I did it for everybody's benefit – to reach our common goal – to be rock stars. I never did anythin' just for me own ego. Like I didn't want the rest of them to dress in sacks while I was gonna dress in an Armani suit. There was never any of that shit. Sometimes I would back off on a decision if it wasn't important to me but if I do feel strongly about somethin' then I won't give up until I have the fuckin' democratic majority.

Ironically though, the name Aslan kind of backfired on us 'cause it came to represent all the prejudice an' bullshit that we'd go through over the years. It was only when I first got into the whole band thing that I became aware of all that Northside/Southside divide. It really sickened me. I've been with people, honest to God, an' I'd bring them to gigs an' whatever, an' they would say to me the only time they ever cross O'Connell Bridge is when they're goin' to the fuckin' airport. I'm proud of where I'm from an' what we are about but it was looked upon as a negative thing.

* * *

U2 had really upped the stakes for bands like us when they put Dublin on the music map after they released *War* at the start of 1983. Although it'd brought a lot of attention to Dublin it didn't do us any favours at all. I doubt U2 realise the amount of pressure that was put on bands like us 'cause of their success.

Suddenly, all these music industry scouts were comin' over from England, lookin' for 'the next U2'. There are some people in the music industry that are good at their jobs but the way I see it most of the rest of them suffer from 'the Decca syndrome'. A guy from Decca Records had passed on the chance of signin' The Beatles in the 1960s 'cause he thought guitar bands were finished. To this day that legend has all these people afraid to pass on another Beatles. But what they fail to realise is that there will never be another U2 – same as there will never be another Beatles or another Oasis. Up to U2 there was no other band like them an' new bands play different music so it's always an intangible quality these guys are lookin' for.

It was an absolute fuckin' nightmare tryin' to remain an individual band in that kind of environment. We'd made a conscious decision that we didn't want to look like we were in a band when we were on stage. I used to never like bands that would walk into a venue dressed like stars, d'ya know what I mean? I always felt that it was very important to wear the same style of clothes on stage that ya wore on the street. I just didn't like bands that would kinda get into that whole dressin'-up for the gig thing.

Unfortunately U2 kinda had the same idea. I mean the two main things that a band are recognised for are their music an' their image, right. So say ya have rock'n'roll an' ya have image an' say they're two sections in a pie chart. If I was wearin' somethin' like Bono was wearin' then I'd be seen as copyin' him, right. So Bono had used up most of the image bit of that section of the pie chart. We'd only this little bit of the pie chart left to work with. U2 also grabbed the lion's share of the rock'n'roll section with their style of playin' the guitars or the drums or whatever. All the attention was on them at the time so we couldn't use anythin' they used 'cause, like, if we'd used a guitar with an echo on it, we would've been accused of rippin' them off. It was really tough workin' against that but the extra pressure made us even more determined.

* * *

When we'd first started giggin' in town as Meelah XVIII we'd depended on our friends an' family to come an' support us. Kathryn went to every one of me gigs. I have to give it to her she was always absolutely 100 per cent behind me. I've seven brothers an' sisters an' some of the older ones would go to our gigs; Joe had nine brothers an' sisters an' the rest of the lads had some family who'd go the odd time. We'd our mates as well, so we'd been able to rely on our home crowd to be in the audience an' we'd had no problem fillin' up places like The Magnet an' The Ivy Rooms.

After all the changes an' rehearsin' we'd been doin' we decided it was time we brought Aslan to the next level. One of the first gigs we managed to get as Aslan was in the Danceline, which was in a place called the Revenue Commissioner's Club up on North Great George's Street. It was a big step up from what we were used to. This guy called Steady Eddie was workin' with this other guy in the Inland Revenue an' they used to run gigs in the Danceline. He was also doin' some work with *Hot Press*. They asked us to do a gig supportin' a band called Toy with Rhythm.

This night was goin' to be very important to us. It was a vital part of the progression I was describin' earlier that we went through from Electron to Meelah XVIII to Aslan. From where we were standin' it was a slow process, like a child growin' into a man, an' it wasn't that obvious but we knew the Danceline was like our graduation into the real music world.

We only fully realised that when we walked out on stage in the Danceline an' played to an audience that wasn't partisan. These weren't all our people out there an' we still fuckin' blew them away. It wasn't just a gang of mates comin' an' clappin' along 'cause they were your mates. Now we'd an audience that would've been critical if we'd been shit. But we weren't – we were really gettin' it together on stage. All the rehearsin' was startin' to pay off an' we were makin' an impression. We delivered the goods that night an' to me it was like a turnin' point in the band. It was the first time I felt like other people were startin' to see it.

That gig was also the first time we were exposed to industry people. The fact that A&R men were comin' up to us after the gig an' introducin' themselves, hammered home the point of how far we'd come. For me it all added up to a sense that we could do this – that we could really be a success. There was times over the years with Electron an' Meelah XVIII that I'd felt almost like some of me confidence was drainin' away. I'd seen how hard this was gonna be. I'd watched other talent fallin' by the wayside an' without even realisin' it, I was probably startin' to lose a certain amount of belief in meself. The Danceline was like a raw injection or reassurance that this could really happen for us.

We went down so well that first night that we were asked to come back an' headline the next gig. The word went out to every fucker we knew an' that Friday night it was jammed in the Danceline – ya couldn't get in the door. The Danceline was one of these places that only a handful of bands in Ireland at the time could get a good crowd in but people were comin' back to see us again an' again.

It was a great place to play in. It was like the way Vicar Street is now. Okay, the Point Depot is a bigger venue with more prestige but I'd rather play Vicar Street 'cause of the intimacy. The Danceline was like that – just a great gig. It became very associated with Aslan 'cause we'd this staunch followin' comin' in to see us. It was a very similar to the buzz when we play Vicar Street now – probably not as many people but they were goin' for it, full fuckin' throttle. There was somethin' about the Danceline – the atmosphere was great, the sound was great, the people were great. It was a very cool place.

I remember the band Something Happens were supportin' us when they were startin' off. I think they were even more surprised by the way people were actin' 'cause they'd that same belief in themselves that we had, but they couldn't understand why they weren't gettin' the same reaction.

I think what was happenin' was we attracted a different crowd into these city-centre venues. Up to then, a lot of the people that went to gigs in Dublin were middle-class, ya know? Workin'-class people stayed in workin'-class pubs an' drank pints of Guinness. But, when we started playin' in town an' that, we brought what would be considered a lower social class of people into places where all these yuppyish kinda people – yuppie is the wrong word 'cause they didn't exist then but ya know what I mean – were hangin' out.

At the time it wasn't cool to play suburban gigs, ya know, out where we were from. That was the buzz. We were doin' what we were told was cool. It was only years later that we started sayin' what was cool an' what wasn't. But at the time we couldn't play gigs in Finglas an' be taken seriously. If ya wanted any respect ya had to be seen an' if ya wanted to be seen by the people that mattered ya had to play in places like the Danceline. If ya wanted someone like yer man the rock critic George Byrne to come to your gig he wasn't going to see ya in some local pub in Finglas, ya know?

All these people who were checkin' us out – the industry heads – were fuckin' astounded. They hadn't seen a reaction to a band like this before. Before Aslan if ya went into the Baggot Inn to see X an' then you went into the Ivy Rooms to see Y, or the TV Club to see Z, the same people would be at all the gigs. If they weren't in the audience, they were playin' on the stage. But we were totally not part of that scene an' our crowd were like a wave comin' in an' that's the way it was – it was an unknown an' when somethin' is unknown, it's hard to quantify, to explain. Lookin' back at it I can kinda see what was startin' to happen but it wasn't so apparent to me at the time. All I knew was that we were a great fuckin' band.

I started to get impatient though – waitin' for the moment when we'd finally be recognised by the record companies. It seemed to me that everywhere I looked, other musicians were gettin' what we deserved. I remember there was one gig I saw that really pissed me off. There was a band called Les Enfants playin' downstairs from us in The Ivy Rooms one night. There were six men an' a dog watchin' their show, while there were hundreds of our fans packin' in to see us upstairs.

That weekend I opened the newspaper an' there was a story about Les Enfants signin' this big huge record deal. I was fuckin' flabbergasted. I was thinkin', 'hold on a minute, for fuck's sake. We're jammin' out places an' these were just after signin' this big deal?' I couldn't believe it.

They were just one of the bands in Dublin that were gettin' snapped up by record companies in the 1980s. All 'round us others like them were signin' these record contracts an' I resented that, or I was jealous of it, maybe, 'cause I believed that we'd more than they had. Bein' totally honest now the singer of Les Enfants was quite sharp. Derek Herbert was his name. But I was thinkin', 'hold on, if this fucker Derek Herbert, who was good, but nowhere near as good as me, could get this huge deal – then what the fuck was goin' on?' It didn't make sense to me. We were the better band, better than all these Les Enfants an' Blue In Heavens, but we were still on the fuckin' sidelines.

It was time to make a decision. I knew in the back of me mind that while I'd a job to fall back on I'd never make the band succeed. I realised that I'd to burn all me bridges so there was no goin' back.

It was tough to give up the comforts of a regular job when there wasn't that many in Ireland but Kathryn was totally behind me; that's a great thing about her. When we sat down an' talked about it the vibe was that she was gonna support me 'til things took off an' when they did she could retire. She'd already given up on goin' back to Australia so I promised her that the day we signed our first record deal she wouldn't have to work again – that was our dream now.

I think it took years for me aul lad to get over the fact that I gave up P & T to do the band thing. He thought I was fuckin' mad 'cause here I was married an' for the first time I'd a decent job as opposed to all the shit jobs I'd had up to then. He didn't mind me doin' the band as a hobby but this was different – this was 'jeopardisin' my future'. He thought I was just young an' foolish an' he saw it as his job I suppose, as a father, to steer me back on track. Here was me da, a man who'd supported eight kids an' a wife d'ya know what I'm sayin'? He didn't like the idea of me bein' supported by me wife while I was pursuin' this 'airy fairy career' that was never gonna happen as far as he could see. It wasn't out of badness or anythin' like that, it was out of his awareness of the harsh realities of life. I mean if I hadn't have achieved anythin' in music I'd probably have been the same with my children. I'd be sayin', 'Lookit, don't even attempt to do it, I tried it, it's not for us.' I do feel that the general kinda attitude with me da was that it was all a pipe dream an' I respected where he was comin' from but me mind was made up.

That Monday I met the rest of the band an' I told them, 'Look, the fact that we have jobs is robbin' us of the hunger to succeed. I'm jackin' in me job. I'm goin' full-time, so whoever's comin' with me . . .'.

Joe quit his job the same day as I did. Tony an' Alan didn't have any jobs so it was an easier decision for them to make. The keyboard player, Gerry, was workin' full-time in Guinness so he didn't want to come with us an' sorta fell by the wayside.

Jackin' in our jobs gave us the time to concentrate fully on the band. There was so much work involved an' meself an' Joe were doin' most of the runnin' around. If we weren't rehearsin', we were goin' up to Johnny Fox, whose aul fella was a printer, to get posters made for a gig an' tryin' to get it done free. We were always scammin' somethin'. We used to do poster runs an' go all round the place puttin' up ads for our gigs. It was a 24-hour, seven day a week job. Like we didn't just meet each other at rehearsals – we were seein' more of each other than we were of our birds.

There was this bloke who'd started hangin' round with us at the time, a fella called Billy McGuinness. I think a couple of the lads knew him from him bein' in a few bands round Finglas. He was a baker an' he'd finish work around lunchtime an' come up to Alan's gaff to watch us rehearse. He became pretty popular 'cause he used to bring up all these buns an' cakes to us when we were starvin'. He was always anglin' for us to let him do some backin' vocals an' he was so enthusiastic that we promised we'd give him a go on stage.

We talked about what we needed to do, right, an' we decided that we'd to get a proper demo of our songs out there. From giggin' 'round the place as Meelah XVIII we'd gotten to know this guy called Dave Meegan, who later became a big producer, workin' with bands like Suede. At the time he'd this little studio in Santry an' he asked us would we come in an' do a demo with him 'cause he wanted some experience as an engineer. We'd no problem with that 'cause we needed the demo an' we couldn't afford to go into the bigger studios in town.

We recorded a coupla tracks for our first demo that we called *Toy Soldier*. I can't even remember what songs were on it but I know they were absolutely fuckin' dreadful. That didn't stop me hangin' around down at RTÉ, at Montrose, tryin' to give it to the likes of Dave Fanning. If you go into RTÉ now as a new Irish band ya have to have your demo recorded on a CD an' presented in a bleedin' gold fuckin' case, d'ya know what I mean? But fair play to Larry Gogan on 2FM. He took it off me one day an' he musta liked it 'cause he played one of the songs from it on his show. So, I have to give it to Larry – he was one of the first to fuckin' help us out. It was probably the first time that any of our songs were on the airwaves.

Hearin' one of our songs on the radio a coupla days later, I knew we were on our way.

'Everybody Hits You . . .'

For the whole of 1984 we played the Danceline almost every weekend. Some of those gigs were early Aslan at our best. People still come up to me now an' again an' mention nights that they saw us in there. It was obvious to us an' to the crowds – that were gettin' bigger every time we played there – that this was somethin' different. We were workin' so hard tryin' to keep the momentum of it goin'. Now all we needed was someone from the music establishment to cop on.

Finally we caught the attention of Dave Fanning. Fanning was just startin' out as a DJ then an' he also ran this massive Lark in the Park in Raheny in North Dublin every summer. If you did the gig an' he thought ya were cool, he'd play your stuff on his radio show. We never really got on with Fanning – I don't think we're cool enough for him – but we were gettin' harder to ignore. When he offered us a slot in the Lark in the Park in 1984 we jumped at it.

It'd be our biggest gig so far – an open-air show where thousands were expected to show up. It was a big fuckin' deal to us. If ya can imagine, you're playin' to maybe 300 or 400 people at a time, even in the Danceline there would've been 400 people at most, an' then you're goin' to play to maybe 15,000 people in St Anne's Park. Instead of havin' to play hundreds of gigs to get to 10,000 people out there, this was a chance to play one big gig to reach even more than that.

It was held on a Sunday in the middle of August an' it was an absolutely scorcher of a day. The place was packed for as far as you could see. There were families out with the kids an' gangs of older people standin' round at the sides an' there were just thousands of young people stretched out in the grass in the sun. It was deadly – it was like our own little Woodstock. We made a big deal outta it.

We'd three backin' singers an' one of them was Billy McGuinness. Billy had kept on hasslin' us to let him join the band an' we'd let him sing backin' vocals on a few songs that we were practisin' in Alan's gaff. He wasn't officially a member but we'd promised him a gig so the Lark in the Park was gonna be his first time on stage with Aslan.

We were all nervous gettin' ready to go on stage but we knew we were well able for it. As performers, ya know, we were always tryin' to do somethin' different at all our gigs. We wanted to make every show stand out in people's minds. We'd decided to experiment a bit an' impress the audience with some stage theatrics. A few days before we'd gone out to this industrial estate in the middle of Tallaght to get some dry ice so we could put on some smoke effects. It was the only place in Ireland that did it an' when we got there we'd had to pack it all in fuckin' newspaper 'til the gig, right. As we took the stage we launched into *Heat of the Cell*, ready to blow the competition away with our dramatic clouds of smoke. One of the stagehands turned on the smoke machine an' the stuff just fluttered away. It was like someone had just lit a cigarette. Most of it had evaporated overnight an' we couldn't even see it 'cause it was an open-air gig. Ah man, it was a fuckin' nightmare – after all our efforts. I just thought 'fuck it' an' got on with it but I was distracted again when I saw me mate Ray standin' at the side of the stage.

Ray was a stuntman who'd worked on the movie set of *Excalibur.* He'd said he wanted to try somethin' even more dramatic by settin' himself on fire an' runnin' across the stage. I'd told him no fuckin' way but he was a bit of a lunatic. We were standin' there just prayin' that he wouldn't come out in the middle of one of the songs with flames shootin' outta him.

Someone musta talked Ray outta it 'cause when we walked off he was still standin' there – not on fire. It was a great buzz comin' off an' hearin' 15,000 people cheerin' us. We were offered the Fanning session after the gig an' we got paid a few quid for it. We blew it on gettin' pissed in the Boot Inn near Dublin Airport an' the next mornin' Billy turned up at Alan's gaff after jackin' in his job. Nobody remembered actually askin' him to join the band but he insisted that someone had so that was it – he was in.

* * *

We started rehearsin' with Billy as our new backin' singer an' he was messin' 'round, doin' a bit of extra percussion. The Fanning session had got us on the radio again but we wanted to do a proper demo to send round to all the other radio stations. First thing we needed was some money to pay for a studio. This guy was hangin' round at the time an' he offered to help us raise the cash. I don't have a problem with anyone 'cause they're gay, ya know, but this fella used to be tryin' to get into me cacks. I suppose to be fair I used to be half lettin' him think that he had a chance, just to get fuckin' money outta him for guitars an' whatever. I would be kinda leadin' this fucker on, ya know? Now I never did anythin', d'ya know what I mean? But I would let him think that somethin' may happen. I didn't give a fuck – I wanted this band to happen. I was goin' to make it happen an' I didn't care how, ya know?

We did this demo of three songs that was called *Breaking Up*. We were tryin' to get it on the radio when we were invited to go on a TV show called *Europe A Go-Go* that was gonna be shown in early 1985. It was like an alternative Eurovision Song Contest that went out to somethin' like 400 million people. They wanted three types of bands to perform on the day – a big ballad band called Auto Da Fe from Dublin, Light A Big Fire, who were a kind of a happenin' emergin' type band at the time, an' us, who were still seen as a garage band.

I think this was the first time this sorta global pop thing was happenin', ya know? It was around the same time that MTV was takin' off. I didn't realise how enormous it was but even if I was aware of it I don't think we would've been intimidated. We were at a stage now that we had confidence in our abilities as musicians. We were findin' our steps an' sure in our commitment.

That's an important piece of advice I give to new up an' comin' bands today. Like I get musicians askin' me for a support slot when we're playin' the Point Depot or whatever. But what they have to realise is, if they haven't got it together, all that's gonna happen by us givin' them a gig is they're lettin' 10,000 people see that they're crap. I don't think some of them realise what a kiss of death that can be. I mean if you see a band an' they're crap you're not gonna go home an' think, 'I'll go an' see them in six months an' see if they're any better'. Once you've established they're crap, you're never gonna go see them again.

We never ever had a gig where we felt out of our depth. We never thought to ourselves, 'well, hold on, we're not up to this'. Anytime we ever did anything we felt we were ready for it. Even this fuckin' massive *Europe a Go-Go* thing, when we performed for 400 million people while we were still rehearsin' in a garage, wasn't goin' to scare us.

It was on the telly at the beginning of 1985 an' they played two minutes of one of the songs from *Breaking Up* with a video of us at the gates of Trinity College. It started off with me seen through the railings walkin' inside the college grounds. It was all very professional an' here we were – these knackers from Finglas – with a video crew followin' us around an' playin' our music to 400 million people 'round Europe. We sat back an' waited for the offers to pour in from record companies around the world – but nothin' ever came out it.

* * *

Yer man Dave Meegan, who'd helped us with our first attempt at a demo, had a friend whose father worked in the airport. He lived in an old farmhouse near the runway an' there was a pigsty, a redundant pigsty, right next door that he offered us as a place to rehearse in. It was good timin' 'cause to be fair I think Mrs Downey musta bein' gettin' a bit sick of us at this stage. We loaded up all our stuff in shoppin' trolleys an' wheeled it all up the four or whatever miles to the pigsty – our new home.

It was an actual pigsty. Ya know, nine-inch solid bricks, filthy an' it fuckin' smelled. It was a tiny room, probably twice the length of an average bathroom an' not much wider. It had this corrugated tin roof an' when it was hot it was stiflin' an' when it was winter, ice would be hangin' off the rafters. I'd have a blanket wrapped 'round me with just the mike stickin' out it would be so fuckin' cold. Now that none of us had any jobs the band became our full-time occupation; we'd be down there, six days a week from nine 'til five, every day. We put in the hours thinkin' it wouldn't be long 'til we were in proper rehearsin' studios. Little did

I know we were about to walk into an A&R fuckin' nightmare that would dog us for the rest of our careers.

What I would term an A&R circus sprang up around Aslan at this time. Representatives from all the major record companies started sniffin' us out, promisin' us the sun, moon an' the stars. It all started after another blindin' gig we played in the Danceline. We were supportin' Toy with Rhythm again. They were a good band – they were kinda like the Human League, ya know? Ed Darragh the RTÉ producer, was in the band – but the crowd was there for us.

There was a review the following week in *IN Dublin* an' that just unleashed a load of A&R interest onto the band. People were comin' up to us an' givin' us their cards. What happens in that line of business is that once one of them hears that such an' such Johnny fuckin' X is into Aslan, they're all like, 'Shit, I can't miss out – they could be the next big thing,' ya know? It's the 'we could be missin' the next Beatles' fear. But of course, they work the opposite way too. As soon as one of them rejects ya' that's it – none of them wanna know – an' that's exactly what happened to us.

The A&R men were insistin' that they meet with our management to discuss a deal but we'd no manager. We needed somebody to represent us 'cause they wouldn't talk business directly to the band. We asked Dick Fagan would he do it. We thought Dick would be great 'cause he'd been involved with bands around Dublin for years. He was also a bit older than us, ya know? He worked in a place called Litton Lane studios on Bachelor's Walk an' he used to let us in there to have a look round whenever it was empty. That's somethin' else we were up to at the time. We'd be in town tryin' to blag our way into recordin' studios at night after the band that was booked in had gone home. There's always those people in the industry who genuinely love music an' don't mind helpin' out young bands. I'm the same; I enjoy helpin' up an' comin' bands that I think have potential, ya know? So, we'd be bunkin' into these places but we had to be careful 'cause the studio would be set up exactly the way the band wanted. We used to have to bring a Polaroid camera an' photograph the desk, the drumkit, even a cigarette if it was left in the ashtray, so that when we were leavin' we could put everythin' back the way it was.

I remember one day leavin' Windmill Lane Studios, havin' bunked in on a U2 session. One of the engineers had let us in an' we'd been there since four in the mornin'. As I walked out the gate of the studio Bono drove in on his way to work. Ten minutes earlier an' he would've caught us.

So we asked Dick could he talk to these A & R fellas for us. He wasn't our manager or anythin' official like that he was just sorta helpin' us out. He's a lovely bloke, Dick, ya know, an' in fairness he was thrown in at the fuckin' deep end. Suddenly he was dealin' with the heavy-hitters in the industry. It all got a bit mad an' he pulled out in the end. Like, one time Dick was supposed to go over to London to negotiate with another company that had shown real interest in us. He's flyin' over to London tomorrow morning, let's say, to meet all the heads to talk 'bout the deal. He was to be there at two o'clock or whatever, but he rings me from Dublin Airport at ten o'clock that morning freaked outta his head. 'Listen Christy,' he says. 'I just can't handle the pressure. I can't go over to London.' We remained on good terms with Dick, but ya know, it was obvious to everyone that it was the end of the road as far as Dick representin' us was concerned. We hooked up with a bloke called Danny Kenny after that.

CBS Records asked us to do a showcase for them. We set up this gig in the TV Club on Harcourt Street for a

Saturday afternoon – this 2,000-seater hall, full production, the works. It was all laid on for these two A&R men from CBS who'd come in to hear us play. We did the gig an' at the end of it yer man from the record company says, 'Yeah, brilliant lads, we're gonna give you a deal.' He says, 'I'll ring ya Monday with the logistics – if youse want 60 grand or whatever, youse want as an advance, no problem. I can sort it.' We were fuckin' jubilant. I fell for it hook line an' sinker but I was never a count me chickens before they hatch type of person so I didn't mention it to Kathryn or anyone else outside the band.

On Monday we got a phone call – 'We changed our minds.'

It was a fuckin' sickener. We were totally deflated an' it wasn't just over the 60 grand. It was more the implication that we'd lost a chance at an international record deal. To us it was a lesson learnt about the insincerity of the music industry. We'd seen these blokes come over from England expectin' things, like tickets for rugby matches an' stuff. If ya didn't come up with the tickets ya were considered small fry an' they wouldn't even come to see ya. Fuck them. Once we got over the shock we were even more determined. I told the others, 'We'll get over it,' an' we went back to the drawin' board.

Hassle with the A & R guys all came to a bit of head after one particular experience dealin' with Chrysalis Records. We'd been negotiatin' a deal with Chrysalis in Ireland for six months. We were talkin' away to them while we were waitin' for the deal to be hammered out. More weeks would pass an' we'd hear nothin' so we'd ring them up again askin', 'Here, what's the story?' So Chrysalis Ireland'd say, 'Hold on, we'll ring Chrysalis England to find out for you' an' Chrysalis England'd ring them back an' they'd ring us back with some bullshit – this went on for six fuckin' months.

I was sick of waitin' 'round for this record deal that looked like it was never gonna happen. So one day, I just got the band into the car, drove over to the Chrysalis offices in the Bluebell Industrial Estate an' I says to them, 'I've a pain in me fuckin' bollix with all this shit.' I demanded that they tell us what was happenin' there an' then. One of the executives, ya know one of the suit an' tie guys, says, 'Well, I'm sorry . . . Chrysalis in England aren't interested anymore.' This is after six months waitin' around. No further examination or explanations – just a bit of a polite fuck off. I remember drivin' home with the others in the car in a fuckin' rage. I just felt like runnin' the car into a bleedin' truck that was comin' towards us.

Now, as I said, as soon as one A&R man passes on a band, all the others start wonderin' why an' they all abandon ship at the same time. We'd let everybody else fall by the wayside, thinking the Chrysalis deal was gonna happen. So by the time the deal fell through all the talent scouts had moved on. We had fucked ourselves up. When A&R men in England heard the name Aslan they'd say, 'Ha, they were around six months' ago.' We were already old news.

I have to take some of the blame. We made some bad decisions. No matter what way you twist an' turn it, we were the ones callin' the shots. We were so concerned 'bout not bein' ripped off an' so careful 'bout who we were goin' to have workin' with us that we were coverin' our arses too well. We were so wary of signin' our lives away that we were makin' all these demands on any record company that approached us. We were sayin', 'No, we want this, this an' this . . .' an' people got frightened off.

The disillusion set in. I couldn't see us progressin'. As soon as the Chrysalis deal fell through, nobody else wanted anythin' to do with us. We went back into the pigsty an' just stayed there millin' it 'round in our heads. We'd nurtured this deal, ya know? We hadn't rushed it. We'd taken our time an' done the whole thing right an' now, all of a sudden, the whole thing was gone. Man, I'd just had enough of this shit, d'ya know what I mean? It was just like the straw that broke the camel's back, let's say.

We'd seen the business for what it was – a fuckin' hypocrisy. We saw people that we considered untalented achievin' shit an' people that were talented not achievin' anythin'. I started realisin' that it really hadn't a lot to do with talent. It was a lot to do with who you knew an' luck.

I remember for example, this other crowd came over to see us. I think they were called Ensign Records. They came into Litton Lane an' there was another band there that had Sinead O'Connor as their singer. As everyone found out she'd a future but the band was second rate. We were the main band that the record company heads were comin' over to see but they walked past us an' offered them a singles deal on the spot.

* * *

All the disappointment was gettin' to me. I was doin' somethin' creative an' if it's not great, well, at least I fuckin' tried, ya know? An' I was dedicated to it, I really was. I mean I even went an' got singin' lessons to improve me vocal scale. I'd kinda taken me voice for granted for years an' now it was actin' up.

When I left the choir behind me in school I forgot a lot of the lessons I'd learned there. I got into the band thing an' I was singin' over loud guitars an' drums. The kinda singin' I was doin' really went against the grain of everythin' I'd ever been taught. I'd been screamin' all these lyrics for the last few years an' I started losin' some of the vocal ability that I had. I'll never forget it – it was like, I dunno, a bird gettin' its wings clipped. I was pretty fuckin' worried 'bout it. I'd been goin' to various singin' teachers for years. I mean to me, gettin' singin' lessons was an obvious move I had to make. Some people think they can just get up on a stage without any trainin' an' sing. Why? I'd never get out on a stage an' try to play a guitar without ever havin' a lesson. If you're goin' to pay somebody to sing, ya deserve for that singin' to be perfect. But now I knew I'd to try an' find a teacher who could reverse the damage before I permanently fucked up me voice.

I had this, what I felt was, beautiful music in me head that I wanted to sing but I wasn't able 'cause I was after damagin' me voice to the extent that I physically couldn't do it. I knew I'd the ability but there was somethin' that was obscurin' it. I used to have the voice when I was younger an' I knew it just didn't go somewhere – I didn't leave it in Galway one week when I was there, ya know? I'd to go an' find someone that could help me to get what was in me head back into me voice.

I went to a load of singin' teachers 'til I found a guy called Frank Merriman who'd a place over Waltons music shop in Dublin. In lessons before the teachers were all like: 'Ah, bloody rock'n'roll – one step forward an' three steps back. You're wastin' my bloody time.' I was sayin', 'Fuck you, I'm a rock'n'roll singer.' Frank had no problem with me singin' rock'n'roll. As far as Frank was concerned, there were two types of singer – good an' bad. He was talkin' my language an' he introduced me to Bel Canto.

Bel Canto is Italian for 'beautiful voice'. It came from the monks in the 16th or 17th century. They'd sing all day an' eventually their voices would seize up, ya know? So they devised a method that the more ya sang, the stronger your voice got – if ya sang correctly.

I have to get into the technical shit now to explain about singin'. Basically how ya sing is, ya have a vocal cord an' it's like an elastic band. When ya take a breath you're after sendin' wind onto that elastic, so it vibrates an' makes a sound. That sound is resonated or amplified by three sets of resonators that ya have – two in your nose, two in your forehead an' two at the back of your head. Some singers don't have a balance between the resonators an' they get what's called an unsympathetic tone. In other words they sound shit. They compensate by shoutin' an' their vocal cord creates phlegm to protect itself from the brutalisin'. Ya can't sing with phlegm in your voice – it actually covers up your voice an' you're fucked. But if ya sing correctly, which is in a sympathetic tone, your voice vibrates an' sheds the phlegm. That's why a lot of singers would do exercises before a gig.

These maestros in Italy went on to develop Bel Canto an' would pick young singers an' train them over five or six years. At the end of their trainin', when these singers started workin', the maestros got a percentage of their earnings. If the maestro didn't produce a great singer he didn't earn anythin' an' he'd have wasted five or six years of his life. So, they'd to have a massive belief in their ability to teach an' to pick the right student.

Frank himself had studied under one of these guys an' became an opera singer. He'd a fantastic voice until he got diphtheria. Unfortunately for him he'd this physical hurdle to get over but fortunately for me he came back to Ireland as a teacher.

Frank told me that the thing about Bel Canto, right, is that it's the opposite of how a lot of other teachers teach. They'll say things like, 'Sing from the diaphragm an' concentrate on your breathin,' ya know? I mean if I'm doin' a gig an' I'm busy gettin' me diaphragm ready an' concentratin' on all this breathin' – how the fuck am I goin' to remember to sing a song? Bel Canto teaches that it's got to be natural. Like when I speak I'm not sayin' to meself, 'breathe after the next word.' If you're thinkin' 'bout breathin' or diaphragms or anythin' like that when you're singin' a percentage of ya is not in the song.

Another thing Frank said was, 'I'm going to 'un-teach' ya about singin'.' Basically what he meant was that all singers absorb other people's ways of singin' an' what happens is you hear these singers that are from say Donegal, an' they have a mid-Atlantic drawl. So what you do is, you strip all that away. Frank said to me on the first lesson, 'We already have a Mick Jagger; we already have a David Bowie – the only thing you have to sell the world is Christy Dignam. We've never had one of them before.'

As soon as I went into Frank I realised he could help me 'cause he wanted to teach me to use that sincerity I'd always felt, through me vocal cords. That's what Bel Canto is all about. Whether you sing or play the tin whistle – if you're usin' the instrument with sincerity, that's what people relate to an' that's what people love. The quality of the instrument is irrelevant 'cause the truth cuts like a sword.

An' ya need intelligence. I worked with a guy in there; I won't say his name, no point in embarrassin' him. He had a brilliant vocal in Bel Canto but he was thick. I'd rather have a penny whistle of a voice an' a good mind to know how to use it than to have a Steinway piano an' no fuckin' brain. I could hand you a Steinway piano but what use is it to ya if you don't have the brain to play it?

Bel Canto increased me appetite for music that had started with me listenin' to me aul fella singin' over the Sunday dinners. It showed me how to sing in a rock'n'roll band without carvin' up me voice. An' it taught me how to recognise quality. Like when I heard Annie Lennox singin' *There must be an Angel* there was a line in it when she stretches out certain words over a few different notes. It was a nice technique an' I kept it in me mind that I'd like to use it sometime. That's a compliment to Annie Lennox. I don't see it as a rip-off, the same way I don't think Barry Manilow is rippin' off Mozart 'cause he plays a piano. I've never met Annie Lennox, by the way, but I'd love to 'cause I think she's fantastic.

I went to Frank for over ten years. The whole time I was with him he was an inspiration an' he encouraged me to chase me dream of makin' it with music. He put me back on track. I owe him everythin' for what he taught me. We've fallen out since over life an' bullshit but I will never be able to thank him enough. As far as I'm concerned he's the dog's bollix.

* * *

After goin' to Bel Canto for a while I used some of the techniques he taught me on the chorus of this song I was writin' called *This is*. In my (humble!) opinion, *This is* is one of the best Irish songs ever. I want to explain where it came from.

The openin' line, *'These are the hands of a tired man'*, was about me aul fella's hands. I remember as a kid I was amazed by me father's hard an' calloused hands. Me aul lad was an upholsterer an' he used these tacks on the furniture an' he used to be able to get the tacks an' really press them into his hands. But the skin was so hard that it wouldn't break. It reminded me of the way cheese goes hard when you leave it out – the transparent tough skin on the edges of it – ya know? His fingers were kinda like that.

The next line, *'This is the old man's shroud'*, is also about me da. I was lookin' at this man who worked from seven in the mornin' to eight at night, six days a week. A very good man an' totally dedicated to tryin' to make a better life for his wife an' eight children – tryin' to raise their social standin'. I wanted to pay tribute to his tolerance of all the bullshit that was goin' on in the world an' the injustices. Here was a man who worked all the hours God sent but nothin' belonged to him. He didn't even own the house he was livin' in. Not one fuckin' centimetre of it belonged to him.

I first realised how cruel that was when I was about 14 or 15. I was drinkin' flagons of cider on the street. I'd only started messin' round with alchohol at the time. I was drunk an' I was singin' all these Wolfe Tones songs, *'Come out ye Black an' Tans, come out an' fight me like a man . . .'* – all that rebel stuff. So, me aul fella caught me an' he brought me in an' slapped the bollix out of me. In my family ya got a slap an' that was it, end of story. Ya never heard about it again. But for the first time in me life, I'll never forget it, he came into me the next day an' says somethin' like: 'I just wanted to tell you the reason you got that hidin' last night. It wasn't for being drunk,' he says. 'I got drunk when I was your age, we all did, but you see that IRA bollix you're singin' about? My father an' two of his brothers died for this country an' d'ya know how much of Ireland I own for their lives? Not even one inch. They went out an' died for Ireland so the likes of Charles Haughey can go an' live in a fuckin' mansion.' I looked at all that an' I remember thinkin' he deserved more.

The shroud in the song is a symbol of poverty. A shroud is not a gilded cloak, is it? It's a shroud. I don't mean it in a depressed way – it represents the bare necessities of what we had to live on when I was young. If ya compare it to now, people who'd be the same workin-class now have way more than we ever had.

There were also huge social changes that were goin' on at the time in Ireland. Some parts of the song are about the very fact that I had the freedom to be able to say what I wanted in a previously fuckin' fervent Catholic country. The line, *'This is the face of a teenage mother'* is about the fact that in the early 1980s teenagers were gettin' pregnant all over Ireland. It used to be the case that Irish girls were sent away in shame to the country when they were pregnant. The teenage lovers in the song *'search for the smiles they shared'* an' I use the word 'shared' in the past tense 'cause they'd had the baby but they were not bein' forced to marry anymore. Either of them could still end the relationship if it wasn't right. Before, people were gettin' fucked into relationships; there were shotgun weddin's, ya know, regardless of whether it was the right thing to do or not.

When I sing, *'These are the feet of a punished pilgrim'* I'm talkin' about all those people who go up Croagh Patrick in Mayo, right, in their bare feet to pay homage to God. Well, that to me is bollix. God doesn't want you tearin' the feet off yerself. If God wanted you to walk up a mountain in your bare feet he would've given ya leather soles an' steel tips in your heels. That's common sense – that's logic.

'Everybody hits you with this feelin'/nobody seems to understand' – there I was just askin' is there anybody out there that understands 'cause when you're a teenager nobody understands what ya mean.

The refrain *'Everybody hits you, everybody knocks you down,'* was how I felt 'bout all the people who were tellin' us we weren't gonna do it, an' how them sayin' that made me want to prove them wrong. It was also about the wider sense of begrudgery that has always existed in this country. Ya know they way the Irish are known for their begrudgery? That's a National trait that I'm not sure many outside observers would be aware of but every Irish person knows what I'm talkin' about. I'd always been aware of all these injustices that were goin' on in Irish society an' that had made me able to empathise with the fuckin' underdogs – it'd given me compassion. An' it made me wonder why, if we all have to go through this shit together, are the Irish such begrudgin' bastards? That sense of belittlin' formed the refrain that just kept repeatin' in me head, over an' over, *'Everybody hits you, everybody knocks you down . . .'*

The first time we rehearsed *This is* I thought the lyrics were good but the melody to me was wrong – it was too fast. When I hear a progression of chords in a music sequence, it'll sometimes evoke an emotion in me. I'll try an' match the lyrics with that sensation. When that happens I'm left with a melody an' a lyric line to go with it. Sometimes the lyrics are far superior to the melody or the melody is far superior to the lyrics. It's a sin then to waste those lyrics on a great melody an' it's a sin to waste that melody on dodgy lyrics. With *This is* I felt the lyrics were great but the melody was not. It wasn't crap but it wasn't good enough. It was way too fast, ya know? It was like a rock song that we were singin' very quickly so we slowed the beat right down an' kept messin' with it an' tinkerin' round 'til finally – we got it.

This is was our first single an' it was everythin' to me to get it right. To me a record is just that – a recordin' of yourself at that particular moment in your life. Ya know the way you want a Mercedes when you're 16 an' when you reach 23 you think an Escort is a nice car anyway? Ya do that all yer life; ya compromise all the way. But sometimes ya don't compromise. Maybe, if it had been our second or third single, I might have had less conviction but this was our first real introduction to the planet. That's why we called it *This is* – *This is* Aslan, *This is* Christy Dignam, *This is* where I have lived, *This is* what I have seen, *This is* me aul fella, *This is*. . . .

I think ya know quality when ya hear it. When a song is finished, ya know straight away if it's any good. Ya might write a song an' go home that day thinkin', 'man, that's the best fuckin' song I've ever written'. After a week you think, 'maybe it's a good song but it's not the best'. But when *This is* was finally written we knew it – man, it hit us right in the face. We'd cracked it. We just had that feelin'.

When we did it properly for the first time I got a shiver up me back. An' I just kept thinkin', 'this is it, this is a cracker'. There's an even bigger reason why it was such a great song. If ya can imagine – you've bein' told for years by the so-called experts that ya can't do this, an' although you believe ya can, there's always that doubt. Then, all of a sudden you've done it – you've written a great song. They can call you a wanker; they can call you whatever, but it's a still a great song.

I got a tape of the original recordin' an' brought it to Bono to hear it. Mother Records was a label that U2 had set up to help out Irish bands who'd been fucked 'round by British labels. The idea was to give them a leg up into the international market. We'd been courted by the record company bullshit an' messed around an' all, so I felt we epitomised everything Bono said about helpin' other Irish bands to get on their feet.

So, I rang him up an' meself an' Joe went to meet him. It was after the release of *The Unforgettable Fire* an' Bono an'

U2 were gettin' pretty big at the time. I'd seen U2 playin' loads of times before an' I'd met Bono around the Dublin scene, at the Project Arts Theatre, the Dandelion Market an' all those places. I wasn't friends with him or anythin' like that – there's nothin' I disliked 'bout him, we were just different kinds of people.

Joe an' meself were to meet him at half-twelve in the Dockers pub in town but Bono didn't arrive 'til half-two. I was fuckin' sick. I know he's a big star an' all but ya still don't disrespect somebody like that. I remember he ordered a sausage sandwich on a batch loaf. I was starvin' an' he asked us if we wanted one but neither me or Joe would take one off him 'cause we were so pissed off waitin' around for him. Anyway, I played him the tape of *This is* an' he says, 'It hasn't got a chorus,' an' it's not this an' it's not that. 'Go back an' do it again,' he says. 'I'll tell you what, I'll give youse a lend of a 4-track studio. Ring Anne Marie in the office tomorrow an' I'll give you the 4-track. Record a gig an' I'll pick you out a song an' blah, blah. . . .'

The rest of the band were up in the pigsty waitin' for us to come back. We were buzzin' comin' outta the place. I was tellin' Joe that this could be our big chance an' Joe was sayin' what would we tell the rest of the band when we got back to the pigsty. It was only when I started sayin', 'We'll tell them . . .' that I realised that Bono had basically told us to fuck off. He was after talkin' to us for two hours an' sayin' nothin' the whole time. It was the big brush off an' I knew we'd to go back to the band an' tell them. I felt fuckin' dreadful.

Sure enough, when I tried to ring U2's office, I couldn't get them for days an' when I finally got on to them their secretary says, 'No, sorry, Paul never said anythin' to me about that,' an' she hung up – end of story. Bono had rejected it.

In the end we recorded *This is* in a tiny rehearsal studio called the Lab. Ya know the way they have 32-track recording studios an' 24-track recording studios, well *This is* was done on a 4-track for 400 quid. We went around to this guy called Jimmy Butler an' his sister Elvira Butler who had this label called Reekus Records. I played the song for Jimmy Butler right, an' he says, 'Leave it here an' I'll have a listen to it again tonight.' But people had told me before that what happens when ya go into a record company is, ya go in an' give them the tape right, an' they listen to it an' if they like it you leave it with them. But then they analyse it to bits an' the next day they say this, this, this is wrong an' all that. So, I told Jimmy, 'No, if you want to hear it again you ring me an' I'll come back an' play it for ya.' an' I just walked out with the tape. So he rang the next day an' asked me to come back in. When I walked in the door he offered to record the single for us there an' then. That was it – happy days.

It was sweet. It was a two-finger fuck you to the music industry. Here were all these bands that had secured big record deals an' released records that had huge production an' top producers an' loadsa money behind them an' we done this Mickey Mouse bullshit thing for 400 quid.

We'd done it on our own an' it was about to become the biggest hit single of the fuckin' year . . .

'Why Can't I Feel No Shame'

Ya know the way at the start of a New Year ya might be out celebratin' on New Year's Eve an' you'd think back over the last 12 months? Ya know, right in the middle of the partyin' ya stop an' think, 'well, that was an all right year' or 'that was a shit year' an' ya wonder if the next one will be any better or any worse. Well, little was I to know at the start of 1986 that it was gonna be the year when me life would be turned around so much that it wouldn't even be remotely similar to how it was before. Maybe the start of the year coulda been an indication to how the rest of it was gonna go – it was definitely dramatic enough.

I was on me way home from somewhere in the middle of January when I heard Kathryn had suddenly gone into labour. I rushed over to the Rotunda Hospital in Dublin an' when I got there I found out pretty sharpish that somethin' was wrong. There was loads of doctors an' nurses in the room, more than I woulda thought necessary for deliverin' a baby. One of the nurses was tyin' the apron thing on me an' she was sayin' that everythin' was okay an' that but I didn't remember askin' was somethin' wrong. I didn't need to ask her what the story was. I could tell that somethin' wasn't right here, ya know?

I went over an' stood next to Kathryn, just talkin' to her. In the background I could hear these beeps. They had a monitor that was takin' the baby's statistics – her vital signs, her heartbeat an' so on. This machine was beepin' away at 120 or whatever it was an' then all of a sudden it started goin' down, 120 – 115 – 112. Everyone sorta stood there watchin' it an' then the next minute the midwife starts goin', 'We're losin' the baby; we're losin' the baby.' Kathryn was sayin' to me, 'What? What did they say?' an' I'm tryin' to keep her quiet an' not let her hear what's goin' on. Basically the baby was in trouble, right. This doctor kinda pushed his way through everyone else an' he had some sorta medical instrument thing in his hand. Then he just leaned in an' whipped Kiera out. I only seen her for a split second 'cause she was wheeled out into an emergency cubicle but I caught this glimpse of a blue body. She was tiny an' she was blue, I swear to God. They were stitchin' up Kathryn an' I was doin' me best to comfort her, wantin' to know what was goin' on. Then the nurse comes in an' says, 'It's ok, your new baby's all right. She's outside.' I was tellin' Kathryn everythin' was fine but I didn't know what to expect when I walked into the other room – I didn't know what state the baby was in, ya know?

There were these eight babies in a row that had all been born within that few minutes in the Rotunda. Every one of them was the same but I swear to God, Kiera just shone. It was like ya know the way ya see those old films where they put the Vaseline on the screen to make it all misty? Honest to God it was like that.

I picked her up an' held her an' in that moment I felt this strange power come over me. Like, if somebody had touched her or tried to harm her I would've killed them immediately. I would've shot the perpetrator in front of a copper an' a judge without even thinkin' about it. An' for that love to hit ya so instantly was somethin' that I'd never expected. 'Cause up to then when you fall in love with somebody it happens gradually. Like, when you meet someone ya fancy ya go out for meals, get to know them an' like them for the person they are. Eventually ya might fall in love – it's a very gradual process. Then she gets pregnant an' while ya know on an intellectual level that there's a human bein' in there it doesn't have an identity, right? So imagine then this baby is born an' instantaneously ya would kill or die for it. Ya love them more than anythin' you've ever loved in the world. It's an unconditional, absolute love an' it hits ya instantly. An' the impact of that was one of the most profound experiences I've ever had in me life. I've tried every drug an' every cocktail of drugs on Earth an' I've never even gotten near the feelin' that it gave me.

It carried me on a wave for days 'til we brought our new baby back to our little cottage in Meath. For a little while it was a bit kinda what do I do here? But Kathryn was just calm about it. We'd our families comin' over all the time as well just checkin' to make sure we were all right an' that.

I think I got into the whole fatherhood thing pretty quick, ya know? Maybe it's that somethin' just clicks with ya an' it comes naturally then for a lot of blokes, I don't know. I remember actually we were all out at the house to celebrate Kiera's birth, a few friends, the lads outta the band, some of our family an' that, when this bloke I kinda knew offered me some heroin for some cocaine that I had. I took a little bit off him an' snorted it in the jacks when no one was around. I remember thinkin', 'that's pretty nice' but I didn't have that much, ya know? I kept it to meself though an' when I came out of the jacks I just went on with the partyin'.

We were all hangin' round out in the back garden. Even though it was fuckin' freezin' it was lovely out there in the countryside an' I was talkin' to Joe about the band. It'd been a big gamble to jack in our decent jobs an' throw our lot in with makin' it with music, ya know? It was a serious throw of the dice but as we talked that night I just felt it – I sensed we were close. I knew we'd some great songs an' we couldn't get much tighter playin' live, plus we'd just recorded our first single. But I'd no idea just how close we were.

A few months later I was drivin' home from practise listenin' to the radio an' right in the middle of sittin' there in the traffic I recognised the first few notes of the next song that came on. I turned it up so I could hear it over the traffic an' there it was – *This is* – Aslan's first single on the radio.

Today, if one of me songs comes on the radio an' I'm drivin' in the summer with the window down I'll turn it off. I'd be mortified if I stopped at a light an' people thought, 'look at that fuckin' eejit, playin' his own CD in his car'. But at the time nobody knew who I was an' when I heard it I blasted the radio up. It just came on – no introduction, straight into the first couple of bars, an' it was like 'wow.' It was absolutely brilliant.

I felt really proud 'cause our song was right up there with the best of them. DJs have a list of 40 tracks or whatever on their playlist that they're goin' to be playin' on their show. At the time they would've had releases from Bowie, Prince an' whoever else. Now, DJs don't say, 'Well, hold on, Aslan only paid 400 quid to record this song, so let's give them a chance an' play it.' They don't give a fuck. Our song was up against the biggest an' the best. It was fightin' records that cost hundreds of thousands to produce an' market, an' the DJs wanted to play it.

This is was voted single of the fortnight when *Hot Press* reviewed it the week it came out. Then other radio stations picked up on it. I think it got to Number 4 in the Singles Charts. I mean, a Top 10 hit single for your first record – it was some achievement. After that it seemed to be on the radio all the time. We were gettin' blanket coverage – I think it was the longest playin' single on 2FM in 1986.

To this day *This is* is still a great song. Any poll they do of the best Irish singles over the last few years, *This is* is always in there. So it's proved itself. I've given Bono loads a stick about rejectin' it over the years an' the story's got a bit out of shape but it happened. Oh yeah, then at the end of the year we actually beat Bono. He'd a song out with Clannad called *In a Lifetime* but *This is* was voted Best Single of the Year.

Almost overnight we became a household name, although we weren't even remotely aware of it 'til much later in the year. I think the first time I really sensed what we'd achieved was when we did a gig that summer in Cork called the Lark by the Lee. We were backin' up Cactus World News an' it was our first big show outside Dublin. It was a massive event, between 15,000 or 20,000 people turned up. There were other small bands on the bill, The Partisans an' Paul Cleary's band, The Blades, an' I can't remember the other names now, but Aslan were at the bottom of the line-up – the opening act. We were to go on in the middle of the day when everyone was still arrivin' or busy gettin' the pints in. But when we took the stage that day in Cork, the place just erupted. We were goin', 'What the fuck?' to each other. I remember near the end of our set we played *This is* an' my God, I barely got a chance to sing the words. The crowd sang along through the whole song an' when it came to the chorus '*Everybody hits you, everybody knocks you down*' I just stood there conductin' while they sang it word for word. It was phenomenal. It gave us such a lift that we blew all the other bands away.

I remember the reaction on the faces of Cactus Word News. Any time ya do those kinds of gigs, when one band is on the other bands stand in the wings lookin' at them. They might be checkin' out the set up or whatever, professional interest, ya know? But not Cactus World News. They'd security on the fuckin' stage so we couldn't look at how they'd everythin' connectin' up. We weren't allowed to see what way the guitarist had set up his amps 'cause he'd created his own unique sound an' he didn't want us robbin' it. We used to describe it as like a screamin', dyin' horse wailing'; it was just masturbation shit. But they were welcome to keep their stupid secrets 'cause we killed them that day an' they knew it.

We were a different band after we came off the stage in Cork that day in June. We had come on as the support act – the bottom of the list – but we walked off as rock stars.

* * *

There's one person that I have to credit with sellin' *This is* to the world when it first came out an' that's Danny Kenny. We'd first met Danny when he was still the manager of Toy with Rhythm at one of the gigs we did supportin' them in the Danceline. I didn't really like him at the start. In fact we got off on a very bad foot.

I had a row with him the first day I met him. One of the record companies had come to see Toy With Rhythm in the Danceline when we were backin' them up. It was their big showcase night an' we were supposed to be there just as a support act. But after the gig the record company heads were kinda comin' after us, askin' did we have a record deal yet an' all that. I was doin' an interview with *IN Dublin* after the gig an' I talked about the fact that we were gettin' more attention than Toy with Rhythm. Now, they didn't fuckin' like that one bit. Danny Kenny came up to me a few nights later an' started givin' me shit about it, sayin' we were steppin' on their toes, ya know? Now, I thought, 'fuck this prick', 'cause he'd an English accent.

Like the mentality I had at the time was I didn't like this English bloke comin' over, tellin' me what I could an' couldn't say in an interview, ya know? So I'd a bit of a shoutin' match with him.

But Danny wasn't stupid. Not long after me first encounter with him he was sayin' to the other lads in the band how he could help us get a proper record deal. I could see that he might come in useful but at the beginnin' of his relationship with Aslan I kinda had a vibe with him 'cause we were still at loggerheads. I suppose the two of us were very driven at that time an' we just clashed.

When I got to know him later I saw that he was actually quite cool. He was a real rock'n'roller, ya know? He was into the whole music scene. But I still didn't trust him entirely. All our dealin's with him were just matey, matey stuff – we weren't agreein' to sign any contracts with him or anythin' like that.

Later he managed Cactus World News an' set up Worldwide Management with another guy called John Reid. Cactus was like their main band – their great hope to make it big. Cactus already had a big deal at that time an' we hadn't, so Danny was lookin' round for us. But the Dublin music scene was still kinda small an' all the bands would've been rivals so when the Cactus lads saw him offerin' us his help there was a bit of friction.

I think it started that day when Cactus seen the reception we got in Cork an' they were a bit worried about the competition. Not long after the Cork gig they split from Danny an' John Reid for whatever reasons. They just told Danny an' John their services were no longer required so the two lads were just lookin' after us.

They were still kinda representin' us in an informal way. There were no contracts or anythin' like that – we just agreed to see where we would go with them. But one day John Reid rings up while we were out in RTÉ doin' a TV programme an' he says, 'Listen, me an' Danny are splittin' up an' youse have to decide who yis are goin' with – me or Danny. End of story.' We're in the middle of doin' a TV show goin', 'What? What the fuck's goin' on?' An' Reid says, 'We've had a row. We're not goin' to be workin' with each other any more so youse have to make a choice between us.'

We were like, 'For fuck's sake.' Here we are, takin' our first steps into the entertainment world an' these guys have a fallin' out? In the end we decided to go with Danny. Like I said, we kinda knew him from giggin' in the Danceline an' that an' he just seemed like he was on the same vibe as us, ya know?

So Danny started lookin' out for us on a 'we'll see what happens' kinda buzz. As it turned out he was fuckin' brilliant at his job. When *This is* was first released it'd started attractin' all this record company interest an' he was the one that was negotiatin' with them. It was Danny who got us our first big record deal an' he guided us through the initial success. I have to give it to him – he was a deadly scam merchant. He elevated us from practically nothin' to being a nationally recognised band, ya know?

One of the first things he did after *This is* had got Aslan's name on everyone's lips was to convince us to put out another single. We decided to release *Loving Me Lately* on Solid Records as a once off kinda deal. Solid was an independent label that was run by Oliver Walsh an' Dennis Desmond of MCD. The vibe was that even though *This is* was a big success we still didn't make any money out of it. But we still had this demo that was left over from when the Chrysalis deal had fallen through.

Record companies would give ya say a couple of grand to go in an' demo material for them an' Chrysalis had given us a grand to go in an' record a coupla songs. When they rejected us we still had the demos an' *Loving Me Lately* was actually one of the songs that we'd recorded on it.

That stirred up even more interest. A bloke from EMI came over an' listened to the singles an' says, 'Well, what else have you got?' We'd spent a year in the fuckin' pigsty, freezin' our arses off, writin' all these crackin' songs like *Pretty Thing* an' *The Hunger,* an' we let him hear them. He offered us a shot at a showcase gig in London.

Danny was in hyper PR mode an' he kept sayin', 'This is it lads, it's about to pay off,' but we weren't so convinced. We'd done hundreds of these showcases to every record company under the sun – Atlantic Records, East West Records, Ensign Records an' the rest. Then the whole Chrysalis and CBS things had happened so we weren't countin' our chickens kinda thing. We did a short showcase gig in London an' that was enough. It convinced the money men to sign a record deal with us. Danny had come up an' delivered the goods on the EMI deal an' it was a real fuckin' achievement as far as we were concerned. We couldn't believe it. We could make our first album – *Feel No Shame.*

I'll never forget the day when we signed the deal with EMI in May, 1987. It was hard to believe sittin' on the plane goin' over to London that this was actually happenin'. All the years talkin' about this moment an' now it had arrived. Kathryn could barely believe it an' I was the same. This was when we would stop bein' a great Dublin band an' become an international act. All those days sittin' on the street outside me gaff in Finglas, thinkin' about becomin' a singer in a band like Slade, an' here I was on me first plane ride to success. All the months of frustration an' bein' told by A&R men youse are sorted, we'll take yis on, no need to worry lads – all that bullshit an' broken promises was over.

We arrived in London an' were brought to EMI headquarters in Manchester Square. We went up to the fourth floor an' we're escorted into this boardroom with a big table an' chairs an' the plush carpets an' all. We sat down an' signed the contracts. Champagne was popped an' we were gettin' all this, 'Welcome on board lads', ya know? I was sittin' there in a room lookin' round at all these Beatles' records on the wall. The likes of Bowie, Queen an' all these other musicians had sat in that same room an' signed a similar contract. Their jumpin' off point was exactly the same as ours. Despite all the fuckin' odds there we were sittin' in the office where these people we worshiped had launched themselves from. Aslan were in the same stable as them now. Since the first day I knew I wanted to be a singer in a great band I'd known I had what it took. But I was still only human. No matter how convinced I was there had always been that pit of doubt in me stomach. It was a moment of affirmation for all of us. That morning I'd sat down with Kathryn an' told her it wouldn't be long now that I'd finally be able to support her an' the baby. She'd already had to give up on the Australia dream an' she'd stood by me when I walked outta the P & T job. All me instincts were tellin' me that me promises were about to come true.

That afternoon I sat down with four lads from the Northside of Dublin an' we signed a deal with one of the biggest record companies in the world – for £80,000.

I tell ya the rest of the lads in the band were all cartwheelin' outta the place. We went off celebratin' that night with the record heads. Everyone was jumpin' through hoops, they were so delighted. But as the night went on I felt like I was just goin' along with the flow. I was fuckin' thrilled as well but I started realisin' that I didn't feel it like they did, d'ya know what I mean?

I was thinkin' back to when I'd started off in me musical career an' all I wanted to do was play in the Baggot Inn. I'd said to meself, 'If I do that I'll be happy.' An' the day came when we did do that but I wasn't satisfied. So then I thought, 'if I ever get a record out I'll be a fulfilled person' an' we did. But I wanted more. I started thinkin' then, 'if I have a big international deal then I'll feel like I've achieved everthin' I wanted'. Now, I'd just done that an' found out that it wasn't everythin' that I wanted. All along I'd passed all these goals that I'd set for meself an' all I'd have was an empty feelin' when I realised 'no, this is not what I'm looking for'. An' I felt exactly the same. It was like I was always tryin' to grab smoke.

I remember sittin' there that night, while all the corks were poppin', an' in the back of me mind I just kept thinkin', 'where's the fuckin' substance here?'. There is a deeply personal reason for me thinkin' like that. It's somethin' I don't think I've ever really understood. All I know is that all me life I think I've had this emotional deficiency that has made me look for fulfilment 'out there' while the whole time I should be lookin' for it 'in here'.

* * *

We went straight into Westland Row Studios to start workin' on our first album. While *This is* was produced pretty much by ourselves an' had only cost 400 quid with EMI behind us we'd our pick of the top name producers in the industry. We decided to get a bloke called Mick Glossop who was Van Morrison's producer. He'd also worked on The Waterboys' album *This is the Sea* an' it was big – a great album. An' he'd also been in the studio with bands like The Skids an' The Ruts, ya know, guitar, punky bands. So I knew he was great for guitars an' I knew from him workin' with Van Morrison that he was gonna be great to do vocals with. So, seein' as how we were a guitar/vocal band he suited our sound an' he really pulled it together for us in the studio.

Mick Glossop was a hard man to work for 'cause he knew how to deal with a load of loose cannons like us. He was in the music business a long time an' he didn't take any shit. He'd worked with a lot of fellas like us, who were after strugglin' in abject poverty all of our lives an' were now all full of themselves.

He thought he needed to keep a tight rein on us an' any sign of what he considered a lack of discipline, like comin' in late or hungover, was quickly nipped in the bud, d'ya know what I mean? But he needn't have worried. We were takin' all this deadly seriously. Like, if I was doin' a vocal in the mornin' I wouldn't be out around town the night before. When Aslan partied we partied but we were all very professional when it was time to go into the studio. This was our first big chance an' we didn't want to fuck it up. I mean this was what we'd been tryin' to get for years an' now suddenly we'd exactly what we wanted. We'd a top producer, as much studio time as we cared for an' the best equipment that the record company could buy.

Alan got his Yamaha 9000 series drumkit which is, ya know, the dog's bollix of a drumkit, Joe an' Tony got brand new guitars an' Billy had got a new acoustic guitar. I actually got nothin' 'cause I was the singer, ya know? Maybe I was given a packet of lozenges or somethin'!

On one level it was great to be goin' in with all this equipment an' all the time to do it but on the other it was a luxury that we just weren't comfortable with. I mean a lot of it is 'the emperor's new clothes' kinda thing. The music industry is awash with so much wealth an' there's loadsa people out there lookin' for an angle to make money out of it. Ya have all these microphone makers an' guitar manufacturers blindin' ya with science. We soon copped on that it was very, very difficult gettin' used to the artificial environment of a top studio. I couldn't really get the hang of it at all. They gave me this microphone that was ultra fuckin' sensitive to pickin' up sounds. In the middle of recordin' a track I'd hit me hand off it an' it'd make a WHOOMP sound an' we'd have to start again. So we wrapped a load of bleedin' foam around it to stop all the noise. I didn't like the way it was on a stand either so I used to kinda hold the mike like as if I was doin' a gig – walkin' around with it in me hands. That's how I recorded all the vocals on *Feel No Shame.*

The others found it hard at the start as well. Tony had this old bass guitar called a White Shadow which musta cost him about a hundred quid, right. It was a fretless bass an' the neck of it was made outta wood an' he used to wear grooves into the fretboard from playin' it so much. But his dream was to get this new Status guitar that had a graphite neck that would never wear down. The only problem was it cost about two grand which was huge money back then. So instead he cut out this picture that he found of a Status bass an' kept it in his pocket.

While we were still strugglin' up the ladder we got to a point where all these other bands around us were gettin' signed to record companies who were givin' them financial back-up. So they used the best equipment while we were still playin' with the same shit we'd had since before the pigsty days. You'd meet them around town an' they'd be listin' off all this great stuff their record company had bought them. They'd be askin' Tony what kinda bass he was playin' an' Tony'd say 'Well, I'm playin' a White Shadow now but I'm gettin'. . .' an' he'd whip out this photograph of the Status an' say '. . . this baby, once we sign.'

He carried around that picture for fuckin' years, showin' it to anybody who was interested. It was the most dog-eared piece of paper ya ever saw. It was almost in shreds by the time we got our deal an' it was our turn to be like kids on a Christmas mornin' with all our gear. Now Tony finally had his new guitar – the one he'd always wanted.

The very first day we're in the studio Tony had to do a bass line on one of the songs. He's so excited that he's there with his fingers flyin' up an' down the fretboard, just delighted with himself. Mick Glossop's in the control room where he can't see Tony an' he says, 'Do that again Tony.' So Tony shrugs his shoulders an' does the bass line again. 'No, didn't get it. Do it again Tony,' Glossop says. An' Tony tries again. Still Glossop isn't happy an' he stops him again. 'Tony,' he says, 'were you out late last night? An' Tony's like 'No, there's nothin' wrong with me.' Glossop walks into the studio an' he sees Tony with his brand new Status bass an' he says, 'What's this?' Tony goes, 'Aw, this is me new bass guitar – it's deadly isn't it?' Glossop takes one look at it an' says, 'It's a piece of shit, fuck it away. Use your old one.' An' Tony had to. He did the whole album on this shit hundred quid bass guitar that he'd been givin' out about for years. He never used the two grand bleedin' guitar ever again. I think he sold it in the end.

* * *

We were in the middle of recordin' *Feel No Shame* when we found out David Bowie was gonna play Slane in the summer of 1987. Meself, Kathryn, Tony an' a couple of mates I grew up with on the road, had all gone over to England the year before when Bowie was playin' in Milton Keynes. It was one of the best gigs I'd ever seen. An' now he was comin' to Ireland for the first time on The Glass Spider tour.

I think I was sayin' before that when we were gettin' Meelah XVIII together we decided to dump all the cover songs in our set so we'd be considered a 'serious' band. We'd all agreed on this except for one song – we couldn't throw out *Five Years* by David Bowie. It was, an' still is, one of me favourite Bowie tracks. Bowie was a massive influence on all of us. Joe was already a big Bowie fan by the time I met him an' in fact, *Five Years* is the song that first attracted Tony to our gigs. He came along 'cause he'd heard we did a good version of it so Bowie was indirectly responsible for Tony bein' in the band, if ya like. Billy an' Alan were fans as well but I loved Bowie. I thought that he was a brilliant performer an' he woulda been an influence on the way I was developin' as a singer on stage. I'd have been singin' along to Bowie's records at home with this image of him in me head. At me own gigs I kinda acted out on stage how I imagined Bowie woulda done it.

So when we heard that Bowie was comin' to play Slane we insisted that we get a support slot on the bill. We were signed with EMI, an' Bowie was with EMI so as far as we're concerned there was already a connection – a way in. We says to Danny, 'Lookit, we don't care if you don't get us one other gig or one other contract for the rest of the year, just get us on to the Slane bill. Cancel everythin' else you're fuckin' organisin'.' We were busy in the studio tryin' to finish the album but it didn't matter. I couldn't emphasise how important it was to us to get this gig. It wasn't that it was Slane – even though at that time it was the only big, open air venue we had in this country an' it was a very prestigious gig to do – we just wanted the memory of playin' on the same stage as Bowie.

I remember even findin' the number for yer man, Lord Henry MountCharles who owns Slane Castle an' ringin' him, sayin', 'Look we want this gig.' But he told me that he'd nothin' to do with it, that I'd have to go to MCD or whoever it was who were runnin' the promotion. So, we just went everywhere an' let everybody know that we would be deeply indebted to them for the rest of our careers if they could help us out.

Somehow, Danny got us the gig. I'm not sure how he did it. I just remember bein' so excited that when the day came we arrived in Slane in the middle of the mornin', hours before we were due to go on stage as the openin' act. We were all hangin' round backstage an' I remember lookin' out to the front of the stage an' there was a few 100 people millin' round, waitin' to get their spot for when the gig actually started.

We got everythin' ready an' then went into our dressin' room an' started gettin' psyched up. We were nervous. I was terrified, absolutely terrified; I'll never forget it. I was shittin' meself. I mean, I'd have been blown away just playin' a gig of that magnitude but the fact that it was on the same bill as Bowie put all this extra pressure on. This was the one gig where we really wanted to deliver the goods. Thousands of rock'n'roll punters had seen all these legends playin' at Slane – can ya imagine what it was like then to be on the same stage as one of them? It was a weird fuckin' buzz. I mean, the fact that I've dedicated me life to rock'n'roll is testament to how much I love it, right, an' here I was livin' it. It was incredible. Almost overwhelmin'. I didn't do any drugs backstage 'cause I was thinkin' about all those people out there who'd paid in an' I didn't wanna fuck it up for them. If we pulled this off I thought then I'd go on a mad coke session but not 'til after.

At the time we used to do a big intro for this song called *The Gallery*. Alan would start off with drums, then Tony an' Joe would come in on guitars while Billy'd be gettin' ready to sing backin' vocals. They'd be playin' for about a minute or two an' then I'd walk on an' launch into the song.

So the band all went out before me an' I heard a big cheer an' it sounded like a very substantial roar. I thought the way the stage was that it was just catchin' the noise off the few punters that were there an' amplifyin' it. Then, it was time for me to go on.

I had me head down as I walked out but when I looked up there were people for as far as I could see, stretchin' out from the front of the stage an' up onto the hill. We'd been there three or four hours before the gig started an' when I was walkin' out I still had this picture in me mind of what it was like when we arrived that mornin'. Now there must've been about 40,000 or 50,000 people out there.

What usually happens at gigs like that is the first band comes on an' nobody gives a fuck – nobody is watchin'. They're just saunterin' around the place. I don't know if all these people came to see Aslan – it might be presumptuous to think that they had but at the time it literally took me breath away. I don't know if this has ever happened to ya when you've been out on a windy day an' ya walk out of a shop an' the wind catches yer breath – for a second ya gasp – that's exactly what happened to me.

The band was playin' away waitin' for me cue an' I could see all of these people in front of me. I was just standin' there thinkin', 'fuck me, we're up here for the next half an hour – no matter what'. I remember havin' to kick meself psychologically outta that 'cause I didn't want to make a show of meself. Of all the gigs I didn't want to mess up it was this gig in particular – we were on the same stage as David Bowie for fuck's sake!

I managed to catch me breath an' I just threw meself into the song. We got through the first few minutes but I started to feel really uncomfortable 'cause we were so far away from the audience. Up to then, except for the odd gig like the Lark in Cork, we'd played a lot of clubs an' venues where the audience could see the whites of our eyes. But at Slane I was probably 60 feet from the nearest person in the audience. There was even another stage between us an' them. It was about two or three feet lower than the main stage. I couldn't connect. I couldn't cross the gap – it was really alien to me to be in that situation an' it totally disorientated me, ya know?

We'd been told before goin' on that under no circumstances were we to go near this lower stage. The idea was that the audience wouldn't know it was there. It was for one of Bowie's stage surprises – in the middle of his set he'd have all these dancers suddenly come on an' dance on this stage. Then he'd jump down an' get close to the audience.

I was still feelin' weird when we started into another song called *The Sands of Time*. There's this really big openin' where I scream '*YEEAAAAGH, I like the look of you/I like your style . . .*' an' then it comes into a part where it breaks down to a guitar riff. Just imagine – Joe's standin' there coolly playin' a few high notes, Tony's bass is keepin' the beat while Alan slows on the drums an' Billy's rattlin' away on percussion. Then it kinda all builds back up again. Alan comes back in on the drums – bash, bash, BASH – an' when the music reaches a crescendo, I scream

'ONE, TWO, THREE, FOUR' an' fuckin' leap into the air. As I jump I kinda half turn an' there's Carlos Alomar an' Peter Frampton from Bowie's band standin' at the side of the stage watchin' us. Now, both these guys are legends to us – some of the best musicians in the world. When our drum-roll reaches a climax we explode back into the song an' this huge roar just sorta rolls across Slane an' rushes towards us. I catch just a glimpse of Alomar an' Frampton high fivin' each other in recognition of what we'd just pulled off. Here are two people who I'd grown up listenin' to an' they were fuckin' surprised an' blown away by somethin' we'd just done. That absolutely flabbergasted me. I just looked over at Billy, shouted, 'Fuck it!' an' I ran over an' grabbed him. The two of us leapt down onto this little stage, ya know, an' got right up close to the audience. There was another huge roar when we did that an' from then on nothin' was goin' to stop us. We were on a fuckin' roll. It was brilliant, one of the best gigs I've ever done an' we all got our memory of playin' on the same stage as Bowie.

We stuck around to watch Bowie an' I remember him comin' from his trailer to the stage. I'll never forget this – everybody in his band, say about 15 people, were all walkin' in a military formation in matchin' grey boiler suits. This wasn't part of their stage outfits – this was just for walkin' to the stage. It was fuckin' weird.

After the show all of Bowie's band just split. They didn't hang around 'cause it was just another gig to them. They were on tour. Like they would've been doin' a gig the night before in Milton Keynes an' they'd be doin' it the next night at fuckin' Glastonbury or whatever. To them it was just another vibe, ya know? But we wanted to stay there for the next three weeks just talkin' about how great the day was, d'ya know what I mean?

That night we all went to the after-gig party in the Pink Elephant. Danny was there an' various journalists an' girlfriends of the band were hangin' out an' we fuckin' partied. We were celebratin' the fact that we'd come through a gig like that.

We were hangin' around in the bar when we got word that Bowie had arrived. He'd these two big, black, monster ex-marines as security guards with him. I don't ask people for autographs 'cause it's not somethin' I like doin' but Billy was gettin' up to go over an' ask Bowie to sign his name on somethin' when one of the security guys stands up an' says, 'Don't even try an' come over here.' It kinda pissed us off a bit, ya know?

Years later we met Bowie at a party backstage after a gig in The Point Depot. These days he's very approachable an' a completely different person so we said to him, 'What was the story with ya after Slane, ya know? We were playing with you on the same bill that day. We pulled out every stop to get to do that gig an' we did well. We thought it was a bit disrespectful that ya wouldn't even talk to us.' But the vibe with Bowie was he was mad into cocaine around then an' ever since John Lennon had been shot in 1980 he was paranoid outta his head. He was over here as an Englishman in Ireland when all the IRA stuff was goin' on. He said he was terrified that he was goin' to be assassinated. An' I think that explains the grey boiler suits that all his band went around in – if anybody, let's say a sniper, wanted to kill Bowie, he wouldn't have been able to pick him out from among this little square of people walkin' backstage.

* * *

We'd had our weekend of partyin' but then it was time to go back into the studio, get our heads down an' finish the album. Glossop was in control again an' it was hard gettin' back to work with him in his role as taskmaster. He was a weird guy, Glossop, he really was.

He was very thrifty even though he would've been on phenomenal money while he was workin' with us. The record company put him up in the Gresham Hotel an' that's where he was livin' for the two or three months that we were in the studio. I remember him tellin' us he went to this bar that he'd found on his walk from the Gresham to the studios for a couple of pints 'cause it was a penny cheaper than anywhere else. This fella was on about bleedin' two grand a day for three months!

But fair fucks to him, he mighta been a hard bastard in the studio but he helped us get the results 'cause when it was finished we'd a fuckin' brilliant first album in our hands. I'm still very proud of it but d'ya know what's weird about the whole *Feel No Shame* thing? Even if we'd recorded *This is* with the same unlimited resources again an' again I don't think it would've captured the buzz of the original 400 quid version. I'm not just bein' nostalgic – ya can't get a better vibe on it. I think it's the hungry boxer thing. We'd recorded the original in a studio that was a studio ya used when you'd no money to use a real studio. An' we were even blaggin' that. That's how much we were on a tight rope. We knew we'd to make this thing work so it was like, 'Let's make the best of this.' I think that – that absolute desperation almost – made it happen, but havin' said that we'd some crackin' songs to put on our new album. Material we'd played hundreds of times through the freezin' fuckin' winters an' swelterin' summers in the pigsty. We'd brought them out of the pigsty an' into the gigs around Dublin. Songs like *Loving me Lately* an' *Pretty Thing* were songs that we wrote about those days in Finglas, hopin' for somethin' to happen.

'All these people hangin' 'round/
Waitin' for the World to change/
All this pressure comin' down/
Life is not a pretty thing/ © Aslan

One of me favourite songs on the album was *Please Don't Stop* which was the first single off it. I want to tell ya a story about that song 'cause it taught me somethin' about how music affects different people in different ways.

Just after the single came out we were at this party, right, an' this young fella came up to me an' says, 'I bleedin' love that song, where'd you get the words for it?' Now, the words of that song go:

'*I'm stumbling down that street/*
I'm out of place/
And I'm an angry man/
A voice without a face/
Help me up/
My feet won't touch the ground/
'I wish you had time to talk' . . .' © Aslan

The vibe of it is about me growin' up in Finglas, ya know? It was about feelin' inconsequential bein' brought up in surroundin's where I felt invisible. Stumblin' through life, always feelin' out of place, right? An' I'm angry 'cause I'm only a voice without any identity an' nobody's goin' to listen to me. *'I wish you had time to talk'* is when I'm askin' for someone to help me in this struggle to become recognised. That's what I meant when I was writin' those lyrics.

But this guy, right, he says he's been comin' to all our gigs an' he says, 'I love that song 'cause I get locked an' me mates carry me home an' me feet aren't touchin' the ground.' I was gonna say, 'That's not what it's about – gettin' drunk an' fallin' up the road with yer mates.' I wanted to explain what the song was really about but then I thought, 'no, hold on, maybe that's not the right thing to do'. I felt maybe I was wrong to try an' impose my impressions of the song onto someone else.

The important thing is that whatever that song meant to him, that's what it was about. An' that's the beauty of music. To me it's like when two people are lookin' at a painting, an' they both think it's beautiful 'cause there's let's say, a blue sea. Now ya might like the blue 'cause when ya were a kid yer ma had a blue dress like that. But I might like the blue 'cause when I was in Spain last year that was the colour of the sky. We both like the painting for the same things but for different reasons. An' that's the same with music.

This fella liked this song; he liked this melody an' the words. Now, what it meant to me when I was writin' it is irrelevant. If that song gives him a bit of happiness, 'cause he thinks it's about gargle, should I ruin that for him by sayin', 'It's not about gargle, it's about this . . .' Should I have the right to do that?

* * *

One day I was on me way into the studio when one of the lads rang an' said, 'Did you see the *Evening Herald*?' I hadn't seen it so then Billy or whoever it was says, 'Ya better pick it up. Somebody's after breakin' into Danny's office an' stealin' the master tapes.'

I stopped the car an' ran into get the paper. There was the story an' it had Danny quoted as sayin' a thief had gotten in through a window an' made off with all the original recordin's of the new album.

Danny's office was over this old antique shop in a buildin' that had a preservation order on it 'cause somebody, James Joyce or whatever, had a shit in it or somethin' like that.

When Danny arrived that mornin' he'd seen that somebody had got in through the skylight. Now there was nothin' there, like it was his office an' it had a telephone an' a fax machine, that sorta stuff but nothin' of any value. He noticed though that an old kinda ghetto blaster had gone missin' so he rings up the *Herald* an' he says: 'Yeah, listen Aslan's office has been broken into. We'd just completed the album an' the master tapes have been robbed.' He was tellin' the reporter all the work we put into it an' how hundreds of thousands had gone down the drain. The fuckin' thing was all over the papers the next day.

It was all bollix. There was a few little cassettes we woulda had lyin' around from some of the sessions, ya know? After a day's work we'd make a cassette just so we could go home an' listen to it. Somebody left a few of them in Danny's office an' it was that sort of shit that was robbed. But Danny didn't make it out that way. He maintained that the original master tapes were gone.

We didn't even know about it – the first I seen anythin' about it was when I read it in the paper. We coulda killed him when we found out it was all a spoof but it got us a load of free publicity just before the album came out. Danny was brilliant at that sort of thing, at gettin' headlines outta some bullshit little story, ya know? He was always lookin' out for ways to get us in the papers. I remember he generated a load of publicity by stirrin' up this row I had with Chris De Burgh.

Chris De Burgh had offered us a support slot for a gig he was doin' in the Point Depot but he wouldn't have been our type of music so we turned him down.

So De Burgh goes on this TV programme called *Anything Goes* an' he says to yer man Aengus wasn't it, with the big hair, 'I can't understand these young bands in

Dublin today. I offered a band called Aslan a supportin' slot in the Point and they wouldn't take it.' Yer man Aengus says, 'That was very silly of them, wasn't it!'

We were all outraged by this – I'm sure Chris De Burgh was offered hundreds of gigs everyday. If he's asked to do a charity gig, let's say for cancer, an' he refuses to do it for a legitimate reason, it's not made a big deal of on national television. We'd made a decision not to support him 'cause he wasn't our type of music. So we hit back 'bout how we thought De Burgh was a sellout 'cause I used to be pissed off at the time when I'd see big Irish stars who I felt didn't contribute to the industry here. I'll never forget it – it made the front page. The papers had a field day with this story about us havin' this big vibe with Chris De Burgh.

De Burgh never forgave us for it either. I remember years later we were in the Burlington Hotel to pick up an IRMA award for *Crazy World* an' De Burgh was there as well, for a Lifetime Achievement Award. He was after collectin' his prize an' he was walkin' back to his table while the whole place is clappin'. He was kinda bowin', ya know, respectfully to all the tables. Then he came to our table and he just looked at us and threw his nose up in the air, ya know, an' huffed off. I just sat there laughin'. The singin' eyebrow I call him.

* * *

We called the album *Feel no Shame* after one of the tracks on it 'cause that was the whole vibe runnin' through it, ya know? We were tryin' to get an image that said be proud of where ya come from, don't be afraid to stand up an' say, 'Yeah, we're from the wrong side of tracks.' See, we wanted to get a picture that almost said, 'Feel no Shame.'

We'd all these people that the record company recommended comin' in to help us with it, art an' graphic designers that were hired to come up with loads of different ideas. We'd tell them what we wanted an' they'd go off to their drawin' boards. But it didn't work out. They were comin' back with stuff that was way off the mark.

Another vibe on the album, like I was sayin' 'bout *This is*, is that it was about the changin' times in Ireland. How we were shakin' off the influence of the Church an' the old traditional views of the family an' that. So I suggested a shot of a father with his daughter for a start. We took a photo of me with Kiera, who was about 18 months at the time, in me arms. It was just a father holdin' his new daughter but it basically captured what the album was about – not feelin' any shame about anythin'. I mean for a man to play a role in his children's life is no big deal now, d'ya know what I mean? But before, men like me aul fella went out an' earned the money while the mother reared the kids. That's just the way it was.

I think it's a great cover. I remember a coupla years later John Cougar Mellencamp used almost the exact same cover for one of his albums. I think the album came out at a time when male values in the home were bein' challenged all over the shop. It might sound high-browed but I absolutely believe that we clicked into this undercurrent of change in Irish society. We identified with it before it was even really tangible.

It's a lovely shot. I'm very proud of it. When we got it back from the designers I just said 'Yes!' I was standin' there with me two babies – Kiera an' me first album – both about to take their first steps out into the world.

Infamy

Feel No shame was released in February 1988 an' went to Number 1 in Ireland within weeks. It was up there ahead of the likes of Terence Trent D'Arby, Wet Wet Wet, Sinead O'Connor an' INXS.

We did our first big interview for *Hot Press* an' there was a snooker club on Bachelor's Walk called The Pierrot Club where we decided to do the photo shoot. When *Hot Press* came out it was just a picture of me on the cover an' I was pleasantly surprised by the band's easy acceptance of that. I was kinda a bit nervous thinkin' that maybe it would be an issue, but in fairness to them, it's somethin' they've always been very cool about, ya know? It's somethin' they understand – that I'm the frontman an' that the media was gonna focus on me. The guy who had done the shoot with us was Colm Henry. I think he's a great rock'n'roll photographer, but he took all these pictures for the article of me holdin' a snooker cue, showin' off me lion tattoo that I have on me arm.

I was cringin' when the article came out right, 'cause me quality control is the people I grew up with. I knew I'd have to go back to Finglas, to me mother's house, an' pass people on the street who wouldn't be long tellin' ya if ya were makin' an eejit outta yourself, d'ya know what I mean?

I think the article started this trend in the press that labelled us as this tough band that you don't mess with. We got the attitude that in between writin' songs an' playin' gigs we were out robbin' cars an' batterin' aul ones. People were sayin', 'Watch your wallets when you go to an Aslan gig.' The music industry ostracised us 'cause we were these tough fuckin' Finglas heads, while the tough Finglas heads ostracised us because we were these nansy pansy musicians. So, I mean where do we fit?

It's somethin' that annoyed me at the time an' then, as the cliché surroundin' us took hold, it really started pissin' me off. It was just somethin' that developed outside our control, as these things usually do. There was nothin' we could do about it.

These were the first signs that from now on, whether we liked it or not, we were gonna be in the public eye. As much as that was just part an' parcel of success an' fame it was a repercussion that I personally wasn't ready for. In the article I remember I was talkin' about the difficulty I had adjustin' to that. While I loved the whole rock'n'roll vibe an' the rock star image with the limos an' the gigs an' all the rest of it, I wasn't prepared for bein' famous. I think it caught me off guard.

The way I thought about it was I couldn't fix a car, right, I couldn't put an engine in a car an' make it go. So to me, the man that can do that deserves a lot of respect an' a lot of admiration. Now, the talent I have is I can write songs an' sing them. In the twisted fucked up world we live in there is more kudos an' emphasis put on the fact that I can do that compared to someone that can make a car go, or build a cot, or whatever it is. But to me, just because that's the case, doesn't mean it's the reality. I don't feel that I'm any better than any of those other people.

So when fans started approachin' me in the street I started to feel uncomfortable. I'd kids comin' up to me ballin' their eyes out an' shakin' an' lookin' for me autograph, an' pointin' me out. I didn't want that. I felt that when ya were receivin' that kind of adulation or that kind of awe then ya had to live up to that expectation. I didn't want to be fuckin' put on any pedestal. I knew I'd a lot of weaknesses an' stuff. I'd as many as the person that was standin' in front of me lookin' for me autograph, so I didn't want to be built up to anythin' in case somethin' happened. An', as it turned out, things did happen when, for a lot of people, I did fall off that pedestal.

Another thing about fame is that it comes in peaks an' dips. When you've a record out you're on the TV, doin' all the shows an' you're on all the magazine covers an' shit like that. But you're famous for just that period of time. Then the album goes out of the charts, the radio play is less obvious an' your fame diminishes in direct fuckin' proportion. You're back to just your ordinary self, goin' 'round giggin' as you always did in a workin' band. You're not in the public eye at that moment so your fame is less obvious, right. Then you have something else out an' the fame starts off again. But you don't feel any different on the three famous days, than on the day the single dropped an' you fell back down into the dip. You're still the same person all the way through, but you're bein' treated completely differently at different times. So fame, to me, is an intangible concept that I've never been able to get me head round.

I also had a lot of self-esteem issues that I wasn't even aware of at the time. This made it even harder for me to accept this new factor of me existence. Someone would be askin' me for an autograph an' I'd be kinda writin' it slowly waitin' for yer man to say, 'Ah fuck off ya prick, I don't want your autograph,' so I could show him a blank piece of paper an' say, 'Fuck ya, I wasn't writin' it anyway.'

I even remember after the release of *Feel No Shame* we'd an official launch kinda thing set-up in the Virgin

Megastore, which was on the quays there at O'Connell Bridge. Danny's office was across the road from it on Bachelor's Walk an' we were standin' on the top floor just before it, lookin' across the river. There was a queue of people from the door of the Virgin Megastore all the way round into Westmoreland Street. I automatically, an' I mean this from the bottom of me heart, didn't in any way associate that queue with us. I thought there was a sale on or somethin' an' that it happened to be coincidin' with our launch. I was just thinkin' that this would probably benefit us, ya know, the fact that this sale was on while we were signin' our album. But when we got over there I realised it wasn't a sale – all these people were queuin' up to buy our album an' get our autographs. It was weird stuff.

I don't know why, but to this day it baffles me. Like, I knew I was in a good band. I believed in the music an' I'd put in all this hard work but the adulation that came with it was not part of the deal. Yeah, I wanted people to come to our gigs an' say, 'That was a great performance, they're a great live band.' Or I wanted them to buy the record an' say, 'That's a great record.' But what I didn't want them to say was, 'Christy Dignam is a great bloke an' he's perfect an' he is this an' he is that. . . .' I just wanted them to like the music. I didn't think that 'cause I was after makin' a great record that it was the equivalent of someone organisin' a great charity event or somebody buildin' a great house or somebody comin' up with a great plumbin' innovation or whatever. Ya didn't have people queuin' up to see that. I felt that I didn't deserve it. To me, it wasn't justified. When I think about it now, I suppose it was a naive thought really, 'cause I always knew deep down that fame goes along with bein' successful but at the time, man, it was mad.

Although the success was a long time comin' an' we'd spent ages workin' for it, it all still seemed to happen overnight. It takes ya by surprise, no matter how prepared ya think ya are. Even now, though it's happened a good few times, an' I'll be there thinkin', 'please God, the next record will be successful,' the surge of publicity will still astonish me. There'll always be incidents durin' the lifespan of any record we release that will wreck me head – the same way as that day when I realised all those people in the Virgin Megastore were waitin' for us. It happens time an' time again. I don't really know what the deal is – I think it's probably 'cause I don't think the fuss is necessary. Of course, there are other people I've met an' that's the only reason they're in the music business. The fame is their drivin' force an' they're successful 'cause once ya have a drivin' force that strong, ya know, you'll succeed.

But for me, success was never a motivator. To this day it still isn't. It's more important that people respect me work an' stuff. Though there's a difference between respectin' your work an' respectin' ya as a human being. When people put ya on a pedestal the respect you receive as a person is tainted by what they expect from ya. I don't think I've ever become comfortable 'bout bein' on that pedestal.

It's funny, like I'd come home after somethin' like the Virgin Megastore where I'd be signin' autographs for three hours with all these kids comin' up to me, roarin' an' cryin', shakin' while they're tryin' to talk to ya. I'd walk in the door an' Kathryn'd be there goin', 'Here, will you hold Kiera,' while she ran off into the kitchen to get a towel. Kiera would've spilled somethin' let's say, an' you're holdin' her while all this stuff dribbles down your cool leather jacket. Then ya have to change her nappy – dealin' with that is gonna ground ya pretty damn quick, d'ya know what I'm sayin? I'd have to come home an' deal with the nitty gritty reality of bein' a new father an' it just knocked me totally out of the buzz of havin' any delusions of grandeur. Any risk of gettin' above me station was totally whipped from under me an' it's a good thing. It's great. I mean, I can't remember any particular examples when I had to come in an' say to meself, 'Hold on, sit down Christy. You're startin' to lose the run of yourself. You think you're somethin' special' – it was nothin' as kinda blatant as that – but if I did Kathryn an' Kiera would've brought me down to Earth pretty sharpish.

I was actually more comfortable comin' home to that family life 'cause I was so totally uncomfortable with me other, public, life. It happens even now where kids'll come up to ya in bits an' I'm tryin' to say, 'Lookit relax, it's all right', ya know? It was harder for me leavin' the house to go into that lifestyle than it was to come home. An' when I was doin' drugs I found it even easier to deal with the bullshit. You didn't feel it; ya were able to just kinda sail through it all.

Another thing that always struck me as weird 'bout success is that when you're on yer bollix an' ya could do with a new set of clothes, they cost you a fortune – but when you're famous you get everythin' for nothin'.

When we first signed with EMI we were given a wage of 80 quid a week – but here we were bein' driven 'round Dublin in limos. We'd credit lines everywhere. We'd a deal with Pepe, ya know, for really cool clothes an' we'd a hairdresser on account. I used to go to these clubs cause all the people who were our colleagues in the music business would be there an' we never needed any cash. It was all about the perception. People seen us as stars because we were behavin' like stars.

We were bein' brought to all these fancy places to eat an' at the time Nouveau Cuisine was in. I remember goin' into this place called Giovannis – I think it was on Grafton Street. We're with all these record company heads, right an' gettin', ya know, a big plate with a little tiny bit of food on it. After the meetin' we had to fuck off over to McDonalds to get a burger on the way home 'cause we were still hungry.

What was really weird was I was still on the dole when the album first came out in Ireland 'cause we were still waitin' to be paid by EMI. I'd been signin' on an off now an' again whenever I was really stuck. We were gettin' organised to do our first tour to promote the album at the time. Billy an' me had to go over to Germany to do a load of interviews for the press 'cause we were gonna be doin' a few shows there. The idea was that when the band started giggin' we'd have all this pre-publicity done. We were catchin' a flight at say 3 o'clock an' I was gettin' me scratcher at 12 o'clock that day. I was picked up outside the dole office on Gardiner Street an' brought straight from there to the airport.

We arrived in Münich, just the two us right, an' there's two fuckin' limos waitin' for us – one each. I was convinced that they thought we were someone else so I was sayin' to Billy, 'They must think we're the Pet Shop Boys or somebody – just say fuck all.' But we figured it out later that while the album was doin' well in Ireland an' was a Number 1 hit that didn't seem like such a big deal to us. When you're based in Ireland you think it has to be Number 1 in Britain or Number 1 in America for it to be considered a fuckin' big success. But to the Germans, we were a hit band with a Number 1 record under us. They didn't care where we were Number 1 – to them it's just a chart toppin' record an' that's all that mattered. They treated us like stars.

We went from the airport an' we were put up in the Münich Hilton. I remember lyin' on the bed, a big four-poster bed, an' they'd a computer pad at either side. Ya could press a button for the lights to come on or another button for the TV, ya know, all this fuckin' gadgetry. I pressed this one button an' I heard a buzzin' sound. I was wonderin', 'what the fuck is this?' Next minute, the roof of the four-poster bed came down, the net curtains pulled across an' a sunbed came on. I had me dole money in me back pocket an' I'm lookin' at a sunbed lightin' up over me head. I was goin' from one extreme to another.

When I signed off the dole I told everyone that I went into the labour exchange an' when she asked me what me new occupation was I told her to fill in 'rock star'. I wasn't bein' 100 percent serious; it was kinda tongue-in-cheek. But it was me nod to all the begrudgers we'd met over the years that'd said it would never happen. An' now it was. I was leavin' a part of me life behind that I'd always hoped I could leave behind. People had always told me life wasn't goin' to change but all of a sudden it was changin'. Now, I could say to them, 'Look, I was right' an' say to meself, 'Your convictions were sound, Christy.'

Ya know, me da never really acknowledged me achievement with the band. For years he looked at it as a hobby, ya know? It was grand for somethin' to do every Tuesday an' Thursday after work but I'd a family to support. Even when we signed with EMI an' we'd some money comin' in he never said well done. But I know he's proud of me.

I remember once me sister tellin' me that he was in Superquinn just after *Feel No Shame* came out an' one of our songs came on the radio. He stopped in the middle of the shop an' said to one of the girls workin' there, 'That's my son up there.' Me sister was kinda goin', 'Aw da, shutup', ya know, she was cringin'. But, I mean, he'd never say that to me. Of course, it was still nice to know he was proud of what I'd done. There'd be the odd time when I did wonder why he just didn't come up to me an' say, 'Listen son, I'm proud of you.' It was only through stories like what me sister told me that I found out I did make him proud. I kinda understand as well 'cause comin' from that generation he wasn't wrong in his opinion that the band was a hobby. I think the thing was me da saw me as a father startin' off with a young family an' he didn't want me fuckin' it up, d'ya know what I mean? His motives were honourable – he was sayin' don't do it 'cause he wanted the best for me. He'd seen how hard it was to make it in the career I'd chosen. Like, there weren't many Irish people before me who'd achieved any level of success in the music industry up to then. So me aul lad had nothin' but failures to go by. He was just bein' realistic. He used to drive us around to the *Black and White Minstrels* when I was a kid an' that would've been his experience of the music business, let's say.

Now though, we'd proved to everyone that we could do it an' we were determined to reap the rewards. Ya can imagine – for years we'd been workin' to get to this level. We'd pushed all our gear in shoppin' trolleys for miles, in hail, rain an' snow, to different places to rehearse. Then there was all the months sittin' in the pigsty an' freezin' our bollix off in there. Now that effort was startin' to pay off, ya know? Of course you're goin' to be bleedin' gettin' in there an' makin' the most of it.

I remember there was another Irish band round at the time, I can't remember their name, but there were two girls in it. They'd just signed a record deal an' they were gettin' lifts in Hiace vans, all around the country. They'd be drivin' home from their gigs while we were stayin' in hotels an' livin' it up. I remember talkin' to them an' askin' them about it. They said they didn't want to spend money an' build up a big bill with the record company. But I was sayin', 'Listen, the way it is, is, if you're successful youse'll be makin' millions so the record company won't mind the fact that ya spent a million gettin' there. If ya don't make it they're goin' to drop ya at the end of the year anyway.' My attitude was milk it for what it's worth while ya can. I'd no qualms about it even when articles sayin' we were gettin' into fights an' bein' arseholes started to be in the paper every other day. I think it was 'cause people saw this rock star image an' were jealous of us an' wanted to criticise it. I felt there was a general attitude 'round that people wanted us to fail.

Another thing was that as much as I enjoyed actin' the rock star, I couldn't get over the insincerity of a lot of people who were involved in the entertainment industry. I'd say that 90 odd percent of people who get into bands are in it solely for the chicks an' the money. So when you're idealistic about the music an' ya take it seriously, this kind of behaviour starts to appal you.

It disillusioned me but there was only ever two things that made me feel like givin' up: the first was sometimes when I listened to someone like David Bowie at his best, I'd think, 'man, I'm pissin' into the wind tryin' to create somethin' that great'; the other times were when I'd to deal with all the bullshit in the music business an' I'd think, 'is this fuckin' worth it', ya know? I'd be wonderin', 'what am I goin' to get out of mixin' with this crowd?'.

It really hit me years later when Aslan split an' I'd to go an' work with some of these people. I just couldn't do it. I couldn't pretend I didn't notice the insincerity of it all. I think it's always existed throughout music history but when I was startin' out I was naive, I didn't know what the fuck I was gettin' into. We'd be hangin' out with journalists, doin' coke with them an' gettin' high. Then it'd be in the paper the next day that we were in some club partyin' every fuckin' night. They never mentioned the fact that Blue In Heaven might also be there or In Tua Nua or Cactus World News. It was always the hard lads from Aslan. The old cliché of all publicity bein' good publicity is bullshit. In our case there was often a very negative side to it. I think I can sum that up with this story:

The *NME* had come over to do an interview with us in Jury's Hotel, out in Ballsbridge. I was excited about it. This was the cream of the British rock press sent over to do a major interview – but the whole time the journalist just talked about U2. All the questions were about Bono an' did I know him an' what was he like an' what was he influenced by, ya know, all this bollix. I was fuckin' sick of it an' the reason I was sick of it was 'cause of U2 we'd to consciously go out there an' work within a restricted environment specifically not to be like them.

Like I remember when U2 did *Sunday Bloody Sunday* an' Bono was into wearin' T-shirts an' boots an' shit. I had a look at what he was wearin' an' had to think of somethin' totally different. I started wearin' a leather waistcoat an' leather cacks. I had me hair pulled back in a ponytail. Then I used to do this thing at the beginnin' of the song *Feel No Shame*, the title track off the album, I'd raise me hands, together behind me head, singin', '*My hands are tied and I can't break free*' an' then all the audience would do it with me, d'ya know what I mean? It became part of our stage show. Then U2's next album came out an' the world exclusive of their new single *With or Without You* was on the *Old Grey Whistle Test.* I'm lookin' at the video, ya know, an' Bono walks out in the leather cacks, the leather waistcoat an' he's stretchin' his hand behind his head. I'm just goin, 'Ah bollix, man, what's this?'

An' now this dickhead from the *NME* is quizzin' me about what I thought of Bono? So I got out a bit of paper an' wrote down a number an' said, 'Look, there's Anne-Marie's number. She's the secretary that looks after U2. Anything you want to know about U2, she'll tell you,' an' I walked out of the interview.

Yer man comes runnin' out after me. His boss had sent him over from England with a photographer to get this interview with Aslan so he would've been gettin' his wrist slapped had he not gone back with it. So he chased me out an' he says, 'Look, I'm sorry about that.' I went back an' he spoke about Aslan. He was very attentive an' respectful. I felt then that I'd done a really good interview an' I was particularly lookin' forward to readin' the article the followin' week.

The *NME* comes out on a Wednesday an' on the Tuesday I picked up *The Daily Mirror* for whatever reason an' I'm lookin' at this headline, '*Young Guns Aslan Slam U2*'. The story went somethin' like, '*U2 claim to be from Dublin's slums. Hot newcomers Aslan get even and spill the beans . . .*' an' then it says '*Read all about it in tomorrow's* NME.'

I was fuckin' stunned.

What had happened was, right, after the interview we all drove to Cork 'cause we'd a gig on there that night. After the show we came back to Dublin with the *NME* blokes an' we went out for a drink. They're over from London, they're in our town, an' they don't know anywhere, so we brought them out for a pint an' showed them a good time. At the end of the night your man was pissed an' he said to me, 'Look Christy, I'm sorry about what happened earlier on. But I know you grew up in the same area as Bono.' When he said that I was like, 'Hold on a fuckin' minute. I'm goin' to tell you now what the story is – I didn't grow up in the same area as Bono. Bono grew up close to Finglas but the area he lived in was a little oasis of fuckin' wealth.' I couldn't believe this shit. 'In fact,' I says, 'where he lives was called Cedar Wood, Ballymun, an' when the Ballymun flats were built they changed it to Cedar Wood, Glasnevin 'cause they didn't want to be associated with Ballymun.' An' the journalist based his whole interview on this 30-second tirade 'Bono doesn't come from where I fuckin' come from'.

I was sickened by it. U2 were on tour in America with *The Joshua Tree* album at the time an' they sent us a telegram sayin', 'What the fuck's goin' on? Why are youse badmouthin' us like this in the press?'

I remember later that year U2 came back to Dublin to play in Croke Park an' I sent into their office for VIP tickets for the gig, which all bands do. They sent me back general admittance tickets – that was their way of sayin' fuck you. At the time we were gettin' well-known an' I couldn't just go to a gig an' stand in the middle of the crowd. It would've been a nightmare. Like when you see bands being VIP'd at a gig it's not 'cause they're bein' uppity – well personally it's not that for me – it's 'cause if they go into the general area they just wouldn't see the gig. You'd be gettin' people comin' up to ya an' givin' ya grief or hasslin' ya or whatever.

I'd mouthed off about the Mother Records thing an' then there was this *NME* thing, so it looked like we were just goin' around bashin' U2. But it wasn't like that. I'd given hundreds of interviews durin' that period 'cause we'd an album out but the one that got the most attention was based on this one fuckin' incident. Altogether I'd spoken for, let's say, 36 hours in that particular period of time an' outta all of that a 30-second rant was printed up an' blown out of all proportion. So U2 naturally assumed that we were goin' around jealous – bein' sour grape fuckers – whingin' about U2, which is absolutely not true.

I ironed it all out eventually with Bono. I explained in other interviews over the years that I'd obviously been misquoted in the *NME* article. Just a few years ago somebody said to me somethin' about havin' a run in with U2 an' I said, 'Ahh, that was years ago. It's all water under the bridge now.' The next day that was in the paper too an' Bono musta read it 'cause he sent me a big case of champagne, with a note sayin' like, 'I don't remember havin' a run in with you but if I did I'm sorry if I upset you. Enjoy the champagne.' So, I have to say that was pretty cool of him.

But that *NME* article was just the start of a whole history of bad publicity I'd have with the press. Incidents like that left an indelible mark on my relationships with journalists. It made me wary an' I realised that I was goin' to have to watch what I said in the future. But even knowin' that, I'm still fucked 'cause I try to be honest an' I try to be sincere when I'm talkin' about stuff. When I get into talkin' about the music we do, 'cause it's somethin' very close to me heart an' somethin' I hold very dearly, I don't bullshit about it. So, if I'm in a total honest buzz about our music an' somebody throws in somethin' personal amongst all that I end up bein' recklessly honest about stuff that perhaps I should have kept me mouth shut about. I still get caught on it 'cause I can't jump in an' out of sincerity an' stay guarded. I can't do that.

I'd be meetin' people from newspapers who struck me as very sincere an' I'd consider them, if not friends, then at least colleagues. As far as I was concerned, we were all in this together. Journalists made their livin' out of me givin' a good interview an' I made me livin' out of them printin' a good story, so we were all workin' together. I thought we were helpin' each other out, kinda thing. We were all in the same business, hangin' around in the Pink Elephant and other clubs, sittin' in the same pubs, drinkin' with them, partyin' with them, but when you're outta yer head yer guard is down. Meanwhile, these people are takin' notes the whole time. They weren't partyin' – they were workin'. I didn't see that. I didn't realise that these people were like that so I was absolutely stunned when it inevitably turned on me.

* * *

I suppose the serious partyin' really kicked off when we started tourin' the album in March 1988. We'd a string of dates lined up across Ireland an' a few gigs in England an' Germany. Me an' Billy had already had a taste of the rock'n'roll lifestyle when we were in Germany the first time an' we couldn't wait to get back on the road.

First off we did a few gigs down the country an' I remember it was a mad time. It really was. It was just the usual stuff that we got up to when we were on the road. We were continuin' on this mad, mental journey that we'd already been on for years. I remember, even before the album came out, we were playin' in Tralee, in a place called Horan's an' it was jammed, ya know? We walked into the dressin' room an' Danny was in there with this bird. She was a cracker, an' as soon as she saw us she went over to a stereo in the corner an' pressed the play button. This music comes on an' she starts to do a striptease right there in front of us. We were just standin' there lookin' at her an' at Danny, with his tongue hangin' out, while she got down to her pelt. Then she just kinda picked up her clothes an' walked passed us out the door. We were like, 'What the fuck was that all about Danny?' an' he told us what he did. He was a smart fucker, Danny. He'd been in the dressin' room with this chick before the gig an' he was sittin' there holdin' his head in his hands, pretendin' to be upset. She asked him what was wrong an' he told her this bullshit story. He'd made up this shit like, 'Look, eh, every night before the gig we fly over these two strippers from Birmingham an' it's kinda become a bit of a tradition for the lads to have a striptease before they go on. But the girls are fogged in at fuckin' Birmingham airport an' they can't make it.' Then he says we wouldn't go on stage unless we got our strip show an' that there'd be a riot, ya know? She was there sayin', 'Is there anything I can do to help?' He says, 'Aw I couldn't ask ya to do that for me,' an' that's when we walked in – right in time for our striptease.

As a singer you do get a lot of attention from girls in the audience but I don't think it's about looks or anythin' like that – it's just 'cause you're in a band. It's that rock'n'roll buzz. Some of them would throw their underwear on the stage an' the roadies would joke about collectin' it all an' settin' up a knicker stall. It was fairly strange for five lads from Finglas an' Ballymun to be gettin' this kinda attention. Some of the lads were like kids in a sweetshop.

We headed off to London after that to do a coupla video shoots for *Loving Me Lately* before joinin' the Northern Ireland band Stiff Little Fingers in Germany. Girlfriends an' wives weren't allowed to go on tour at that early stage so here we were – five young men on our own together havin' a fuckin' ball, ya know? We'd come from a very Catholic country where there wasn't a lot goin' on. Ireland years ago wasn't the Ireland it is today. We didn't have all the pubs an' clubs an' shit yis have now. So we were after goin' from livin' an' bein' reared in a kinda workin'-class background straight into the jet set kinda lifestyle. We were in a rock'n'roll band an' we were determined to live it up.

We became the old rock'n'roll cliché by thrashin' our hotel rooms. I remember walkin' in one night an' there wasn't a stick of fuckin' furniture in the room. Everythin' was gone – the bed, the TV, everything. I went into the bathroom an' there it was – all piled up in a heap in the bath with the taps on. Another time I came in an' the TV was hangin' out the window an' it was still plugged in, so if I pulled out the plug the fuckin' thing would go. If I lifted up the TV an' took the strain of it the plug would whip out an' I wouldn't have been able to hold it. I'm sittin' there in a dilemma, goin', 'What the fuck!' It took me about 15 minutes to edge the thing back in the window.

We even tried to get Danny Kenny. He used to have this little pony tail, ya know, them little rats' tails, that people wore in the 1980s? It was a big long yoke. I used to hate the thing an' I wanted to cut it off him when he was asleep. I was goin' to leave it on his chest so that when he got up outta the sack it'd fall on the floor but he always fuckin' woke up anytime I went near him.

In between gigs we'd be drivin' across the country for hours, bored in the back of a van. We played cards everywhere we went. We'd this one game called Switch an' whoever lost would have to do a forfeit, d'ya know what I mean? Like one time I had to queue up in a busy shop in Dublin an' ask for 20 smokes. When the woman behind the counter asked me for the money I had to start sayin' at the top of me voice, 'D'ya not know who I am? I'm Christy Dignam from Aslan, surely I don't have to pay for cigarettes here.' The whole shop was just starin' at me while outside the window those fuckers were breakin' their bollix laughin'.

Another time we were drivin' through Portlaoise on a Saturday afternoon an' Joe had to get out in the middle of the main street, in the middle of the day, an' sing, *'You ain't nothin' but a hound dog . . .'* an' start doin' all these Elvis impersonations. Alan lost a good few times. One time he'd to go out on a leash an' be walked up the street in Cork, with his cacks around his ankles, by one of the roadies.

But there was one roadie, Gerry, who'd never got beaten in the cards, never ever. We were all sayin', 'You'll lose someday Gerry – we'll get ya back then ya bastard an' give ya a special punishment.' An' of course his luck ran out in Germany. We were lookin' out for a good forfeit for him to do an' one day we found the perfect one. There was a middle page spread of a Manchester United player, half-naked in a fashion magazine. Gerry had to spread it out on the floor in the dressin' room, lie on the ground beside it, leanin' on his elbow, an' pretend he was wankin' off to it. Then we sent this big German security guy in to get two cans of beer out of the fridge. We were all standin' in the corridor behind him when the guard opened the door an' walked in. There was Gerry lyin' on his side right, his cacks pulled down around his ankles, yankin' the bejasus outta himself. Of course once he did the forfeit he jumped up an' started tryin' to explain to the guard, ya know, 'Listen this is just a game of cards we play'. The guard was lookin' at him, probably goin', 'Yeah, course it fuckin is', ya know? But Gerry kept makin' it worse by tryin' to explain it, gettin' himself in deeper an' deeper.

All this stuff was part of bein' on tour. There's a lot of pressure in the music business an' a lot of hard work on the road, so we worked hard an' partied hard. I felt we deserved it. Think about it – I'd gone from soup kitchens to the fuckin' Münich Hilton. What else are ya gonna do? Are ya gonna be gathered an' collected an' make the right decisions? Fuck off. Rock'n'roll is not about that.

People might consider some of the behaviour excessive but I make no apologies for any of it. If I wanted me life to be any different I would've become a solicitor or a doctor or whatever. I loved the excess – that was what rock'n'roll was about for me.

While we were on tour I was doin' every drug ya could mention – acid, hash, an' there was a lot of coke goin' round. Now, to me, drugs weren't even necessarily part of bein' in a band or anythin'. It just gave ya an excuse to use them. I think ya get a certain leeway 'cause you're a musician. I was never a big drinker 'cause I never enjoyed the buzz of gettin' drunk. I didn't like alcohol, probably 'cause both me grandfathers had died of alcoholism. So I did drugs instead. An' when I took heroin, I knew I was home.

I'd been dabblin' with heroin a coupla of times in the two years before we went tourin' with Stiff Little Fingers but that's all it was – a bit of dabblin'. I was doin' a little bit here an' there. I was snortin' it an' that but it wasn't all the time. It was only whenever I came across it kinda thing. I wasn't payin' attention to how often I took it. I didn't even think I had to. To me, it was like the way I took coke – just randomly.

I was very ignorant of the whole heroin scene. I didn't know anythin' about it. To me a heroin addict was someone puttin' a needle into their arm an' lyin' in a fuckin' alleyway. It wasn't someone that was rockin' in a band. As far as I was concerned, there was a big difference between someone who was gonna snort a little bit an' stick a needle in their veins, ya know? I didn't see that big a danger in it 'cause up to that point nothin' else had come back an' slapped me on the arse, so I didn't think that this was goin' to. I'd tried all these other drugs an' had some kinda recreational handle on them. I thought heroin wouldn't be any different – that was the first big mistake I made.

Then I got sick. The band did a few dates in Germany an' we were goin' back to Ireland to finish off the rest of the tour. We were still in Germany when I started gettin' pains runnin' through me muscles. I had all these aches rackin' me body but even worse I had this absolute feelin' of desolation inside me. It was a horrible, horrible feelin'. It was like a huge depression. It's very difficult for me to try an' adequately describe it. It was like, if ya can imagine, you've just heard your whole family has been wiped out in a massive disaster, your spouse or girlfriend has been fuckin' around havin' an affair behind your back an' she finishes with ya an' your business partner has just ripped ya off for every penny you own. If ya can imagine all those things put together an' all happenin' to ya on the same day – think of the depression that would send you spirallin' into. There's absolutely no way ya can see yer way out of that.

I'd no idea what was wrong with me – nobody did. I thought I was comin' down with some mad bug or virus. We rang a doctor an' he came to the hotel an' examined me but even he couldn't help me.

As soon as we flew back into Dublin Airport we were picked up an' brought straight to Waterford for a gig that night. I managed to get through the show but I remember after it Danny Kenny tellin' me I'd to go off an' sign a load of autographs. I was sayin', 'No, fuckin' way. I can't, I'm absolutely in bits.' There was a few vibes with the rest of the band, like they were kinda blankin' me a bit, but I didn't pay that much attention 'cause I was in bits. All I wanted was to get into bed. I went into me room an' shut the door.

This mate of mine had come down to Waterford with me an' he was waitin' in the room when I came in. He took out a bag of heroin an' we started smokin' it – BOOM – that was it. Whatever I was feelin' was gone – all that sickness an' aches an' pains an' the desolate fuckin' hell I was in suddenly vanished, just like that. I was sittin' there, me head floatin', tellin' him about the state I was in leavin' Germany an' how I was feelin' great now. He turns around an' says, 'Relax, you were just strung out pal.'

An' that was it – that was the first time I realised I was addicted to heroin.

The Ace of Spades

It wasn't a huge leap for me to go from smokin' hash to doin' heroin, ya know? I was already in that drugs sub-culture, so it was only a matter of time before I came across it. Now I know this might sound really stupid an' naive but when I did try it there was nothin' obvious to scare me off it. When I first took heroin it was just startin' to come into Dublin. There weren't addicts hangin' out on the streets like there is today. I couldn't look at them an' say, 'Bollixed if I'm touchin' heroin, look what it did to those people', d'ya know what I'm sayin'? Anythin' I knew about heroin I'd seen on TV, on fuckin' *Starsky and Hutch* or whatever.

How I first came into contact with it was I used to score hash off this Hell's Angels biker bloke over in the Mount Pleasant flats on the Southside – I think those flats are gone now. One day, when I was about 20, or even 19, I can't remember exactly, I went over to get some smoke. He was asleep an' his bird says to me, 'There's no hash here, only skag.' I was afraid to reveal me ignorance an' say, 'What the fuck is a skag?' So I said, 'Yeah, I'll take that.' So that was it – I'd bought me first ten spot of skag, ya know?

I remember lookin' at this little bag I'd got for ten quid an' comparin' it to what I woulda got in hash. It was just a tiny bit of powder. So I had to ask her what do you do with it an' she said, 'Just snort it, it's a lovely buzz,' kinda thing.

There I was one day goin' off to buy some hash an' I'd ended up comin' across heroin. This is somethin' I always felt about the legalisation of hash. When you're lookin' round for soft drugs like hash, you've to go into the criminal underworld 'cause it's illegal, right? An' that increases the risk of ya bein' exposed to harder drugs like heroin, which was exactly what happened to me. If I hadn't had to go to some dingy, scruffy, little flat somewhere to score me hash, there's probably a chance that I wouldn't have encountered heroin. That's the way I look at it.

It was me younger brother's birthday at the time an' he wanted to go out an' do his first drinkin' session so a couple of carloads of us drove out to Donabate. We were goin' to stay the night, pitch up tents an' have a big fuckin' barbecue an' that. I remember drivin' along the beach an' we'd stop an' I'd run up into the dunes lookin' for a flat spot to pitch the tents on.

So, I'd get out an' look around at all the dunes an' think, 'nah, this is no good'. An' I'd get back in, drive a bit more an' have another good look. Eventually I seen this lovely flat bit of grass so we stopped an' put up our tents. It was gettin' dark at this stage so we built a big fire in the middle of it, fried burgers an' had wine an' hash an' all that.

At one stage durin' the night, though, while all the others were around the fire, locked outta their heads, I took out the bag of heroin an' looked at it again. I'd had this bag of skag in me pocket the whole time but I hadn't told anyone about it. I'd worked out it was actually heroin an' I just instinctively knew not to go blabbin' about it, ya know? As little as I knew about heroin I was still aware that there was a stigma attached to it. I was holdin' it up so I could see it thinkin', 'man, it's a fuckin' tiny bit of powder'. I remember thinkin' again what a bad deal it was for the money as I poured some into the palm of me hand.

I lifted it up to me nose an' took like a sharp intake of breath through me nostril an' the little bit of gear disappeared. I sat back down an' this time, compared to when I first smoked hash an' got nothin' off it, this time I felt somethin'.

The only way I can describe it is that for the first time in me life, I felt normal. I'd always been vaguely aware of this emptiness inside me, that made me feel distant from everythin' an' everybody I'd ever been with – even within me own family. I just felt dull inside. I'd achieved all these little goals in me life but as I crossed each one off the list all I was left with was a hole. I was never satisfied. I was always frettin' around the edges of me accomplishments. I could recognise what was goin' on around me but inside, inside I was dead. In place of what I presumed were real feelin's was this gnawin' hole in the pit of me stomach. But I wasn't so acutely aware of it 'til I took this bit of heroin an' the hole just slowly evaporated.

I was lyin' down on the grass, in front of the fire an' lookin' out over the sea. I was warm, safe an' at ease with meself. I was fine. That's the best way I can sum it up – I was ok now. I'll never forget it. The feelin' I got from heroin was the opposite of what people describe as bein' high or stoned on drugs. I just felt like now I knew how Kathryn felt when she woke up first in the mornin'.

As we went on with the party I kept thinkin' to meself, 'that was a really sweet buzz', ya know? I kept it to meself, 'cause I realised I'd broken a taboo. Like I was sayin' before how ya read all this stuff about heroin an' how it's so dangerous an' it kills you. So when ya do it an' ya wake up the next mornin' an' everythin' is grand – you're not dead, you're not lyin' in an alleyway strung out, you're not a fucked up junkie – ya think, 'well, this is bullshit what people are sayin' about it'.

We ended up havin' a serious session that night an' the whole lot of us were out of our heads. I remember wakin' up the next mornin' at about 9 o'clock. I was in me tent, fucked, when me brother came in an' said, 'Christy, c'mere, you better come out an' have a look at this.' So I crawled out of the tent an' looked around. If ya can imagine, right, we're on this little flat piece of grass, dunes all around an' at the top of one of the dunes I seen about four or five golfers standin' there lookin' down on us. We were on the green of a fuckin' golf course. There's about a four-foot high circle of cinders from this fire we'd built in the middle of their green. There's bits of burgers, bottles everywhere, tents – the place was completely trashed. So we just legged it to the cars an' got back to Finglas as fast as we could.

So I was back home an' I was still thinkin' about how it'd felt after I'd taken the gear. I hadn't become instantly addicted to the stuff. I wasn't rushin' out to buy more, ya know? That was another one of the myths that was goin' around later. I didn't turn into a ragin' psychotic junkie, lookin' for his next fix. If somebody had said to me then, 'Christy that's it – ya did the last bit of heroin in the world,' I wouldn't have cared less. I would've done another bit had there been more but I didn't, simply 'cause I didn't have any more, not 'cause I was scared of it. I was no longer wary of it either.

I think the next time I did it wasn't 'til years later. It was around the time Kiera was born an' I got some off that bloke in exchange for some cocaine. So I did a little bit with this bloke but it was probably a few months after that before I tried it again. An' then I remember Kathryn's brother had come home from Australia an' he wanted to set up a business. At the time aluminium windows were big money an' I kinda had a lot of experience in that from workin' in the windows factory so I told him I'd help him set it up. I used to go down to the Glasnevin Industrial

Estate to get materials an' there was a bloke who worked in a factory there an' he was a heroin addict. At lunchtime I'd be hangin' around an' I just got talkin' to him. One day he asked me if I wanted a smoke an' he took out some tin foil an' burned a bit of heroin on it. I'd be up there every other day an' if he was around I'd go up an' hang out with him out the back of the industrial unit an' smoke a bit of gear. That's how I gradually got into heroin.

I started buyin' a bit off this guy, just a bit of a gram for a Saturday night, sorta thing. Then I was doin' it every other weekend, ya know? I'd get a bit for Saturday night an' I'd still have a bit left over on Sunday. Then, without thinkin' about it, I'd get more on Saturday to have some for Sunday an' Monday, d'ya know what I mean? Then I was doin' it twice durin' the week. Ya have to understan' that this was over a very long period of time, maybe two years or so. I didn't become addicted to heroin over the course of a few weeks or a few months. It was a slow, shallow slide that I wasn't aware of 'cause it was so gradual.

Heroin is very widespread now but back in the eighties Dublin was riddled with it. There were marches all the time on dealer's flats, the Concerned Parents Against Drugs were very active an' ya could get a bad hidin' if ya were caught in the wrong area havin' anythin' to do with heroin. There were only a few places that ya could go into to get it an' it was more difficult for me 'cause I couldn't anonymously go in an' score. By this time I was too well-known. So, I started hangin' round with people who were doin' heroin an' who were part of that whole scene.

There was this one bloke that I used to get to score for me. When he went off to the flat complexes I'd give him money to get himself some as well. I was like the goose that laid the golden egg for him. We made a good partnership. That bloke's dead now – he overdosed. A lot of people I knew who started usin' heroin round the same time as me have died since then. They've overdosed or they're in jail or HIV positive or somethin'.

When me usage did go up I still didn't see that as somethin' that I was makin' happen. I seen that just as somethin' that was happenin'. I was comin' across heroin more regularly all right, but I thought it was by chance. It never occurred to me that I was actually makin' meself run into it. With hindsight, of course, I was actively seekin' it out but I didn't know it at the time. I didn't know that these were the first signs of addiction.

Drugs work on a psychological an' emotional level. I'd say to meself: 'I know this is a dangerous drug an' as soon as it starts becomin' a problem, I'll stop. I'm not gonna be like all these other fuckin' people that were caught out – I'm too smart for that. What I'll do is, I'll use it occasionally an' as soon as I see it becomin' a problem, I'll stop immediately.' So ya tell yourself that lie. An' for a while you do manage to do that. Ya stick to this occasional, sorta casual use until it becomes more frequent as time goes by – but ya don't really notice that progression until later on.

Initially though, when you start to take heroin, it gives ya a little kick to your creativity 'cause it changes your perception an' your perspective – at the very beginnin'. It gave me an air of confidence when I was writin' stuff or when I was bein' a father, or a husband or whatever. It made me feel good about meself in what I was doin' 'cause it killed all the doubts. An' that confidence actually generated its own cauterisin' effect on the hole I was tellin' ya 'bout – the emptiness in me stomach. I was goin' round for years with this uncomfortable, gnawin' feelin' inside me but the first time I took heroin the hole was gone. Then I woke up one mornin' an' I'd that gnawin' feelin' back, but now I'd a choice – I could either endure the pain an' emptiness or get rid of it. It's nice the odd day to rid yourself of the discomfort of just bein' alive an' it became very seductive knowin' that I could find peace of mind in the bottom of a bag.

Ya have all these feelings, tellin' ya to do it an' they're hard to resist. When I did heroin I used to feel like the ace of spades – the best lover on earth, the best songwriter, the best front man, the best friend, the best. . . . Eventually though that fuckin' effect goes but it doesn't happen for a while. At the start it's all good. By the time you realise it's not happenin' an' it's not workin' anymore, it's too late – you're fucked.

Meanwhile, the band were drinkin' till the cows came home. I wasn't into that drinkin' buzz – I never was. There was just this one little thing I did an' that was a bit of heroin every now an' then. That was my buzz. The way I saw it at the time was it wasn't a big fuckin' deal. What I didn't see was that I was slowly driftin' away from the rest of the group – me friends an' me family.

I went from bein' part of a band, socially an' professionally, where everythin' was done together an' for the same, common goal, to separatin' from them 'cause of the stigma attached to the drug I was usin'. I was bein' secretive an' lyin' to them. There was a dishonesty now 'cause I'd to hide stuff from them. An' 'cause you're on heroin, ya gear your life towards usin' an' ya replace your friends with unsavoury people.

I'd been good friends with those lads in the band but a gap developed. If I ever felt alone what I'd do is I'd go out an' get a bit of gear an' that would kill the loneliness – instantly. Instead of dealin' with all the emotional stumblin' blocks that ya come up against, ya avoid them by replacin' them with heroin. I mean, the logical thing to do would've been to go to someone like Kathryn or Joe an' tell them, ya know? It's easy to say that now but at the time I didn't think I'd a problem – I really didn't.

* * *

But it all caught up with me that night in Waterford. I suppose it was inevitable. I was distraught when me mate told me in the hotel room that I was strung out. I was absolutely stunned that I'd let meself get inta that position. The first thing I thought was, 'I'm gonna have to knock this on the head. I have to get meself together now. I'm goin' to sort this out', right, but before I had a chance to do anythin' about it, the shit hit the fan.

The other lads in the band had seen me in a fuckin' jocker in Germany an' just gettin' through the gig in Waterford. One minute I'm dyin', ya know, I've the worst bleedin' pneumonia on Earth. Then five minutes later I'm the ace of spades, brand fuckin' new, d'ya know what I mean?

They came up to me after the gig an' said, 'We know who those scumbags are who you're hangin' out with an' we know what's goin' on.' It was the first time I was confronted about it an' it stopped me in me tracks. Up to then I thought I was so clever that nobody even noticed what I was doin'. I thought nobody had a clue. To me, realisin' I'd a problem came out of the blue but obviously it didn't for them; they'd been watchin' me an' seein' this comin' for some time.

There's a lot of work involved in bein' a drug addict an' that would've been the lead up to why the band got pissed off. You're in a situation where ya might have a big gig on an' after the show ya have to go to a restaurant to soft soap these guys from the record companies. They're goin' to decide your careers but the way I saw it was, I had a choice. I'd say to meself, 'If I don't get gear I'm goin' to be of no use over here at this meetin' 'cause I won't be able to keep me head. I need to go off, get the gear an' when I arrive back I'll be the ace of spades, the best fuckin' negotiator on God's Earth.' So ya say to yourself, 'It's goin' to take me half an hour to do this', an' ya make up some excuse as to why you're goin' to be half an hour late. Ya head off to get some gear but the guy that has it isn't there so you have to wait for him. Ya know you're not goin' anywhere 'til he arrives. Everythin' else is put on hold 'til ya score an' ya arrive back an hour an' a half later.

Even on a day-to-day basis, I'd be arrivin' late at a rehearsal, right, an' givin' a dodgy excuse for where I'd been. I'd rub underneath the car an' manky up me hand, sayin' I got a puncture on the way over. After the rehearsal one of the lads would offer to give me a lift to collect me tyre from the garage an' I'd say, 'What tyre?', before rememberin' I'd told them some bullshit story an' sayin' somethin' like, 'Ah yeah, I'll collect it later,' sorta thing.

Sometimes I didn't get any gear an' I'd have to go in sick. I was supposed to show up for practise or whatever at 9 o'clock but I'd kinda hunt around 'til 11 o'clock tryin' to score. If I didn't get any I'd eventually have to go in sufferin' from withdrawals. But then I'd be leavin' an hour or so later with another dodgy excuse to get out.

It got to the point when I'd just two things to do every day – get to rehearsal an' get meself straight. But if it was goin' be a throw-up between the two of them there was no fuckin' competition about which I was gonna choose. That was me reality. I wasn't goin' anywhere till I got gear an' I justified it to meself by sayin', 'Well, I'm gonna be no use to them if I go in sick anyway.'

When I did score I'd have a quick smoke in the car before I went into work. I'd be walkin' in thinkin' I was the picture of fuckin' health. Half an hour later I'd have me head in me lap an' me eyes half-closed. At the same time ya think you've everybody conned 'cause you feel so good an' confident within yourself. Ya think you're on top of everythin' but ya don't realise that everybody is just, out of probably embarrassment or fuckin' pity, avoidin' confrontin' ya.

That was the routine for just one day, d'ya know what I mean? Now think what it would be like dealin' with that for 20 days. Sometimes I made an excuse an' I might get away with it but how many other times did I do that to the band an' they knew exactly what was goin' on? They just got a pain in their bollix with it.

The other person I'd to hide it away from was of course, me wife, Kathryn. It was a bit easier to keep me addiction hidden from Kathryn 'cause she was out durin' the day. I'd be off doin' all me connivin' an' scorin' before she came home from work. She'd come back in the evenin' an' I'd have gotten sorted that day an' I'd be fine. I don't think she noticed but if she had her suspicions she didn't reveal them to me. I think there's a big difference between suspectin' somethin', even if you're 99 percent sure, an' bein' absolutely sure. An' that one percent of doubt will put ya off takin' action 'cause once ya acknowledge a situation exists like that, a situation of such critical importance, yer bringin' it to the forefront an' ya have to do somethin' about it. She woulda had to deal with all the repercussions that confrontin' me woulda brought. It probably seems incredible that I thought I could get away with it for so long but this was nothin' compared to how much further I slipped into addiction. I mean at this stage I was only dippin' me toes into the fuckin' water.

There was a bit of a showdown that night after the gig in Waterford. A coupla the lads basically came to me an' laid into me. They were sayin' things like, 'What the fuck are ya up to?', ya know? 'We're workin' our bollix off an' you're goin' to fuck it all up by hangin' 'round with them scumbags. Ya think we're not wise to what's goin' on?' But I thought they were over-reactin' to a minor situation 'cause as far as I was aware I was not lettin' this heroin buzz interfere with things. Everythin' was bein' done; everything was bein' achieved. Anythin' we'd ever gone for or ever wanted we were gettin' – we'd gone for a record deal an' we'd got it; we went for the Bowie gig an' we'd got it; we wanted to get on the Stiff Little Fingers tour an' we'd done it. I was thinkin', 'what's the problem here? What are they whingin' about? So what if I'm takin' a bit of gear, so fuckin' what?'

I was in denial of the whole thing. But, of course, I felt some regret 'cause at the end of the day music was somethin' I loved an' I didn't want to hurt any of the band – they were me mates. So when I sat down with them the next day I promised I was goin' to pull it together an' sort meself out, ya know? The events of the last 24 hours were enough to convince me that somethin' was goin' wrong. Here I was after bein' confronted by me mates 'bout me heroin buddies just hours after findin' out I was strung out. They'd no idea of the extent of me addiction – but I was startin' to think that maybe I was after bitin' off more than I could chew.

* * *

I genuinely meant it when I said I was goin' to get it together an' stay off the gear. I didn't want to jeopardise our future an' I believed the band when they warned me that it was in jeopardy. The confrontation in Waterford just confirmed in me mind that okay something had gone wrong an' that I was gonna have to fix it. I thought, 'now it's just been verified for me that it's a problem, I'll stop'. But that was when I gradually began to realise that heroin is not the fuckin' inoffensive, recreational drug that I'd thought it was. I'd no idea how hard it would be to just stop. I was so fuckin' naive. Like, I'd bein' doin' heroin on an' off for what – two or three years? An' there I was thinkin' it was just a matter of makin' a decision an' that would be it. I didn't even consider bringin' Kathryn into the whole mess 'cause I assumed that I could nip the problem in the bud. How wrong I was.

By all outward appearances we were a band that was about to set the world on fire, but internally we were startin' to fall apart – well, at least the rest of the lads could see that but I couldn't. At that point I still thought I'd this heroin thing sussed an' I pulled meself out of it to a certain extent. I stayed away from the people who were all part of the heroin scene – the dealers an' users that I was hangin' round with. We'd a few more Irish dates before we finished up to get ready for our first American tour an' I just concentrated on gettin' through them.

The momentum from the success of *Feel No Shame* propelled us along for the rest of the tour an' every night we walked on stage we were greeted with a fuckin' roar of excitement. It was crazy – people were runnin' up onto the stage, grabbin' me an' stage-divin' back into the audience while we launched into song after song from this album that was at the top of the charts.

But, no matter how hard I tried the smack still niggled away in the back of me mind. It never went away. It's like bein' told ya can't have sex, ya know? If I said to you when ya were younger, that ya could never have sex, an' I drummed it into you – ya can never have sex, ya can never have sex – an' you never do, then if ya go to your grave never havin' had sex, it's not goin' to be as big a deal to ya. But if you've had sex an' then you're told ya can never have sex again, havin' already tasted the joy of it, then it's a different story. It's more difficult to resist. I had tasted the joy of heroin, ya know?

We finished the tour in the summer of 1988 an' all the hullabaloo died down. Everyone stopped fuckin' scrutinisin' every move I made an' the heroin thing wasn't mentioned again. But things had changed in the band. I'd started to feel a bit distant from the others an' now that we'd had a row over the reason things were not good.

In the meantime, we'd gone home to get ready for the tour in the States an' I slotted back into that family buzz again. I thought about tellin' Kathryn what had happened in Waterford but I just couldn't. We were happy at home. We'd moved into a new house in Valley Park in Finglas 'cause we'd had a few problems out in the cottage. I was away giggin' all the time so Kathryn had to spend a lot of time there on her own with the baby. There was no central heatin' in the house when we'd first moved in an' we were stayin' in her mother's while we were gettin' it put in. One night there was a huge storm an' when we came home the next day there was these two big elm trees lyin' in the driveway. The end of one of them was lyin' on the roof where our bedroom was. If we'd been in the house when they came down on top of it we'd have been fuckin' destroyed. We got the gaff fixed up then an' we'd a skip outside in the garden. A few days later I was off doin' a gig an' this bloke knocked on the door an' asked Kathryn who owned the skip 'cause he said he wanted to take some of the wood outta it. She was just sayin', 'Yeah, go ahead', when he tried to push her back into the house an' come in after her. She started shoutin' me name, pretendin' there was someone else in the back an' he legged it. After that she wouldn't go back to the house on her own so we moved down to Valley Park. I missed the cottage but I was more relaxed havin' Kathryn an' Kiera near our families.

I struggled to stay off the gear while I was at home but within a day or two I was off scorin' again. I'd gotten a shock in Waterford but I'd kinda gotten over it. I'd say to meself, 'Right, now I know how dangerous heroin is, I'll just take it an odd time.' An' it was so easy to start believin' the same old lie again – that I could control it.

I describe the lure of heroin as like that of watchin' a beautiful woman in the distance. Every time ya take heroin ya see this beautiful woman, right. An' each time ya take it ya get closer to her. But the closer you're gettin' the more ugly she's startin' to appear, ya know? By the time ya actually get close enough to realise she's a fuckin' evil old hag, you're ensnared – you're physically addicted – an' it's too late to do anythin'. You're runnin' to a standstill 'cause at this stage you're just takin' gear to stop havin' withdrawals. You're takin' gear to stop yourself from bein' sick. You're not takin' it to be stoned or to have a good time; you're takin' it just to stave off the withdrawals an' the agony they bring.

Years later I studied an' read everythin' there was about heroin to try an' understand me addiction. I mean heroin is made from morphine an' morphine is named after the Greek God of sleep, right? An' heroin really does put your reality an' all your pain to sleep. The reason why withdrawals are so severe is 'cause we've an endorphin gland in our brain that deals with all the aches an' pains that we get everyday. Like, when you need to excrete toxins ya get that little pain in your stomach that's goin' to turn into a severe cramp if ya don't go for a shit. This endorphin gland releases your own kind of body morphine to kill that pain. If ya bang into somethin' or stub your toe this endorphin gland deals with all those little things. So when you're usin' morphine or heroin, which is morphine-based, you're tellin' this endorphin gland, 'I don't need you. I have me own source.' The gland becomes redundant an' stops workin'. When you stop takin' the morphine or heroin, this thing is dead so all those little aches an' pains that are supposed to be dealt with are runnin' unchecked into your brain an' you're left in fuckin' agony.

So you're livin' with a situation where you're strugglin' with all these symptoms an' this desolate feelin' inside an' ya know, ya know the whole time, that you have this little bag of powder that will sort it out – instantly.

Ya start reasonin' it out, ya know? Ya say to yourself, 'If I do some now then I'll be able to get this day over with an' do what I have to do.' That frees ya up to deal with the addiction the next day. But then you've got work commitments or whatever so you can't take the time off that you need to go through withdrawal. So you keep sayin', 'Right, I'm gonna to do it tomorrow.' You develop a 'mañana' mentality – I'll do it tomorrow, I'll do it tomorrow, I'll do it tomorrow, I'll. . . . In the meantime you're gettin' in deeper an' deeper an' deeper. You'll go on doin' that for years an' years, an' while you're puttin' it off the addiction is gettin' worse an' worse.

It's a very, very, clever, fuckin' cunning disease. I didn't realise I had a sickness. I thought I was unfortunate enough to have run into some drug that had addictive qualities an' maybe I'd underestimated how dangerous it was. I refused to consider meself a drug addict even though I'd realised I was addicted to heroin. It's a bizarre distinction when you read it here in black an' white but it's a fuckin' vital one when you're tryin' to protect yourself from the knowledge that you've got a serious drug problem. Let me try an' explain that.

Like, there are alcoholics to this day livin' in this country who have lost their marriages, maybe a couple of marriages, an' their jobs, 'cause of alcohol, 'cause of heavy drinkin'. But they're successful business-wise so they can afford to keep drinkin' an' they'll still not admit to themselves that they're alcoholics. They see an alcoholic as the guy sittin' in a doorway on O'Connell Street with a bottle of wine in his hand. I saw a drug addict as the equivalent to that in drug terms. A drug addict was someone out there sellin' their arse or somethin', tryin' to get the price of the next hit. The picture just didn't fit me.

The Bust

The last gig we did before we headed off on our first tour of the States was the 1988 millennium concert in the centre of Dublin. It was a special day. Dublin was 1,000 years old an' to mark the occasion we were asked to headline a free concert at the Ilac Centre, just off O'Connell Street. We played to thousands of people – our people – an' it was like a kinda thank you to all the friends an' family for the support over the last year. If there's one picture that I think captures Aslan at our peak, before everythin' disintegrated, I would have to say it's a photo that was taken of us on stage that day. For me personally the photo symbolises the stark fact that I was goin' in opposite directions at the same time in me personal an' in me public life. The gig was a turnin' point for me an' Aslan in a year that would see us become massive stars before throwin' it all away.

That show still has a resonance for me that I remember to this day. A few kinda biggish acts like Mary Coughlan an' some other bands, The Fountainhead an' that, had already played durin' the day so by the time we took the stage later that evenin' the atmosphere was charged. Ya could just feel the expectation comin' off the crowd. I mean we were a band with two Top 10 singles in the charts an' a Number 1 album an' here we were ready to go on stage in our home town in front of 15,000 people, out celebratin' the fact that their city was 1,000 years old. As we walked on I remember thinkin' it was even better than the buzz we'd got at Slane. I glanced out over the crowd as I reached for the microphone. I could just make out the skyline of the buildins' behind this massive audience. A deafenin' chant went up "ASLAN, ASLAN, ASLAN . . .'. I looked over at Joe an' he'd a massive grin on his face. I was tryin' to shout over at him before the first song but he couldn't even hear me.

We launched into one of our openin' songs, *Let Loose in Heaven*. It was written as a dedication to Phil Lynott after he'd died a coupla years before. We got Brian Downey, Thin Lizzy's drummer, to come out on stage an' play the song with us – the crowd went wild.

This was a personal tribute from me to Lynott. I'll tell you why I held Phil Lynott in such high regard – apart from the obvious reason of his talent. Years before I was bringin' one of our first demos to every record company an' manager's office I could find in Dublin. I was only a kid at the time an' just startin' out, it musta been in Meelah XVIII, an' I was always walkin' round with this tape of our stuff in me pocket. I went into the Westland Studios on Westland Row to try an' get someone to listen to it an' there was Thin Lizzy – sittin' in the hallway, waitin' for a meetin' with someone.

Phil Lynott was standin' there, this long, skinny character with a huge bush of black hair on his head an' he started talkin' to me. He was kind of givin' me advice an' just yappin' an' tellin' me what I should do with the tape an' who I should bring it to, ya know? Here I was at the very, very beginnin' of me musical career an' they were huge at the time. I thought, 'fair fuckin' play to him for takin' the time to offer me encouragement'. I thought that was very, very cool, ya know? It left a big impression on me an' I still admire that about the man. I was devastated when Phil died. When it all came out about me own drug abuse a lot of armchair psychologists said I was tryin' to fulfil a prophesy of followin' Phil to the grave which, I have to admit, might have had a bit of truth to it.

So, the Ilac gig was to be our last show before we headed off on our first tour of the States. Danny had organised for us to play a string of dates across America to coincide with the launch of *Feel No Shame* in July. We were gonna play in New York an' Boston before stoppin' off in Toronto. Then we were gonna head over to the West Coast an' San Francisco, San Diego an' a few other cities. I remember we got paid 47,000 quid for the millennium gig right, but by the end of that day we only had about 700 quid left. Not only did we have to pay the police an' the security people, an' all the rest of it, but we also splashed out on a fleet of limos for our families. I had a limo go pick up me mother an' me granny from Finglas, me granny was still alive at the time, an' bring them to the gig. Here was me mother, who'd had a really hard life an' stuff like that, an' she was able to look out at the neighbours from the windows of a chauffeur-driven car, d'ya know what I mean? Me ma was kinda the same as me da in that she never really let on if she was impressed by all this fancy show business lark but I remember her face gettin' outta the limo. She was just beamin'. To me, the cost of that in money terms was totally irrelevant.

There's another reason why this gig was important to us. At that time we were signed to EMI Britain an' when you're signed with EMI there are three labels you can go with when it comes to marketing in America – Capitol, Manhattan or EMI America. They've to decide whether they want to take ya on. So all these Americans came over to see the band an' they're all there at this gig, checkin' us out. They couldn't have seen us at a better time – playin' to 15,000 people on a very proud day in Dublin's history. At the end of it we were gettin' into our limos an' we could still hear the crowd singin', '*Everybody hits you, Everybody knocks you down . . .*'.

After the gig we all went to the Trocedero Restaurant in Dublin an' laid on a big spread for all these huge Americans, ya know? We were givin' it all the soft-soapin' but we knew after playin' such a blindin' gig that it was already in the bag. Sure enough, when we were all standin' up after dinner, the guy from Capitol, a fat bloke with a huge belly an' a ponytail reached over, shook me by the hand an' says, 'The next time I see you boys will be Stateside.'

That day it seemed that all our troubles were behind us. We were already mega in our own country. We'd just finished a successful European tour an' now we were gonna become superstars in the States.

I kissed Kathryn at the front door before gettin' into a taxi for the airport. She was smilin' at me an' wavin' Kiera's little arm goodbye to her daddy. I got to the airport an' met the rest of the lads. Waterford seemed to be far behind us an' we were on a really good buzz, messin' around the departures lounge waitin' for our flight. When you're on the ascent nobody knows how far it's goin' to go. As I was gettin' on the plane I remembered I'd left me camera behind. I just thought 'fuck it, I'll bring one the next time'. I assumed it would go on forever.

I'd no idea that the millennium gig would be the last time we would play together as a band in Dublin for five years an' one day. Lookin' back on it now, when you're outside an' removed from the immediate situation, it's obvious what was goin' to happen. At the time, though, when you're in the middle of it all, ya don't really see all that. Everythin' was just part of the roller coaster.

* * *

The American tour was hugely successful. We got a great reaction wherever we played. I remember on the first few dates we were playin' support to a guy called Graham Parker. Now, Parker was massive in the States at the time an' this was his turf but after the gigs people were askin' us for the encore – an' we were only the openin' act. It was fuckin' great.

Sometimes we'd to work a little bit harder to get the audience into the same mood as an Irish one. I mean, in Ireland we were stars but in America we were an unknown entity so we'd to kinda win them over. I found the Americans a bit more conservative than the audiences at home. We'd be playin' in bars an' that an' in some places they're very strict about the age so the audience would've been a lot older than we were used to. Plus, Parker was an old kinda rock'n' roll head, so we were playin' to his audiences a lot of the time.

It was cool though. Like sometimes the challenge of winnin' them over made ya a better band. It's great preachin' to the converted but at the same time it can be more fulfillin' when ya go into a gig where they're waitin' for ya to impress them. They're all there lookin' at ya cynically an' sceptically an' by the end of the set if they're bleedin' eatin' outta your hand it's a great buzz.

It happens at a lotta gigs where the audience don't really know us. Ya start off the show an' you're workin', workin', workin', 'til there's almost like a shift in gear an' then you've got them. You're in the zone. It wouldn't be so obvious at gigs at home where we had a lot of support 'cause the audience more or less was with us from the beginnin'. American audiences are also a bit jaded 'cause they've seen everythin' already. I mean ya get artists over there that were huge a few years ago an' they're on their way back down the popularity stakes while you're on your way up. Ya find yerself on the same level an' so they're

Sittin' in the Haunted Cottage in Ratoath, County Meath.

Me mother-in-law, Bessie, givin' me advice on me weddin' day.

Performin' at the weddin' with some mates.

Playin' with Conor Goff at an early Dignam and Goff gig.

Playin' in Horan's, Tralee – just after the 'strip show' in the dressing room. © Brendan Landy

Singin' *Crazy World* with Kiera at the Finglas South Band Show in 1993.
© Darren Kinsella

Billy an' meself jammin' at the show.
© Darren Kinsella

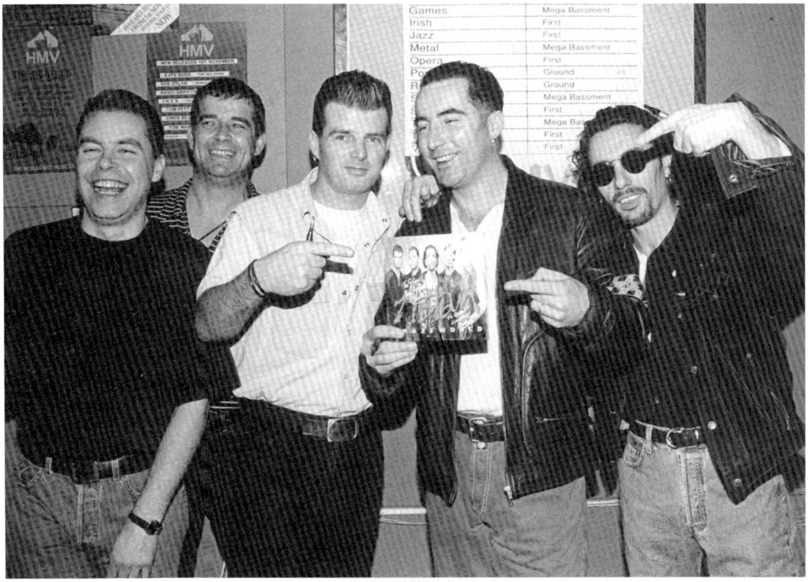

The launch of the *Crazy World* single in September 1993.
© Darren Kinsella

Playin' another great night at the Point Depot.
© Darren Kinsella

Dancin' with me mother Theresa.

Me an' Kathryn, 2003.

kinda goin' around playin' the same circuit that you are. The audience are jaded by the time ya come along an' ya have to try very hard to get over that.

We went on an' did our own shows after supportin' Parker. We were playin' in these venues that we'd grown up hearin' about. We played The Roxy in New York. It was a very prestigious gig over two nights an' we sold out both nights. It was the American equivalent of the Marquee in London. I remember playin' in a place called the Fillmore East in Los Angeles where all these legendary acts had performed in the 1960s – The Doors, Jimi Hendrix, Eric Clapton. . . . We walked in an' there was all these old posters for those gigs: *'Ladies and Gentlemen – Live on stage at the Fillmore East – The Doors'*. There I was on the same fuckin' stage, treadin' the boards of these heroes of mine, 20 years later. It was mind-blowin'.

We'd come to the land where rock'n'roll was born, ya know, an' we here we were, these young Irishmen, selling rock'n'roll like we were sellin' sand to the Arabs. When I went over first I'd a bit of an inferiority complex as an Irish musician takin' on the home-grown acts. I thought that the bands would be cooler; they'd be better dressed; they'd be better song writers; they'd be better rock'n' rollers. . . . But when we got there an' performed the response we got was so appreciative an' so respectful that I was actually taken aback by it initially. An' then I started seein' that 'cause we were Irish, audiences in the States actually expected us to be good. We'd come from a huge musical heritage in Ireland that had produced the likes of U2, Sinead O'Connor, Van Morrison an' all these people. The fact that we were now up there in that roll call was like a further confirmation that we were a great band. I remember thinkin' here I was in the land of rock'n'roll an' the people who live in it are tellin' me that what we're doin' is right, so fuck those pricks from bleedin' Bally fuckin' mun who said I was a wanker for wantin' to be a singer. Just look at me now. We were fulfillin' all the expectations an' sometimes surpassin' them. It felt good. I hadn't been livin' in cloud cuckoo land after all by believin' we could achieve all this.

I was in flyin' form durin' those gigs an' I started to get more confidence 'cause people were kinda worshipin' us. I could live with that an' almost expected it, ya know? An' I was developin' me stage persona even further. I was always tryin' to work towards makin' that connection with the audience – gettin' in there among them an' encouragin' them to sing along. It was payin' off – we were creatin' this real buzz in the place an' people were goin' for it. But as soon as we came off stage I experienced the same problems I had at home copin' with the fame in me public life.

On stage was me alter ego – that was Christy, the singer of Aslan. He was what people expected at an Aslan gig but that didn't necessarily mean that when I walked off after a show that I felt the same way. It's important to understand that distinct difference. When I'm on a stage that adulation is important. It's part an' parcel of bein' in a band an' I enjoyed the whole rock'n'roll thing, the buzz of it, the excitement, but I don't expect it after the show, when I'm just tryin' to be Christy.

The US tour was goin' great but if I thought I was gonna get a break from drugs for a while I was sorely fuckin' mistaken. Yeah, I'd escaped from the heroin scene in Dublin but there was a lot of drugs in America as well – a lot of cocaine in particular, ya know?

I was usin' a lotta coke on that tour. I was lashin' into it to keep goin'. Tourin's a fuckin' hard job – ya do a gig an' after bein' on stage for an hour or whatever, ya have to do the interviews an' talk to the record people who are dealin' with ya in that town. Then you're gettin' to bed at four in the mornin' an' you're up again at nine to drive to San Diego from LA. When ya get there you're settin' up your gear, doin' another gig an' on an' on. Cocaine is a stimulant so it was givin' me the energy to keep goin'.

An' 'cause I was out partyin' with the rest of the band it actually improved relationships for a while. We were bridgin' some of the gaps that'd appeared between us. I was reconnectin' with them in a lot of ways – doin' these great gigs an' then goin' back to someone's room an' we'd be partyin' like mad an' we'd be high fivin' each other. We were gettin' on with each other an' I was happy with that.

Musically, the American tour couldn't have gone any better so by the time we were goin' back to Ireland I felt like we were back on track as a band. But I quickly found out that I wasn't one of those people that can use drugs an' then knock them on the head when they want to. They're like people who overeat at Christmas an' who then go into the gym an' work it all off. I came back from America even more fucked up than I was goin' over an' I couldn't just stop. I couldn't say, 'That was a mad buzz an' now it's time to get back to work.' I was in the throes of heroin addiction. The cocaine I was barrellin' into me just staved off the worst of the withdrawals but as soon as I got off the plane I dived back into the heroin scene. Within days the band was finished.

* * *

One of the first things I wanted to do when we got back from the States, apart from score some heroin, was sort out our manager, Danny Kenny.

The thing with Danny was, right, up 'til then we'd still been workin' on a gentleman's arrangement with him. There were no contracts or anythin' like that. It was all just verbal agreement – that's just the way it worked.

But when we started gettin' really big Danny was eager to have proper contracts signed up 'cause he was afraid that EMI or one of the other big record companies we were dealin' with would find out how much money was goin' through his office. The band was a fuckin' gold mine an' he knew there was nothin' to stop someone comin' in an' makin' us a better offer as manager. I really don't think we would've done that but I suppose there was always the possibility that it could happen.

Then, when we came back to Ireland, Danny started talkin' about drawin' up an official contract an' gettin' us all to sign it. I just didn't think that we should be with Danny anymore. Danny'd worked well gettin' us signed an' he'd helped us get where we were now, there's no doubt about that, but I thought that at this level he was gettin' in above his head. The rest of the lads didn't feel the same – they were convinced that we should sign with Danny. So that whole issue about what to do about management was bein' discussed at the time.

In the meantime we'd gone back into the studio to start layin' down tracks for the next album for EMI. I remember August 13, 1988, was a Saturday afternoon. On me way down to join the rest of the band at rehearsal I dropped into a flat on Clonliffe Road to buy a bit of gear. I was runnin' a bit late so I was just gonna leg it in, grab two deals an' have a smoke in the jacks in the studio later on.

The bloke I was gonna see was called Pascal Boland an' he was from Finglas, same as me. When I started scorin' I knew a few people dealin' in Finglas an' they were all workin' for Boland. He was always a hard fucker, Pascal, ya know? Ya had to be careful around him. At this time he was one of the major players in Dublin's heroin underworld. He was probably supplyin' most of the Northside with smack.

I remember I pulled up, knocked on the door an' yer man threw the keys down. I let meself in the hall door an' walked into his flat. Pascal an' another guy were lyin' on two single beds. He handed me this batch of 10 quarter-grams of heroin an' I was lookin' through them to pick out the two nice ones when I heard a key in the door.

I says, 'Is that a key in your door?' An' he says, 'No, that's next . . .' an' he didn't get the word out of his mouth when the fuckin' door came in on top of me. Within seconds I was on the ground, me hands pulled behind me back an' handcuffed. I remember someone put a fuckin' gun up to me head.

They were plainclothes cops – the drug squad – an' I was caught up in a raid on the gaff. Now, I wasn't used to this sort of thing. 'Cause of the profile I had, I couldn't walk around scorin' where I wanted. People knew me. I had to be careful, ya know? At the same time the fact that I was well-known also worked in me favour. Like, I'd probably get a better deal than most people'd get 'cause I was a bit famous or else I'd be able to knock into a dealer at times when it wouldn't be cool for anyone else. So I was kinda benefitin' in that sense from havin' a familiar face.

But the fame also meant that cops knew who I was as well. First, they dragged me outta the room an' into the hallway. One of them, he looked like the boss, recognised me straight away. He says: 'Right Christy, tell us where the rest of the gear is. Those two are scumbags, you're alright. So tell us where the rest of the heroin is.' He was sayin' things like, 'You've a career ya don't want to ruin,' an' all that 'Just tell us where the smack is an' we'll let you go', sorta thing. They searched the whole flat but they only found the 10 little quarter bags that had gone on the floor when the door came in. I didn't know if Pascal had any more heroin in the flat an' that's what I told them. So I was like, 'I don't know anythin'. I don't know what the fuck yis are talkin' about.' He obviously assumed I wasn't tellin' the truth 'cause he started gettin' really pissed off an' was shoutin' at me that I was gonna have to take me chances with the other two. Then he leans in close to me an' he says, 'Right, you, you're gettin' done with them.'

At the end of the search they put the three of us sittin' together on the floor. They hadn't found anythin' else. The boss copper goes, 'Right, this is the way it's going down.' He turns to yer man Pascal, who owned the heroin an' says, 'This is your heroin, your flat. You know, we know an' you're gettin' charged – end of story. But if ya don't put your hand up an' say it's yours, I'm goin' to charge the three of yis an' you're all goin' down. You're gonna get charged one way or another so it's up you.' Credit where it's due – Pascal put his hand up. I was hopin' that they'd let me go there an' then but we were all handcuffed an' brought down to Fitzgibbon Street Garda station.

All that was goin' through me head was, 'oh fuck, I was supposed to be down at the studio an hour ago'. Ya have to understand as far as I knew the band didn't even know I was back dabblin' in smack. An' now this – this was serious shit. I was after fuckin' up big time. Big time. I was convinced that everythin' was over. Like the band was gonna be finished, me family, me career an' I was gonna end up in jail. All those things were goin' through me head while we were been driven' down to the cop shop. I kept sayin' to meself, 'Ya prick; ya fuckin' dickhead. How the fuck could ya – ya were warned this was going to happen.' I'm a realist ya know? I knew I wasn't gonna bullshit me way out of this one.

We were brought into Fitzgibbon Street an' they'd Polaroid cameras there to take photographs, mug shots ya know? Nearly every fuckin' copper in the station is comin' down to get their photo taken with me. I was just tryin' to be sweet 'cause I didn't want to get charged. I was been as accommodatin' as possible. I just wanted to lick arse an' get the fuck outta there.

So, they charged yer man Pascal an' after a few more questions they finally let me an' the other bloke go. I left the station an' got down to the rehearsal fuckin' hours late. I didn't say anythin' about what'd happened. I just made another one of me bullshit excuses an' started breathin' a bit easier. I was thinkin', 'I'm after getting away with it, thanks be to Jesus'. I felt like I was after winnin' the Lotto. An hour prior to this an' it was all over an' now, all of a sudden, I'm singin' into a mike in the studio as if nothin' had happened.

I knew the general gist of the law, ya know, that if you're not charged there an' then you're probably not gonna hear any more about it. So I got on with the session an' thought, 'man, ya were poxed there, ya wanna be more careful in future'. But, ya know, Dublin's a small place. What I didn't know was that a cop who was based in the station knew a friend of a friend of the band an' he came across the photos an' got wind of what happened. I think that's how the band found out.

* * *

A week later we were due in for more rehearsals an' meself an' Alan arrived in the studio at the same time. But the rest of the band weren't there. I was thinkin' was there somethin' I'd forgotten, maybe a photo session or somethin'. Alan said he didn't know where they were either.

So I rang Danny Kenny in his office an' I says: 'Here Danny, do ya know what the story is? Only Alan an' meself are here. Where's the rest of them? We're supposed to be in the studios today.'

Danny goes, 'The lads are here with me. Come over to the office.' I says, 'What's wrong?' an' he goes, 'I'll tell ya when you get over here.'

So we went over to Bachelor's Walk but when we got there the lads were gone. Danny was sittin' behind his desk an' he basically just came out with it. He says, 'Lookit, the band is fed up with ya an' they just told me to tell ya, you're out. That's it, you're finished.'

I was in absolute shock. I just thought, 'fuck me what's this all about'. I wanted to talk to the band; I wanted to hear from them what the fuck was goin' on. So I says to Danny, 'What d'ya mean I'm out? Where's the rest of the band? I wanna talk to them.' He says, 'Well, they've gone back to the studio an' they don't want to talk to ya.'

Alan had walked in behind me an' I turned round to him an' said, 'Nice one Alan, you could've fuckin' told me!' Then Alan goes, 'I swear to God, Christy, I don't know what the fuck is goin' on.' Alan admitted that they'd been talkin' 'bout what had been goin' on with me all right, that they knew I was back on gear an' shit like that but he swore he didn't know there was goin' to be a big decision that particular day. I believed him 'cause he was after turnin' up that mornin' in the studio the same as me.

So anyway that was it. I didn't say anythin' else. It was very brief. Danny just said that's it, end of story, good luck. It was very cold, very passionless. I mean Danny had been lookin' after us right up to when the split happened. I knew him really fuckin' well. He'd been with us through some of the most important times an' now's he's just lookin' at me goin', 'You're out.' It's debatable whether he'd any influence in the spilt but regardless of whether he did or not I feel today that he failed as a manager. As far as I'm concerned the music business is run by accountants an' lawyers, right, an' a manager's job is to work out deals to earn ya money. But his ultimate responsibility is to keep the band together. He's there to iron out the creases an' I don't think Danny Kenny did that. So I just looked at him an' said, 'Right, fuckit' an' I jumped in the car an' flew back to the studio.

The three of them were there – Joe, Tony an' Billy – an' I says to them, 'What the fuck is goin' on?' An' they said, 'Did Danny not tell ya?' I said 'Yeah' an' they said, 'Well, that's what's goin' on – you're out. We want you outta the band.' They were very clinical about it. There was no explanation, no excuses. They just came down an' said the same stuff as Danny. It felt like the same – that's it, end of story, good luck – fuck off. I don't think they felt very good about themselves doin' it but it didn't stop them.

Everythin' I'd worked for was fuckin' gone – just gone, ya know? There was no negotiation an' I knew they meant it. This wasn't some little fuckin', 'Snap outta yer buzz, yer bein' given a fright here'. This wasn't to give me a kick in the arse or warn me – it was nothin' like that. This was of end fuckin' story.

I remember drivin' home an' bein' absolutely, utterly disgusted. Over all those years I felt I was the drivin' force in the band. It was my fuckin' band but they'd taken all that off me – all the equipment, all the money an' the record deal. It was gone. It was all theirs an' I was left with nothin'. I hadn't a pot to piss in. I was literally on me own. I was just an ordinary fuckin' Joe soap again.

I drove out of the laneway where the studios were in Ringsend, turned up towards Pearse Street an' passed Shelbourne Park an' that's when it hit me that I had to tell Kathryn what the fuck had happened.

I'd told Kathryn for years that she wouldn't have to work for a livin' for much longer an' when we'd signed the deal I'd told her this dream was just about to be achieved. We'd a mortgage that she was payin' on her own an' now I'd to drive home an' tell her that instead of her being able to just give up work, she'd to continue workin' an' leavin' Kiera with her mother. I'll never forget that – that was a truly horrible feelin'. I knew she wasn't gonna start losin' the head or anythin' like that. It was just the fact that I knew I'd to go home an' tell her that broke me heart. I just felt like a complete fuckin' loser. I thought, 'I've fucked up big time,' d'ya know what I mean?

Just to compound the crap was the fact that I'd to tell her it was over drugs.

Paper's Cut

I don't know if there're many people who've had to come home from work one day an' tell their spouse that they've been fired an' not only that but that they'd been fired 'cause they were addicted to heroin. I'd to break it to Kathryn that the band was finished an' I'd also to tell her I was a brass monkey – junkie. So she'd to deal with all this comin' at the same time.

I got home an' I rang her in work an' told her she had to come back now. When she arrived I cried in the kitchen as I tried to explain that I'd thrown me career away but I think it was the drugs thing that killed her. I'd have smoked hash in front of Kathryn, like an' she might've known that I did the odd bit of coke here an' there. She probably accepted that it was part an' parcel of bein' in a band but she'd no idea of the extent that I'd gone to with the heroin.

To me, it's a measure of her as a person that she was just there for me. Kathryn always has been, ya know? I'm sure there've been times when there was no way that I could've been as understandin' as she was, had the situation been reversed. It was all a massive shock for her – it was for both of us – but she never threw it back in me face. She never said, 'What the fuck are you after doin' to me? You're after fuckin' me up here.' But obviously she was frightened an' she made me promise her that I'd get help. I just sobbed there in the kitchen with her an' swore I would.

After a couple of days sittin' at home mullin' over everythin' that'd happened in me head, me shock an' sadness turned into anger. I was thinkin' of all the times I'd sat outside RTÉ with our demo tape, tryin' to get someone to listen to it. I was thinkin' of the day I knocked on Alan's door to ask him to join the band. I was thinkin' of when I'd to tell me mate Mick McKenna to get off bass 'cause I wanted Tony. Even though I knew Mick would say, 'If ya get me off the bass I'm leavin' the band,' ya know? I couldn't stop thinkin' about all the friendships I'd lost, all the things I'd done to get this band where it was an' now it was just fuckin' gone – just gone.

I'd grown up with these lads, spent hours of every day with them in a freezin' pigsty, gone on stage with them from the Towers in Ballymun to the Fillmore East in LA. If God had've appeared to me, ya know, the day prior to the split an' said, 'Right, Christy, I've got a bit of bad news one in five people have to get cancer an' there's five members in the band so I'm afraid I have to give it to one of youse' – I woulda took it. I woulda took the cancer for any one of them. So, to have that commitment to somebody, that loyalty, an' to have them do that on you was impossible for me to deal with. The only thing I couldn't do for them, an' it was the one thing they wanted, was to give up the gear.

I'd said in interviews before that when the five of us got together, all five elements of Aslan, a sixth thing, an X factor, happened. I personally believed that not one of us was replaceable in the band. We were all an integral part of the chemistry an' I knew from the start that if we changed any element of that, then the chemistry wouldn't work. Like, ya might think a drummer is not that important an' that he would be the easiest to replace, ya know? People watchin' a band might think it doesn't matter a fuck who's playin' drums. Like if a gun was put to your head an' ya were told one of your band members had to go, the drummer would probably be the first, the bass player would be next, then maybe the guitarist, but the singer would be the last. So for me to have believed from the very start that nobody was replaceable in the band an' then for them to think they could get away with replacin' what was probably the most integral part, was ridiculous really.

But they obviously didn't see the importance of me in the band, as a singer or as a friend. They were sayin' that me voice was in shit an' that I couldn't sing anymore but I don't know about that. Maybe, the drug takin' would've had an effect on me voice eventually an' maybe it was gonna end up in shit, but if it was that obvious to me an' everyone else that me voice was gone I wouldn't have been as surprised as I was when they fucked me out.

The sackin' had come outta the blue to me. I didn't know 'til later that they knew about the bust I got caught up in. It was never said to me at the time that that might have been the reason. But ya have to remember that I was driftin' around with all me concentration on where I was gonna get me next fix. As far I could see everythin' was goin' ahead with the band. I didn't have to worry about whether everythin' was workin' out. We'd created a fuckin' brilliant first album, done a successful American tour an' we were in the studio recordin' our second album, ya know? The new album was shapin' up, the songs were goin' well. I was still turnin' up at the studio for work, an' even though I was late half the time, I didn't see that as a reason on its own to be sacked. The thing was I wasn't listenin' to anybody at this stage – the band, me friends or the record company.

The way I was viewin' it was, here we were in a rock'n'roll band an' what I was doin' was rock'n'roll behaviour after all. I found out much later that even the record company had gone to them an' offered to send me to a clinic or to put me on separate transport to the gigs. They were tryin' to keep the peace but obviously, from the band's perspective, it had gone beyond the point of no return.

Lookin' back on it, I don't blame them for takin' the stance they took as such, right. I was outrageously fuckin' incompetent an' I wasn't as productive as I should've been. I was detrimental to the band at that particular stage. As far as they were concerned, an' I'm just basin' this on what I know of them as people, their vibe would've been that I'd already been given me warnin' after the gig in Waterford. So yeah, all those things are true, but at the time I was thinkin' they shoulda had the balls to stand up an' say they took that stance 'cause they seen their careers goin' down the tubes an' they wanted to try an' save them. I thought that was the real reason I was fired.

I'd no contact with the band for years after that. They never called me up to say howya feelin', or, are you short of a few bob or anything – but then I didn't call them either.

* * *

One of the toughest things about bein' famous is that all the bad things, as well as the good, are aired in public. An' of course it was inevitable that the papers got wind that somethin' was up. So the next minute the phone starts ringin' an' all these journalists are askin' me: 'What's goin' on Christy? We heard ya were sacked. What happened?' I just kept me mouth shut. But there had to be a story given out right? An' the story put out by the management was that we'd split over music an' personal differences.

The followin' day, on the front page of *The Star*, was the headline, *ASLAN: IT'S THE END*. There was a photograph that had been taken of the five of us together but they'd put this tear effect down the side so I was separated from the rest of them in the picture.

The basic vibe of the article was that I'd left the band over musical differences an' that Aslan were finished, which was not what the other lads an' the management had wanted at all. They were tryin' to pass it off that I'd left the band an' Aslan was goin' to continue on uninterrupted. I was like a broken string on a guitar that you just replace, ya know? It was no big deal – ya just get another one. So, I think they were a bit fuckin' upset that the papers had taken the angle that Aslan was finished.

An' that's when all the shit started to circulate – the papers were gettin' in touch with me an' I was told that the management had gone to them, off the record, an' said: 'Lookit, Christy's in bits. His voice is gone an' he's fuckin' strung out on heroin.' Journalists were sayin' to me that they'd been told that I was mimin' at that big gig in the Ilac Centre 'cause me voice was in tatters an' that Joe had to do all the singin' – stuff like that – which was all absolute bollix, by the way.

But this is what the journalists were tellin' me an' they were sayin', 'Look, we know it's over drugs, we were told it was, what's your story?' So I rang this lawyer bloke I knew in England. We'd some dealin's with him for band stuff in the past, an' I just asked for some advice. I says, 'Lookit, the papers have got hold of this story an' journalists are comin' to me with this, what'll I do? Will I deny it or admit it?' The lawyer's attitude was somethin' like, 'If you deny it Christy an' they have evidence that you're lyin', they'll slaughter you.' He advised me to go for a damage limitation kinda buzz.

I decided to do an interview then with this journalist from *The Star*. I admitted to him that I'd dabbled with heroin but that it was all in the past an' it wasn't anythin' to do with the split. I said I'd done it in a dark period in me life an' I wouldn't advise anyone to ever do it – it was a fuckin' stupid mistake I made. I told the paper: '*It's a horrible drug. I would never recommend anybody to touch it. It is absolutely destructive an' nobody can handle it.*' That's the angle I went for – I was honest an' up front about it in an effort to get it out there an' be done with it.

A couple of days later, I was at home an' the phone rang at about 3 o'clock in the mornin'. It was Kathryn's ma an' she said the police had been up at her door lookin' for where I lived. Now, Kathryn's mother was an old lady. She was really upset an' didn't know what was goin' on. Then they came down to me – within half an hour they were at me door – but it wasn't the police. They were journalists pretendin' to be the cops, usin' the same tactics – flashin' badges, lettin' on to be the police, sayin' they'd cameras outside the house, recordin' me an' all this carry on. They were givin' it all this, sayin' that they'd heard I was one of the main fuckin' financiers of heroin on the Northside of Dublin, an' what did I have to say about it. But I wouldn't even go out to the door, ya know? Me brother was stayin' with me at the time an' he went out to tell them to fuck off.

On the Saturday of that week, say maybe two days later, I walked into me local shop. It was directly across the road from where I lived in Valley Park in Finglas. I used to like goin' over there 'cause I was a bit of a local celebrity an' I always got a 'how's it goin?' or whatever from the friendly aul wans in the shop. But when I walked in this day they were all lookin' down their noses at me. They didn't even answer me when I said hello. I was thinkin', 'what the fuck's goin on here?' 'cause it was obvious they were lookin' at me like I was a piece of shit after walkin' in the door.

I was just about to say somethin' to them when I glanced down at the floor, where the newspaper section was, an' there, on the front page of *The Star* was *CHRISTY SOLD HEROIN* in fuckin' huge *THE POPE MUST DIE* headlines. There was a full-page picture of me beside it.

I nearly collapsed. I couldn't even pick up the paper. I just got the fuck outta the shop an' sent me brother over later to buy it. I was absolutely stunned when I read the article. I just couldn't believe it.

This was the same newspaper who I'd just done the drug story with an' whose reporters had come to me only a few weeks before that beggin' for an exclusive, 'Christy the rocker at home with his family' kinda feature. They'd come to me home an' interviewed me with me family an' took photographs of us sittin' together on the couch – me, Kathryn an' Kiera. After the interview the journalists had been like, 'Listen Christy, thanks a lot. We really appreciate you givin' us this interview.' I actually saw these journalists as colleagues, d'ya know what I mean? I thought we'd become mates nearly, ya know? We were in a self-servin' industry – we were helpin' each other out. Like I was assistin' their careers by givin' them stories an' they were helpin' me by givin' me the publicity. So for them to turn around an' do this, I just couldn't believe it. Like I actually thought, 'no they obviously didn't do this, somebody else done it'. I couldn't believe that they worked for the same paper that'd hung me out to dry.

I knew that I'd fucked up but I didn't give a shit so much 'bout me 'cause, as far as I was concerned, I'd made me bed. I'd involved meself in this lifestyle an' the downside of it was, sometimes people like these journalists were gonna do shit like this. I'd involved meself in drugs which meant I'd left meself vulnerable to this sort of thing. But me wife an' me daughter, me mother an' father an' me brothers an' sisters had nothin' to do with this lifestyle yet their name was bein' dragged through the mud. An' that's what killed me more than anythin' else.

The effect that all this was havin' on them was difficult for me to comprehend, ya know? A lot of me brothers an' sisters were still in school an' they used to come down to me every second day lookin' for autographs for their schoolmates. Then they were readin' all this shit in the papers 'bout me. All of a sudden this brother that was kinda handy to have to, let's say, provide some minor celebrity, was now a fuckin' liability. They never said, 'God Christy, we're so disappointed,' or anythin'. I mean they didn't' have to say shit like that, ya know, 'cause I knew they musta been embarrassed. It musta been impossible for them to back me up when it was all there in black an' white – regardless of whether it was true or not.

The article was not only a slur on me character but an attack on me own family. They weren't just writin' 'bout me, they were writin' about Kathryn an' Kiera. Like in *The Star* with the *CHRISTY SOLD HEROIN* front page you opened up page two an' three an' there was the story. It was spread across three fuckin' pages of *The Star* that day with massive headlines like *ROCK STAR WHO WAS LIVING A DOUBLE LIE*. On page 3 there was a picture taken the day they'd done the 'family man of rock' thing an' it was of me, Kathryn an' Kiera, all sittin' on the couch together downstairs. But d'ya know what they did? They used a photo from that session which would've been one of the ones where I was blinkin' or had me head turned the wrong way an' made it look like I was outta me head sittin' there, beside me family. An' I remember people sayin' to me later, 'Ya know, if they were gonna write this shit 'bout ya why the fuck did you pose for the photo, you an' yer bird, an' all?' They thought I stood in for the photo that day – they didn't realise the photo was for an interview that was done weeks before that.

The paper also picked up on the Clonliffe Road bust an' said it '*. . . was the last straw for his mates in top group Aslan. He was sacked on Tuesday.*' *The Star* insinuated that this was the drug ring that I was supposed to be financin'. They quoted this man, whose identity they were keepin' secret, who claimed he'd been with me when I sold heroin. The unnamed man was quoted as sayin', '*I have seen him* [Christy Dignam] *take money for drugs . . .*' an' '*Christy has supplied me with drugs. . . .*' It was fuckin' ridiculous. I'd been in the middle of recordin' me second album with me band. The day I was busted, I'd been rushin' into the studio so where the fuck was I goin' to get the time to finance a drug empire? The raid happened on a Saturday after we got our wages on a Friday night. We were still on 80 quid a week at the time which was the equivalent price of two quarter grams – so that was me whole week's wages I'd had on me that day goin' in to score. But people saw us as this rich rock'n'roll band, playin' all these big gigs. Newspapers like *The Star* made us out to be worth millions when, in reality, we hadn't a pot to piss in. I mean yeah, the band was makin' a fortune but we were all still bein' paid a weekly wage. That was it.

The only reason I'd been let go by the police that day was 'cause they knew I was only there scorin'. If the cops had suspected for a second that what the journalists were writin' now was true or if there'd been even one per cent of a chance that I'd anythin' to do with financin' any drug ring I wouldn't have made it out of the police station. I definitely wouldn't have made it back to rehearsal.

I'd thrown down the paper in horror as I read all this shit. Then when I picked it back up again an' started readin' more I realised it was worse than I thought. It went on to claim that I was seen handin' over money to people goin' to England to get heroin. Then they went on an' described how you smuggle it into the country. Now, they didn't say I was smugglin' heroin into the country but they made out by insinuation that this was all part of the story. The unnamed woman said:

> '*Christy passed money through me, about £1,700, for a courier taking the next flight to London. I knew the money was for buying drugs and I knew when the courier got back they would be divided up.*'

But there was one cruelty in the article that hit me even harder than anythin' else. They described me sittin' in a '*foul-smelling room*' while crouching by me knee was '*. . . innocent little Ciara.*'. There was another line an' basically, what they done was, they blew it up real big on the page an' put it in italics to emphasise the point. It read, '*Christy smoked heroin in front of his baby Ciara, then he said* . . . "This is good stuff".' I'll never forget how much bollix that was. I've never, ever taken drugs in front of me daughter – it's somethin' I wouldn't ever do. Who the fuck would do somethin' like that? An' this bullshit that I was supposed to have said, '*This is good stuff*', – it was like somethin' outta an episode of *Kojak*. Irish people don't talk like that. I mean when we got fuckin' good heroin we might say, 'This is nice gear,' or 'This is lovely gear.' Ya wouldn't say, 'This is good stuff man.' It was complete comic book nonsense that was made up by somebody imagining what a junkie might say. I just couldn't believe that bit – sayin' I was blowin' smoke rings with me daughter sittin' there. They made me out to be fuckin' Beelzebub.

Just imagine, right, I considered some of these people me colleagues. I'd helped these people out in the past an' I'd become close to them an' I just kept thinkin', 'why would they do this?' Why? Was it out of fuckin' malice? Was it for money, for filthy lucre? I just couldn't believe it – I still can't believe it.

As soon as I got over the shock I got in touch with some solicitors in Dublin an' we talked about takin' a libel case against *The Star*. But me first step was to issue me own press release which I did the followin' week, denyin' everythin' in the story an' sayin' I'd be takin' legal action to prove it. The statement was picked up by a few of the papers an' printed but I mean, the damage was already done.

Somebody wrote later that I was one of the first victims of the British tabloid invasion of Ireland, ya know? I was an example of how fascination with celebrity was creepin' into the Irish media. If there was an upside to all of this then it was that a lot of other journalists that were around at that time, working for the likes of *The Irish Independent* an' *The Evening Herald*, people like Damian Corless an' George Byrne, that got behind me an' supported me.

It seemed like a lot of people started to take me side after *The Star* thing came out an' this actually worked counter-productive to what Aslan's management had wanted at the time, ya know? Some of the reporters could see the irony of the split. They knew Aslan an' knew what we were like. They were fuckin' there with us. They'd watched us all sittin' in clubs together partyin' an' fallin' outta taxis an' into more parties. They'd seen all this behaviour an' could see my side of things.

I started doin' more interviews, tryin' to undo the damage that'd been done. All along the line I was bein' absolutely honest. I think I was indirectly tryin' to explain to everyone who knew me, me parents, me family an' friends, what the whole thing was about but then that was slanted an' turned an' fucked over. I just eventually lost me way, ya know what I mean?

It was a terrible, terrible time. Even now, I can't even fully fathom what it was like. I was just lost. I was like a balloon blowin' round in a storm an' everywhere I'd land I'd 'cause more pain to meself an' everyone around me. It was fuckin' horrible an' I just didn't know who to trust or who to talk to so I just retreated into a shell behind me barricades.

* * *

I'd stopped usin' heroin immediately after the band split but when *The Star* came out an' exposed me as a junkie an' accused me of dealin', it all got too much an' I was off scorin' again. I still thought nobody would know that I was back on the gear. I was even convinced that I was foolin' Kathryn. I would drop her into work in the mornin' an' then I was free for the rest of the day to go off an' find gear. I'd be comin' home stoned outta me box an' when you're stoned ya think you're perfectly normal. Ya don't realise your sittin' there with your head in your lap, noddin' off an' burnin' cigarette holes in everythin'.

Kathryn could see what was goin' on – she knew I was back on the gear an' she begged me, for the sake of our marriage an' for Kiera, to get help, so in October of 1988 I agreed to sign meself into the Rutland treatment centre in Dublin.

Ya have to be clean to go into the Rutland so I got off gear, passed their tests an' signed up for a six-week course. I'd never been in a treatment centre before an' it came as a bit of a shock. The Rutland is up in Knocklyon, near

Tallaght, an' it looks like a big mansion house, with the big gardens an' all. It was lovely on the outside but while you're in there you have chores to do, ya know, like sweepin' the floor or peelin' potatoes, or makin' a bed or whatever. An' I remember thinkin', 'this time three months ago I was fuckin' giggin' in Los Angeles, in New York, an' now I'm in a drug clinic cleanin' the fuckin' toilets'.

The reality of me new life was gettin' harder for me to accept. I kinda grew up knowin' that I wasn't an idiot, d'ya know what I mean? Now I was thinkin', 'how the fuck did I end up in here bein' treated for drug addiction?' Okay, I was ignorant of the whole heroin thing when I'd first taken it but I'd seen all the American movies about addiction an' cop programmes like *Kojak* when I was a kid. I shoulda known where heroin would bring me. I'm not stupid an' it was there for me in black an' fuckin' white, so why did I do it? I'm not thick, so I had to keep askin' meself how did I let it happen. I kinda went into a lot of self-searching, ya know? I was readin' psychology books an' everythin', wonderin' what was the reason for all this an' tryin' to find out how could I stop. I became a student of addiction, learnin' how it affected the body an' the mind.

For the first week you're not allowed any contact with the outside world. Ya can't make phone calls or take phone calls or see anyone – no family, no friends or visitors. But every Tuesday they had what's called 'Confrontation Day' where they bring up the spouses or the partners of the people in treatment. So ya have seven or eight people in a group an' the seven or eight husbands, wives, mothers or fathers or whatever, would come up an' we'd all be sittin' in this room. The idea was the relatives would confront the addict with the reality of what it was like to live with them durin' their addiction.

It takes a lot of effort to break through the denial that addicts throw up around themselves. I remember leavin' the first session in tears an' me an' Kathryn huggin' outside in the grounds of this place. An' she was sayin', 'Come on, stay with it, you're doin' the right thing. We'll get through this together.' Now I'd been off the heroin then for a while an' me feelin's were startin' to come back, me sexual libido had slowly started to make an appearance. When we all went back into the room, all I could think about was grabbin' Kathryn an' gettin' outta there to have some time with her. Meanwhile, all these wives of alcoholics are recountin' what their husbands had done to them or what they didn't do for them. I'm listenin' to all this thinkin', 'for fuck's sake, in comparison I did fuck all'. I was thinkin', 'I must be the best addict on Earth'. Then the counsellor says to Kathryn, 'What was it like livin' with Christy before he came here, Kathryn?' An' she started talkin' about when I went back on the gear after *The Star* came out an' says, 'He'd come over to me when he wanted to make love but I felt like he was goin' to put his heroin hands all over me an' I'd nearly vomit all over him.' An' I'm sittin' there goin', 'What the fuck?'

There was another break for lunch an' I stormed out. When Kathryn caught up with me an' asked me what was wrong I just turned an' spat at her, 'How dare ya talk to me in front of people, like that.' Tears sprang up in her eyes an' she just turned an' walked off.

After lunch we went back into the session an' the counsellor says to Kathryn, 'Kathryn, you're very quiet, have ya not got anythin' to say?' Kathryn looks at him an' says, 'I'm not sayin' anythin' in front of that bastard, he just tore into me outside.' So the counsellor calls me out an' he lashed into me. But Kathryn was right, ya know? That's the way it was. It'd just come as a shock for me to hear that this was how she felt 'cause I hadn't really even been aware of what I was like. When you're in the middle of an addiction ya think nobody has a fuckin' clue what you're up to. But nobody was fooled.

While I was in the Rutland, there was times when other addicts – I was the only heroin addict in there, but there was a lot of alcoholics – had these moments when they were tryin' to get to the root cause of why they were there. Now an' again, suddenly – Badoom – it all came out an' they realised that their fathers or mothers had come home when they were kids an' beat them up or whatever had happened to them. An' I remember thinkin', 'I wonder what happened to me when I was a kid – how come I'm a fuckin' junkie?'. I never had any of this horrific childhood. Me old fella didn't come home an' beat us up every Friday night. Like, sometimes we'd nothin' to eat but it wasn't 'cause he drank all the money, it was 'cause we'd no money.

But I remember the first Sunday I was home after finishin' the treatment. I went up to me parents' house an' I was tryin' to explain to me da about what had been goin' on in the Rutland. I said to him, 'Look, there coulda been somethin' that happened to me as a kid that instigated this whole addiction thing.' An' I remember him lookin' at me like, 'are you sayin' I didn't hug you enough as a child or I didn't do enough for you?', with confusion in his face. I was tryin' to explain why I was an addict, lookin' for forgiveness, an' here I was gettin' meself in deeper an' upsettin' him even more. I thought, 'aw fuck me, that's not what I wanted to say, that's not what I meant at all'.

I left the house in bits an' as soon as I walked out the door it was like a fuckin' hammer hittin' me in the face. Lookin' back on it I musta blocked it all out from the age it happened to the age of 16 an' again for the rest of the years until then. Suddenly, all the terrible details came floodin' back. I was rememberin' meself comin' home one day when I was 16. I remember this local bloke was just sittin' on a wall, lookin' at me with a kinda cheesy grin on his face. As I walked past I turned round an', I don't know why, I just said to him, 'D'ya remember when we were kids?' The minute I said those words I just seen his face goin' white. Then I said, 'Remember ya used to bring me inta your house?' an' it'd all come back to me then for the first time.

When I was about 6 he'd sent me up for a bottle of cola from the shops. When I came back he'd said come in. So I walked into the gaff. All the doors were shut an' he went round, slowly lockin' them.

Then he stripped me off, took the laces outta me shoes, tied me up an' fuckin . . . had his bleedin' . . . did his business with me. An' it didn't just happen once – it wasn't an isolated incident. It happened a few times. I was tellin' nobody 'bout it 'cause I inherently knew it was wrong an' I thought I was the one who was doin' somethin' wrong.

Then, when I was about 9 or 10, I told me best mate at the time. Later that day he says: 'Look I was tellin' me brother, me older brother, 'bout what happened to ya an' he thinks he can help ya. He wants to see ya when he comes in from work later on.'

I called into me mate's gaff that evenin' an' went upstairs to the brother's room. He would've been in his mid-twenties. He says to me mate, 'Listen, you wait downstairs, he won't talk in front of ya.' An' the minute his little brother went out yer man fuckin' done the same thing to me.

Although it only happened the once with him, I thought, at the time, as this little kid, that I was the prick-teaser. I started thinkin' then that I'd a hand in all this, d'ya know what I mean? I thought after that then that I was doin' somethin' wrong. I was convinced that I was makin' this happen somehow, ya know? Okay, if it happens once yer kinda unlucky but if it keeps happenin' you're gonna start thinkin' that ya are instigatin' it. I felt I was leadin' these fuckers on or I was temptin' them in some way that I wasn't even entirely sure of.

The last time I'd thought about all this was when I was 16 an' I'd said, 'D'ya remember when we were kids. . . .' A week or two later, there was a For Sale sign there in his garden an' he was gone. He'd legged it – outta the gaff. I never told anyone 'bout what had happened. I was obviously too fucked up over it an' I didn't wanna deal with it.

Lookin' back on it, it wasn't like I made a decision to block it. Like, it's not somethin' that ya kinda consciously remember blockin' out 'cause then you're actually rememberin' it on a different level, d'ya know what I mean? It just went out of me memory naturally. I'd even forgotten about confrontin' that fucker when I was 16. It was somethin' that I just didn't want to think about. Eventually, if ya don't give somethin' much thought in your daily life, it gets pushed to the back of your mind. I think maybe, psychologically, ya have a choice when somehin' like that happens to ya. Ya can either visit that place every day of your life an' fuckin' drive yourself to a nervous breakdown or ya can refuse to even think about it.

I know this sounds weird but while I didn't acknowledge that it had happened, I always kinda knew in the recesses of me mind that there was somethin' wrong. All through this period, I did have to deal with the consequences of the abuse in me daily life, but I wouldn't have been consciously aware of why I was the way I was 'til I kinda started focusin' on what might have happened to me.

me family down an' now I was tryin' to deal with the abuse I'd suffered. I was not only exposed as a junkie scumbag but I was labelled a dealer of heroin. People have been killed, kicked to death on the streets, after they were accused of bein' a dealer. That's the thing that got me. I never had a problem admittin' I had trouble with drugs an' I was always totally honest about bein' a heroin addict, even though it took a long time to come to terms with that. But everybody in Dublin was lookin' at me an' thinkin' I was a dealer. I'd no money an' I couldn't get work. I was tryin' to get some solo gigs but people wouldn't employ me 'cause they didn't want to have some scumbag, junkie dealer in their club.

I couldn't deal with the shit anymore. I just remember thinkin', 'here, fuck this man', an' I got into the gear then big time. It was the only solace I had. It was a way of lockin' all of that shit out. It was the only friend I had at that moment. Now, I know it's a cliché but that's exactly the way it was.

Less than two days after I'd walked out of the Rutland clinic I was scorin' heroin again.

Takin' Care or Business

You're never goin' to find what you're lookin' for by usin' heroin. Ya take heroin hopin' to fix somethin' that's wrong with ya inside but it's just not goin' to happen. An' it takes a long time to figure out that one simple truth. I remember someone describin' it to me that takin' heroin is like gettin' into a ring with Mike Tyson or someone. He knocks the bollix out of ya, smashes ya to bits; you've to go to hospital an' get yourself all fixed up. Then when ya come out of hospital havin' recovered ya say, 'Right, the reason Mike Tyson got me that day was 'cause I wasn't usin' me left jab properly.' So ya go back into the ring an' he knocks the bollix out of ya again an' leaves ya in hospital. Ya spend a couple of months there, ya recover an' come out again, except this time you're sayin' to yourself, 'I used me jab that time but I didn't realise that after the jab I should've used a right upper cut as well.' So ya go back into the ring an' he knocks the bollix out of ya again . . . When are ya goin' to realise that Mike Tyson is a better fighter than ya? An' it's exactly the same with heroin – when are ya going to admit to yourself that heroin is bigger than ya?

I've had a lot of time to suss all this out in me mind which, sometimes, can be counter-productive in that ya intellectualise the addiction. Ya tell yourself the lies that 'cause ya understand it all ya don't have to go through the same bullshit as everybody else who is strugglin' to get off gear. It's a 'they didn't do the research that I did' kinda attitude. Ya convince yourself that ya know how to beat it an' that's the deception that keeps ya' trapped.

I tried givin' it up so many times before I went into the Rutland an' each time was as sincere as the last. I'd stand back an' watch it happenin' again an' again. I'd have all the determination I could muster an' I'd say, 'Right, that's fuckin' it – I'm stoppin' today.' But the thing is I'd to try an' maintain that same resolve over a sustained period of time. An' then you're goin' into withdrawals an' they get more severe as the days pass. You're tryin' to hold on but at the same time you're sufferin' all this pain an' abject depression, an' ya know that there's this tiny bit of powder there that'll stop all that shit an' it all starts gettin' too much. So what ya do is ya say, 'Right, I'll just smoke a little bit to sort this out. I'll just smoke it for a moment so that I can catch me breath an' get the strength to go on,' but once ya take it that one time you're back to square fuckin' one – an' ya just keep doin' that. Ya keep goin' back to the 'mañana' mentality – I'll do it tomorrow, I'll do it tomorrow, I'll do it tomorrow. . . . It was an endless cycle.

Ya see the thing that makes it hard for ya to stay away from the gear is that you're frightened. Basically what it is, is, ya have all these demons but you've found a way to staunch the manifestations of those demons by usin' heroin. So, ya have to have a very, very good reason to throw away the one thing that's stoppin' those things – the pain an' the hurt the heroin is causin' has to be bigger than the pain an' hurt that you're hidin' with the heroin.

I think what has to happen first is ya have to hit you're rock bottom before ya can start hopin' to mend yourself. That's what alcoholics talk about when they describe hittin' their rock bottom before they start the recovery process. Like, for me, goin' into the Rutland Centre that time was one of me first big serious attempts to knock it on the head. An' although I'd stopped when I went in there I kinda knew even then, deep down, that I wasn't gonna stay stopped. At that time I did it for the wrong reasons – 'cause the shit had hit the fan an' everythin' was pilin' up on top of me. I just did it to shut everybody up. It wasn't 'cause I wanted to stop. I remember, even while I was in there, passin' the time just waitin' for it to end so I could get out an' score. I spent the rest of the time delvin' into all the reasons why I was usin' heroin an' I was kinda openin' all these old wounds. So when I went out into the world I was left fuckin' raw an' I wasn't able to handle it.

The only two things that'd stopped me from havin' a complete death wish was me family an' havin' Aslan. When I came outta the Rutland a lot of the reasons I had for kinda keepin' a cap on the problem no longer existed. I didn't have a band to be hidin' it from. With me music gone all I had left were me family but I felt I'd let them down by losin' Aslan an' not fulfillin' all the promises that I'd made to them. With nothin' left to hold me back I just plunged off the edge.

When I look at the progression of me addiction now, I was only at the beginnin' of it then. An addiction is a disease an' all diseases are progressive so it was inevitable the way things were goin' to go. I was still just smokin' gear when I came out of the Rutland but it was just the tip of the fuckin' iceberg compared to the way it went. The downhill spiral led me into depths of addiction that would nearly cost me the last thing I had – me life.

* * *

As soon as I was free of the Rutland I was back out lookin' for gear. To hide it from everyone else I quickly developed a split personality – Christy the junkie an' Christy the family man who was gettin' his shit back together.

So what I was doin' was comin' home pretendin' everythin' was back to normal. It was kinda like I'd had a bit of a major mishap but I was back on me feet an' startin' new again, ya know? An' to a certain extent I was. I was thinkin' about gettin' another band together an' a few ideas were runnin' around in me head about how to get me music career back.

For a good while everythin' was grand at home, everythin' was cool. I was comin' back in the evenin' an' from 6 o'clock on I was tryin' to be a respectable father, ya know, an' a dedicated husband. But it was a double existence. Durin' the daytime, I was out there livin' the life of a junkie.

I couldn't tell Kathryn, I mean, what was I gonna say? I didn't want to hurt her, ya know? I wanted her to be happy. I was after lettin' her down so many times I just couldn't face doin' it again. I was trapped. At the start it was easy to keep up the pretence. Me an' Kathryn might be out somewhere an' she'd say to me, 'We're doin' so much better now. I'm so glad you're off the drugs,' an' I didn't have the heart to tell her I wasn't. What could I say? I couldn't just come out with, 'Actually I'm a ragin' junkie.' So, I just built up this fuckin' alter ego almost, to live this schizod life. From then on it was just a matter of tryin' to juggle both of them an' to keep the two of them separate all the time. I had it all worked out. When to do a bit to keep me straight for the rest of the evenin' an' how much to do so I wouldn't be noddin' off with lit fags in me hand, burnin' the couch.

When you're a heroin addict, life is like a nightmare in reverse. If you've ever had a nightmare ya might wake up, realise it was a bad dream an' think, 'Jaysus that was scary, thanks be to fuck that's over'. But when you're addicted to smack it's the opposite of that. The only time ya escape from yer addiction is when you're asleep. But while you're asleep your body's not gettin' any heroin. As soon as ya wake up an' open your eyes, you're in the height of withdrawal, d'ya know what I mean? That's what usually wakes ya up an' that's why the first thing ya do when ya get up in the mornin' is go out lookin' for gear.

I'd be wakin' up at 11 o clock after Kathryn was gone to work. I'd pull on me jeans an' try an' figure out where I could score. I was goin' down to buy off this regular guy I knew but regular guys only last a certain amount of time in that business. They either get busted an' jailed or they run out of gear, or their supplier runs out. So ya spend 90 percent of you're day runnin' round lookin' for a fix. You're goin' to friends of friends or ya go to a bloke that used to score with ya an' he says, 'Well, before when I couldn't score, I knew this bloke in Clondalkin . . .'. So now ya boot over to Clondalkin but this fella hasn't got anythin' but he says he knows someone else, a bloke who might be carryin' an' on it goes. . . . By this time it could be 5 o'clock in the evenin' an' I'd be in the fuckin' height of withdrawal again.

Ya start off takin' heroin for the buzz an' all that, but eventually you're just takin' it to stand still. It's like bein' on a treadmill – as the withdrawals start creepin' up on ya the treadmill's gettin' faster but then ya take some heroin an' it slows down to a manageable pace an' you're at walkin' speed. You're fine an' you're takin' care of business. But as the day progresses, it starts to speed up, gettin' faster as each hour passes 'til you're in that frenzy an' ya have to get more gear to slow ya down again. An' then you're takin' care of business, takin' care of business. . . .

But sooner or later smokin' it wasn't goin' to be enough. It was only a matter of time before I started injectin'. I'd always said I'd never use a needle to inject heroin. I was still only smokin' it when AIDS became this big epidemic an' I knew the dangers of sharin' dirty needles. Plus, to me, ODs an' all that were related to usin' needles. I'd never heard of anybody who overdosed just by smokin'.

But the day came when I'd to inject heroin for the first time – for purely economic reasons. At that time it was takin' a quarter gram, which was a 40 quid bag, to stop me from gettin' sick. It would take at least two, sometimes three of these, just to get me through the day. When I was first fucked outta the band I'd a bit of money stashed away but I'd to sign back on the Labour an' that was basically what I was survivin' on. I mean Kathryn was workin' an' payin' the bills an' all but I could hardly go to her an' say, 'Here, have ya got a few quid – I need to score.'

One day I only had 20 quid. There was another bloke with me an' he had about the same. So we'd 40 quid between the two of us an' we knew it wasn't enough to get both of us together. Then he says, 'Well, ya know, if ya have a jib, ya don't need as much injectin' it as ya would if you're smokin' it.'

So, we got a quarter between the two of us an' yer man had a brand new diabetic works. It was still in the package an' all, so I knew it was clean. I was still very nervous though, 'cause for years I'd rejected the idea of usin' needles. I used to look at other addicts an' think, 'man, I'd never use a needle. How can them cunts use needles?', d'ya know what I mean? I actually saw meself as different to them.

I didn't have a big physical revulsion of stickin' a needle into me arm, ya know? I just had a vague fear like a lot of people have. To this day I can inject meself no problem – I remember when I was in hospital a while ago with pneumonia the nurse couldn't find a vein so I'd to inject meself 'cause I knew where the veins were. But if anybody else comes near me with a needle I'd fuckin' flip – I'd be so nervous. But the first time I'd to let this bloke do it for me 'cause I wouldn't have been able to get the veins – it takes practise. When ya start shootin' up people are usually doin' it for ya 'cause ya wouldn't be able to do it yourself. The first time ya inject into yer arm is usually out of necessity – you're sick, ya have to do it an' there's nobody else around.

Now, this is dangerous territory in that I don't want to be bleedin' glorifyin' heroin to anybody or makin' out that it's somethin' that it's not. If I'm gonna tell ya now 'bout what the feelin' of using a needle is like, I want to qualify it an' put it in the right context. I don't want anybody thinkin' that I'm sayin' how great heroin is – not because I give a fuck about any backlash – but I'd hate to think I would be encouragin' someone to take heroin, that'd kill me. But basically the way I look at it is, there's no point in denyin' that heroin gives ya a euphoric feelin'. Otherwise, why would anybody fuckin' do it, ya know? The thing is there's a huge price to pay, d'ya know what I mean? An' that price is addiction, AIDS, death an' all the other things that go with takin' heroin.

When ya smoke heroin in the middle of withdrawal ya have all those horrible feelin's that I described before. It's only over a 10 or 15 minute period that the heroin starts to soothe them 'til eventually you're covered with this euphoric feeling – this anaesthetic – an' there's no pain. It's such a gradual thing that it takes about 20 minutes before you realise you're not sick any more, but that euphoric feelin' only takes seconds when ya inject it.

Ya have your bag of gear an' ya put your heroin in the spoon. Ya put a bit of citric powder on the heroin, but ya have to be careful what you use for citric acid. When the

AIDS epidemic hit, a lot of clinics an' needle exchanges started supplin' clean needles an' citric 'cause, I mean, people are goin' to use heroin, so there's no point in lettin' them destroy themselves with dirty works. Before that people were usin' vinegar or Jif lemons for the acid, an' there was a preservative in the Jif lemon, which was apparently makin' people blind an' shit, ya know?

Ya add a drop of water to your heroin an' citric. Within a few seconds, that's gonna all break down 'til it goes from white to a brown-like, tea-coloured liquid. Ya cut a bit off the filter of a cigarette an' ya put it into the liquid an' get your needle. Ya suck the liquid through the filter so now it's in the chamber. Ya tie a tourniquet on your arm, right, an' your vein comes up. Ya put the needle into your arm, pull back the plunger an' a drop of blood will come into the chamber, which shows you're in the vein.

I'm dyin', I'm so sick while yer man's doin' all this, right. I'm fuckin' shakin' an' aches are runnin' through me. Then he pushes the plunger an' – instantly – I'm outta me head. It's pain relief on the spot. It's so sudden – that's how quick it hits ya. It's just 'BAM'. So ya can imagine, that's why ya often hear about people who overdose an' they still have the works in their arms. I couldn't believe the difference in the feelin' I got from injectin'. When I opened me eyes me first thought was that I regretted waitin' this long to use a needle. All I could think about was all that heroin I'd wasted by smokin' it. An' once you've used a needle then it's like the time ya first took heroin – you've broken another taboo.

* * *

I have to admit that for a while any musical ambition I had took a back seat to heroin. I was scroungin' round a few old contacts an' names in the business, checkin' out a few avenues where I thought I might get a break, even if it was to go solo. But most of me days were spent gettin' me next fix. An' that meant divin' even deeper into that criminal underworld that most people only read about in Sunday newspapers.

One of the worst things about drugs, right, is the people who ya have to deal with. Some of the people I came across when I was scorin' heroin were the lowest scumbags I've ever met. There is no honour among junkies. They really would fuckin' do ya if it gave them half a chance of scorin' enough gear to keep themselves from gettin' sick. It was all smiles an' concern when ya were in it together an' the chances of gettin' some gear that day were good but if they'd to choose, you'd come a poor fuckin' second.

There were loadsa times, hundreds, when I was badly ripped off. To this day I can't look at chicken soup the same way. You'd be dyin', sick with the withdrawals an' after runnin' round for hours you'd manage to score. You're like, 'Aw thanks be to Jaysus,' an' then ya find the nearest place ya can get some bit of privacy to shoot up. Ya go to a jacks in a pub or wherever the fuck you're gonna go. Ya go to the quickest place ya can, bust open the bag an' get this smell. Ya stare down at the powder an' ya know instantly that it's not heroin. It's chicken soup or bisto – that's just horrendous. You've spent all your money an' now ya have to go off an' start lookin' all over again, tryin' to blag some on tick. I hated all that shit. But there was one thing I hated more than gettin' burnt an' the fuckin' backstabbin' – I hated havin' to lick arse to scumbags an' wankers.

I was goin' down scorin' off this bloke in Glasnevin. This would've been the followin' year, about 1989 or thereabouts. When I got there he said he hadn't got anythin' an' he'd have to go off an' get it. So I says, 'How long will ya be?' An' he says an hour or somethin' like that. I was after buyin' a car before the band split up so it was still new lookin' at the time an' he spots it parked out on the road when he was leavin' the gaff. He says, 'Give us a lend of your car an' I'll only be 20 minutes.'

Now, I was sick, ya know? I'd no choice. I had to stay on his good side so he'd come back. I handed him the keys an' he fucks off with me car an' me 80 quid for the gear in his pocket. I went into the Addison Lodge, ya know, down near the Botanic Gardens an' I had a coffee. I only had about three quid left on me 'cause I was after givin' him all me money, right? I was havin' a coffee an' half an hour passed, an hour passed, an' I had to get out. I couldn't sit there with just one coffee all day. This was at 11 in the mornin' an' when it came to 12 I had to leave. I walked round the corner an' stood on Moby Road, where I could see his house. An' I just stood there watchin' out for him to come back. So 12 o'clock came an' went, 1 o'clock, 2 o'clock, 3 o'clock, 4 o'clock passed an' I was still standin' there. By this stage I was in bits, in the height of withdrawal – strung out to fuck.

The next minute I heard a siren in the distance an' it was gettin' nearer. When I looked up towards Harts Corner I seen this police car comin'. It was an unmarked car, ya know, a dick car with the lights stuck on the roof. It was bootin' down towards me an' I says to meself, 'Jaysus there's some fucker gonna get tore out of it.' Next minute the car suddenly swerves in on top of the footpath an' they open the doors so I'm pinned up against the railings an' I can't run anywhere. They jump out, drag me into the car an' they bring me down to Whitehall Garda Station, which was a fair fuckin' distance away.

They told me some aul wan in Neighbourhood Watch or somethin' had seen me standin' there all day an' thought I was casin' some houses so she called the cops. They didn't know who I was 'til I gave them me name an' then they just said, 'Right', an' they strip-searched me an' all that. But I'd nothin' on me so they fucked me outta the station.

I started walkin' back to yer man's gaff. I was really dyin' by this stage. I could barely walk 'cause I was shiverin' so much an' me legs kept crampin' up. I had to stand an' lean against the wall a few times. By the time I got there it was dark but I seen me car was parked outside. Now, all I wanna do 'cause of all the shit I'd gone through, is go in, grab yer man, tear his liver out an' shove it up his arse, d'ya know what I mean? But, I know if I do that, I'm not gonna get me gear an' I'm fuckin' really sick now. So I'd to go in an' kowtow to him when all I wanted to do was kill him. So I walked in an' he says, 'Ah howya, Christy? Eh, I didn't get anything . . .' An' I had to just sit there an' swallow it all.

That was just one time I was stopped by the cops. I could tell ya about hundreds of times 'cause it became part an' parcel of me life. It was a hazard of the profession, if ya like.

I was always fairly lucky as far as avoidin' gettin' busted with gear was concerned. I'd a few close calls all right but I was never caught with anythin' on me. I remember one day, it musta been in the summer of 1989, I was in town with another lad scorin' an' we went back to me car to shoot up. I had the gear on the spoon an' I was gettin' it ready when next minute a police car pulls up beside me. The copper rolls down his window an' looks over, just inches away. I'm sittin' there with the gear on the spoon in one hand while I'm rollin' down the window with the other. The cop starts askin' me name an' was this my car an' all that. I'm talkin' away, ya know, 'Yeah, this is me car, yeah, yeah, the insurance is in date, no worries . . .'. The whole time me mate's kinda goin' in me ear, 'Dump the gear, Christy, for fuck's sake, dump the gear,' but I was terrified of spillin' it. If the cop had made a move to get outta the car I'd a just tipped it, ya know? But I wanted to see for how long I could avoid doin' that. I wasn't droppin' that fuckin' spoon unless I absolutely had to 'cause what was in it was more important than any cop at that moment.

After a few more questions they fucked off in their car an' me an' me mate are left sittin' there, takin' deep breaths. Finally, me mate turns around an' he's like, 'Ya mad bastard, ya shoulda dropped it.' But I'm lookin' at him, with a grin on me face, goin', 'Ah, yeah, but then what?'

When ya become a junkie ya have to develop an ability to avoid bein' caught with drugs by the police 'cause they only have to be lucky once. Ya have to be lucky all the time. I was so well-known as a junkie in Dublin that I couldn't pass a police car without bein' stopped an' searched for drugs, that's how bad it was.

There was times when I'd be drivin' up the road an' I'd have gear on me, in me bag in the back of the car, say an' for no reason I'd stop an' I'd take it out of the bag. I'd have it in me hand, gettin' ready to throw it. An' I dunno why I'd have done that but all of a sudden I'd be pulled in by the police an' I'd be able to hide it somewhere. Whereas if I'd a left it in the bag I'd have been fucked 'cause they would've looked into the bag an' opened it. Loads of times shit like that happened an' I can't explain it – it's like a sixth sense. You're always aware 'cause you're doin' somethin' illegal but it doesn't explain how ya know that this is the day they're gonna stop ya.

It's some sort of self-preservation isn't it like, some sort of instinct? You're really paranoid an' careful 'cause you're an addict an' that does save ya 90 percent of the time but loads of people I know were caught at least once with somethin'. An' I'd often wonder how I got away with it. There were times Kathryn'd say, 'Just have somethin' to eat before ya go,' an' 9 times outta 10 I'd say, 'I'll eat it when I come back.' But the day I'd say, 'Right, I'll sit an' eat it',' I'd get a phone call that the gaff I was goin' to was raided.

The thing is even with the self-preservation an' everythin' it gets to the stage when you're so desperate to stop bein' sick that you'll disregard the warnin' signs an' take risks.

I remember sittin' outside Tolka Park football pitch just a few months after the cops stopped beside us in town. There's a place round the back where ya can pull in at the side of the road. But it's kinda open, ya know? It's not the best place to park an' not look suspicious. Me an' this other lad had only just scored our gear, ya know, but it had taken us all day to get it. So we were sick an' like I was sayin' when you're sick ya want to get it into ya as quick as ya can. There's no such thing as drivin' around lookin' for a nice spot. So we pulled in off the side of the road so we could do it in the car. I says to me mate, 'Right, I'll watch out while you're doin' the business.'

As he's busy gettin' his works out an' preparin' the heroin I'm watchin' out, makin' sure no police cars drive up. So he shoots up an' then I'm like, 'Listen, you watch out while I'm havin' mine.' I have the needle ready an' I was just tappin' on me arm to get the vein up when I hear, WHACK, WHACK. I look up an' there's the police on the bonnet of the car, lashin' their batons off the windscreen. I'm sittin' there, a gizmo in me hand full of gear an' I'm lookin' at these two cops tryin' to get in. One of them jumps down an' tries to pull the door off the fuckin' hinges. The other's still beatin' the window. I'm thinkin', 'if they arrest me now I'm fucked'. I knew if I left the heroin in the gizmo they could charge me with bein' in possession. I just go POW with the syringe into me leg an' I push the plunger. Me mate had already done all his so I just lean over an' open the door.

We let them drag us out an' arrest us 'cause we knew there was nothin' they could do – all they had were two empty needles. They obviously knew damn well what we were doin' but there was nothin' they could charge us with. They brought us down to the station an' did the usual strip-searchin an' questionin' but they had to let us go – what else could they do? Obviously they tore the bollix out of us but I was gettin' used to that. It was just par for the course.

I didn't give a shit anyway. I was fuckin' high an' they didn't have anythin' on me.

* * *

This is the way me life went after I got kicked outta Aslan. I knew that this heroin problem was gettin' worse but at that time I didn't know what else to do. I'd already been through treatment an' it didn't work. I'd managed to pull off this mental two-way existence of feedin' a habit by day while comin' home to be with me family by night. I was scared. I was genuinely thinkin', 'this is gettin' serious an' I need help', but I was afraid to say anythin' to anybody, even Kathryn, 'cause I'd kinda built up this big lie for the last coupla years that I was fine. I couldn't just turn round an' say, 'Listen, the last two years or whatever have been bullshit. I'm more fucked now than ever.' I'd been tellin' her an' everyone else that I'd been cured so I was determined to keep it that way.

If there was just one thing that was gonna save me now, it was music.

One Man's Dream

I was fightin' an on-goin' daily battle to keep me drug habit under control an' some days I won. Some days I made it through the day without doin' heroin. Some days I was just like everyone else an' I'd swear that this was the day me life was gonna change. An' then other days I slipped an' fell an' I escaped into the arms of me habit again – on, off, on, off, on, off. . . . Every time, I'd swear this was the last time I'd put a needle in me arm. Then the next time I did it I seemed to swear with even more determination to rid meself of the terrible sickness sweepin' through me – on, off, on, off, on, off. . . .

I knew I couldn't let the struggle become the only purpose to gettin' through the day. I needed to have another go at makin' it in the music industry – not only to save me career but to save me sanity as well.

It'd been a hard decision to make 'cause I'd to re-immerse meself into a world that had just fuckin' crucified me but in a way the choice had already been made. I wasn't trained to be anythin' else. I never studied in a college to be educated in some other profession that I could fall back on. I never had a job that I could return to an' be able to say, 'Ah yeah, fuck the music, this'll do me for the rest of me life.' I didn't have anythin' else goin' for me apart from me talents as a singer. So, in that sense, I didn't have any other options – we'd to pay the mortgage, I'd to look after me daughter, an' I'd a drug habit to feed. As well as that, I still wanted music in me life despite all that'd happened. I didn't have a plan but I never really had a plan anyway. Even with Aslan I'd no real idea. I mean we came out as a band an' I wanted it to be a successful band. I wanted to see how far we would go. Each level of success was received with a feelin' of justification that we deserved to get where we were. It was still a surprise though when we reached each of those levels 'cause I'd seen so many others that were very talented but didn't achieve anythin'. But world domination was never important to me. Now, I just wanted to get out an' prove that me voice wasn't fucked an' that I still had the talent to make it on me own. It was important to me as well that people could see that the papers were wrong, the ones that'd said I was burnt out, d'ya know what I mean? So all those things were lightin' a fire under me arse.

Also, Aslan still had each other, a manager an' a record deal, so they'd the potential to become really successful. Now, I'm only human, you can be fuckin' sure I was sittin' there goin, 'I hope they go down the tubes . . .' I remember they brought out a single called *Strange Love* which was one of the songs we were writin' together when I had the split with the band. It was their first release with their new singer Eamo Doyle. I remember they played it on the *Late Late Show* one night. I sat down to watch it an' I was fuckin' delighted when they were on 'cause, I have to be honest, they were shite. I was thinkin', 'man, yis eejits, yis'. I was relieved when I seen this guy singin' with them 'cause I just knew he hadn't got anythin', ya know? He'd no voice, he'd no style. He was nothin' to do with Aslan an' I knew it wasn't goin' to work out for them.

In the meantime I was findin' me feet back on the public stage after a coupla lucky breaks at the start of 1989. It seemed like as soon as I'd made the decision to get back into music fate had stepped in an' moved things along for me. Me first chance had come when I got a phone call from a guy called Tim Martin askin' me if I wanted some free studio time.

Tim was the bloke who'd been the engineer on the *Feel No Shame* album. He was in workin' on Terence Trent D'Arby's new album *Neither Fish Nor Flesh* in Windmill Lane Studios when D'Arby's bird had a baby an' he'd to fly home to England earlier than he'd expected. D'Arby had read somewhere that I was tryin' to get a solo career goin' an' he knew Tim had worked with me before so he told Tim to ask me if I wanted to use the studios while he was with his bird. He already had the studio block booked, all paid for, so it woulda been goin' to waste. I thought that was a very decent thing to do. I mean I didn't know Terence Trent D'Arby at all. He just made an offer to help a fellow musician who needed it, ya know? Studios are expensive places to use. They can cost thousands every day an' it was money I didn't have. I didn't have fuck all at the time so I jumped at the opportunity.

I knew I was gonna get back into music some time an' the fact that this happened so soon after I decided to do it made me believe that maybe I could get a new band together. I approached Oliver Walsh in Solid Records an' he said he was prepared to release a single for me if I could get it down in time. Now I only had three or four days in the studio so I got in a coupla session musicians, a guitar player an' a drummer an' that an' I recorded a song called *One Man's Dream.* We'd only about a day left in the studio before D'Arby was due back when Oliver Walsh rang me an' asked what I was gonna put on the B-Side. I hadn't even thought 'bout it. Most of the other guys had already gone home for the day but I looked into the TV room an' found Fred Malone, one of the session guitarists still sittin' there. He came back into the studio with me an' strummed a few chords while I wrote down the lyric lines for this song that was in me head. We both just sat there goin' over it an' in a day we managed to record the basics of a song I called *Chasing Shadows.* That was meant to be the B-side but Walsh liked it so much he listened to it that he wanted to make a double A-side single.

While they were pressin' the single I played me first solo gig at McGonagles. I asked a coupla musicians I knew to back me up on the night. I put up all these posters around town billin' it as The Chrsity Dignam Band. It was funny, I remember I was on the Labour at the time an' I went in one day to get me dole money an' yer woman behind the counter said, 'You're Christy Dignam off the posters.' I said, 'Yeah', thinkin' she might be a fan or somethin' but then she says, 'So technically you're workin'.' I was goin', 'Eh, eh, . . . it's just one gig, . . .' but that was it – I had to sign off.

When it came to the night I was really nervous 'cause I didn't know if anyone was gonna turn up, ya know? I'd been this big star with Aslan but I didn't know if that fame was enough to carry me through on me own. It's hard to explain, ya don't really see it the way other people see it, ya know? Ya don't realise the extent of yer fame. As far as I was concerned I was famous 'cause I was in Aslan but on me own I was just Christy Dignam, d'ya know what I mean?

So when I walked into McGonagles that night I didn't know what the fuck was gonna happen. I thought a few mates might come to the gig but I didn't know if anybody else would bother showin' up. I arrived at the venue an' I asked the guy at the door if there was many people inside. 'Christy,' he says, 'It's jammed.' I couldn't believe it. It was packed.

When I went down on the stage everyone in the place just started clappin'. I played a few of the new songs I'd written an' a coupla Aslan numbers. The place went mental. Half way through the gig I realised I was gonna pull this off.

By the time I was finishin' the last song I'd completely relaxed an' I was enjoyin' meself. I think the crowd recognised that an' they gave this long applause at the end. I was backstage in the dressin' room an' they were still callin' out for more after five minutes so I got back out an' did a coupla other songs. I'll never forget it. It was me first time on a public stage without Aslan an' the reaction I got convinced me I was doin' the right thing. I started thinkin' about maybe gettin' back out on the road, dependin' on how well the single did. It was due for release in March.

Around this time I got a phone call from EMI askin' would I be interested in auditionin' for the British band Marillion. Their lead singer Fish had just left an' the record company asked me would I go over to London an' rehearse with them for a weekend. I wasn't really into their music at all but I went over anyway, just to keep EMI sweet, ya know? They were a big label so I wanted to keep in with them an' maybe redeem meself in their eyes after the shit with Aslan.

I jammed with them for the weekend an' I musta done okay 'cause they asked me to come back an' do more rehearsals with them. Now, I was gonna go along with that but they also mentioned that I'd have to go on tour with them if I got the job. At that stage I said sorry, but I wasn't interested. I explained to them an' to EMI that I wanted to get me own solo career goin'. I didn't want to be part of someone else's band.

I was lucky in that there was a few other offers goin' round that I could've taken up if only for the money 'cause I was still broke then. Another record company, I can't remember their name, were talkin' to me about recordin' an album of classical songs sung by various singers an' that would've made a bit of money but I wasn't into it. It didn't suit what I wanted to do. I didn't want to be walkin' back into a situation that I couldn't control, especially after what had happened before.

It wasn't that I thought I had too much talent to waste on projects like that. I don't think like that. It was just, ya know, I knew what I wanted to do an' I didn't want other musicians to be in control of the situation an' push their opinions onto me.

Solid released *One Man's Dream* an' *Chasing Shadows* as a single in March. It turned out that *Chasing Shadows* was one of the most successful singles I'd ever done. It got a great response an' was played on the radio a good bit. I was fuckin' delighted, obviously, but to be brutally honest I wasn't even aware of how it was goin' down with the music heads. After I'd split with Aslan an' all the shit happened with the *Star* I just lost interest in what the press said about me. I didn't read reviews any more – good or bad.

I'd to do a few gigs around Ireland to follow up on the success of the single. The problem was I'd worked with these experienced session musicians to record the songs in the studio right, but goin' on tour was different. I wanted to get a few young fellas who were just startin' out 'cause they'd have more enthusiasm for life on the road, ya know?

I started lookin' round Dublin's music scene again for fresh talent to make a new band. It was kinda like all those years ago when I went searchin' for the right people to be in Aslan. I wanted to avoid accomplished musicians who had their own way of doin' things. The idea was I was gonna mould these new guys.

While I was still checkin' out a few musicians here an' there I was invited to play a gig out in Mountjoy Prison. I said yeah but I was shittin' meself 'cause there was a guy in there that was 'after' me. He was this fella from Ballymun where I used to have to go to get gear. He was a big fucker, ya know? Junkies were all little skinny yokes, but he was massive. He was also a real hardened criminal – a fuckin' animal, an' people tried to stay away from him.

A few months before I'd been out in Ballymun to score an' I met this junkie I knew. She was on the game, ya know, an' she'd been up all night makin' her money. She'd 120 quid in her hand, dyin', sick, waitin' for somebody to arrive with gear. I was standin' at the corner an' as I was talkin' to her I seen yer man comin' up the side of the flats on me left, where she couldn't see him. He's standin' round the corner, she's around the other side, an' yer man just swings round with his fist an' smacks her straight into the face. She was just this skinny little bird, ya know? She kinda crumpled up in a heap on the ground. He just leaned over an' took her money. He glared at me an' strolled off with the cash in his hand while I went over to help yer one off the ground. Her face was in bits an' she was bawlin'. She was all right though. She was more messed up over losin' her heroin money than getting the dig in the face. It sickened me but what could I do?

A coupla days later I'd to go out there again to pick up some more gear. I remember it was late on a Sunday an' there was nothin' much goin' on. There was no dealers about. Most of us had been hangin' round for hours an' by this time there was 12 or 13 people hopin' this one fella would arrive with the gear. Then this hardened criminal showed up again. He sat down with the rest of us, took out this knife an' started pickin' an abscess off his hand with the blade. I'm tryin' to quietly move away from him 'cause the story was he had the virus, – that he'd HIV.

Next minute he just flies up an' puts the knife to me throat. I swear to God, I could feel it diggin' into me skin. He's after stickin' it in this open sore on his hand so all that's goin' through me head is, 'if that even breaks me skin I'm fucked', ya know? So he says, 'Right, give me yer money.' There's 40 quid in me back pocket so I says, 'It's there, in me pocket, just take it,' tryin' to be cool so he won't stick me.

Nobody was gonna help me, ya know? They didn't want anythin' to do with it 'cause they needed to keep their own money, d'ya know what I mean? He let me go an' told me to go an' fuck off. I'd been there since 12 o'clock that day, dyin'. This was about 4 in the afternoon an' I'd been sittin' all that time in the freezin' cold. Now me money was gone so I couldn't even come back an' try an' score later.

As I walked off this was goin' through me mind an' I thought 'fuck that' an' I headed straight over to Ballymun Garda station. I went up to the desk an' I says to the copper, 'I'm after bein' robbed over at the flats an' I'm after havin' 40 quid taken off me.' The copper recognised me, ya know, an' he says, 'So what? Youse junkies are always out there robbin' each other.' I was like, 'Hold on a minute, I'm after reportin' a crime to you. Are you tellin' me you're not goin' to do anythin' about it?' He goin' 'We'll arrest the guy, we'll go to court an' you won't bother turnin' up. It's always the same with you lot.' Then I says, 'I will turn up in court.' I just wanted me money back, ya know, I needed to score. I'd no chance of gettin' money anywhere else. So he says, 'You're promisin' me you'll turn up in court if we find this guy?' an' I says, 'I swear, I will.'

He's lookin' at me like I was bullshittin' him but finally he calls in another copper an' they bring me out to the cop car an' we all get in. The police drove across the road with me in the back seat 'til I spotted your man still sittin' there in the same spot. He hadn't mugged me an' run off or anythin' 'cause he thought he'd nothin' to fear from me. He just looked up kinda casually when the police car arrived but the minute he sees me gettin' outta the car I seen the shock on his face. I told the Old Bill that he was the one who'd attacked me an' they arrested him an' put him in the back of the car. I went over to the copper as they're puttin' him in the back an' asked could I get me money back. But the copper says, 'Oh no, we need it for evidence. You'll get it after the court case.' I just thought, 'aww no'.

I never heard back from the cops about it an' I'd kinda forgotten about it 'til after I'd agreed to do this gig in Mountjoy Prison months later. Say the gig was on a Wednesday, I remember gettin' the paper on the Tuesday, an' the reporter in the court musta copped me name on the charge sheet or whatever 'cause it said yer man had '*. . . pleaded guilty today to robbin' rock singer Christy Dignam in Ballymun. . . .*' Turned out this fella got 10 months – in the same prison I'm playin' the next fuckin' day.

I went up to the prison an' I asked the screw up there what the story was with this guy that had got sent down. I was worried that he was gonna come after me. But the screw says, 'Don't worry Christy, he's on such an' such a wing. We'll make sure they're not comin' down to see the show.' The whole time I was there I could hear the other prisoners singin' all this shit, 'He's comin' to get ya; he's comin' to get ya. . . .' As it turned out the gig went down great with the lags in there but I was shittin' meself on the stage in case yer man was in the audience. But the screw kept his word an' I never saw him again.

That was a once-off gig I did meself for the prison an' after that I started tourin' with The Christy Dignam Band. It was made up of all these unknown musicians that I'd found an' done some work with over the last few months. It was very successful.

I've always relied on a very stringent quality control that I apply to anythin' musical I do. There were times when I did let the standards slip a little bit in me solo career – I'm only realisin' that in retrospect – but I think me music still had a generally high standard. As far as I was concerned that justified me gettin' back on a stage an' performin' for people. At the end of the day I wasn't askin' people to ride me, ya know? I wasn't askin' them to be me best mate. I was tryin' to sell the music, not meself an' I felt I was deliverin' the goods in that area. I think a lot of people could see this an' appreciate that it was a difficult time for me – releasin' meself back into the public domain with untried musicians, tryin' to put me music back out there.

A lot of the gigs were jammed out an' these were the same venues I'd been playin' with Aslan. So, as a solo artist, I nearly continued on at the same level that I'd been at when I left Aslan.

Meanwhile Aslan were doin' a tour at the same time. I was gettin' to their venues a week after them an' hearin' there was 30 people at their gig while I was playin' to 2,000. Obviously, ya know, I was happy about that, relieved that my tour was more successful. I'd be lyin' if I said I wasn't secretly thrilled.

I'd played a gig with Aslan in 1988 in The Marquee in London, which is a very prestigious venue, an' we'd sold out two nights. Then I heard that when the rest of the band went back to do it themselves, the whole crowd started shoutin', 'CHRISTY, CHRISTY' in the middle of *This is* an' fuckin' bottled them off the stage.

So all these stories started filterin' back to me an' it was all sweet music to me ears. I know that makes me sound petty. I could be all politically an' morally correct here an' say I was delighted for them, that I felt they deserved the success, that they'd worked their bollix off for it but no, I was still disgusted with them. I wanted them to fall on their arses. It's true, it would've killed me had they gone on to world domination while I was still playin' an acoustic set in the Baggot Inn. That would've pissed me off no end.

There was still a lot of bitterness long after the split – it was the loss of the friendships that hurt me more than anythin' else 'cause these were all people that I'd considered me best friends. Like I didn't consider the betrayal of journalists, who I'd seen as work colleagues, anywhere in the same league as the betrayal I felt after the band fucked me out. The band weren't just colleagues; they were me best mates. These were people I'd grown up with. These were people I'd shed all the tears with an' they knew every vulnerability I had – that's what hurt more than anythin', ya know?

Lookin' back on it, I think I did hope in the back of me mind that some day, maybe, we could get back an' sort it out, ya know, continue on where we'd left off. But obviously if they were goin' to be successful with this Eamo Doyle then they weren't gonna feel the same way. The first real spark of hope that we'd get back together probably didn't happen for me 'til I seen everythin' fallin' apart for them. I'd said in an interview just prior to us splittin' up that it wouldn't work if any particular element of Aslan was changed an' when that happened at least I could say, 'See? I was right.'

As for me, I was findin' me feet with The Christy Dignam Band an' I was gettin' more exposure. I was invited onto *The Late Late Show* to perform in 1990 I think it was, an' that's where I met another guy who'd be responsible for changin' me musical career – again.

* * *

I'd been playin' around the country with The Christy Dignam Band when I went into RTÉ one night to sing *One Man's Dream* on the *Late Late*. As I was leavin' this guy called Neil Joyce approached me with a business proposition. Neil was a doctor who was also involved in a few bands round town. He was workin' for the promoters MCD at the time, organisin' gigs an' that. He came up after the show an' congratulated me, sayin' I was doin' really well. Then he said he'd this idea that he thought could work for me. He'd an affiliation with this musician called Conor Goff – they were friends, ya know – an' he said Conor was doin' a successful tour in the States but he was comin' back. Neil asked me would I be interested in meetin' yer man Conor an' maybe settin' up a band together.

Now I knew Conor Goff 'cause he'd had a few bands around Dublin before then. I think one of them was called Conor Goff an' The Crash. But me initial reaction to Neil's suggestion was no way 'cause Conor was into a completely different type of music to me. Conor was more of a rocker; he would've been more into Bon Jovi, let's say. We were from two different schools of music, ya know? But then, when I started thinkin' about it, I wondered if, 'cause we were from two totally different musical backgrounds, the chemistry of those two elements would create a third element that would be somethin' unique? I started thinkin' that maybe the artistic conflict would be a positive thing so I said I'd give it a go.

I still had the Christy Dignam Band goin' on at the time for the *One Man's Dream / Chasing Shadows* tour. When Conor got back from the States, he came in to see us play but he wasn't happy with the band. He insisted that they'd have to go if I wanted to hook up with him. Now they weren't the best musicians in the world. They were good enough an' all but I didn't have a fuckin' unbridled loyalty for anybody at the time. I mean 'cause of what had happened with Aslan I wasn't prepared to make any sacrifices for other people an' I wasn't goin' to get cosy with this band either. I'd learnt from the past that emotionally, gettin' close wasn't the right way to go – if ya wanted to stay emotionally bleedin' secure ya had to keep yer distance.

So meself an' Conor agreed that we'd look out for other musicians an' we got another band together of people from other groups, which is somethin' I always said I wouldn't do. I didn't want to play with musicians that'd already been around the block a few times but Conor insisted that we needed an experienced band behind us if we were gonna tour together. So we got in Cactus World News's drummer, In Tua Nua's bass player an' so on. Thinkin' back later I remember feelin' that it was a big mistake 'cause it would compromise the quality of the music. But I went along with it probably 'cause it was handier for me to let somebody else do all the thinkin' an' deal with the business end of things. That was always too much for me, so I let him take over I suppose. I mean like Conor was well aware of what the story was with me an' heroin but it wasn't a big deal to him.

We'd a set that was a mix an' mash of songs. We played some Aslan songs an' I also had the two solo songs I'd written *Chasing Shadows* an' *One Man's Dream*. Conor brought in a coupla other numbers but a lot of the stuff we were writin' ourselves. We started doin' a few small gigs round the country in 1990, callin' ourselves Dignam and Goff.

Not long after I'd started out with the Dignam and Goff band the legal action I'd taken against *The Star* for libel finally came up in court. When they'd printed that story callin' me a dealer I'd released me statement to the press denyin' it but I still wanted to get a retraction from the newspaper. So I'd asked a Dublin solicitor to take the case. It was important to me, for so many reasons, to clear me name. I had to do it for meself – as I've said, I'd no problem admittin' that I was takin' heroin but that whole allegation that I was dealin' just appalled me. I wasn't profitin' from drugs in any way. If anythin' I felt I was a victim of drugs. Even in the worst stages of addiction I'd never, ever, get anyone else heroin; even if they'd begged me to. It was the one principle that I'd always been very adamant about. It was just somethin' that I held onto in me mind that separated me an' me habit from the mentality of the pushers.

I also wanted to prove to me family that the dealin' report was all bullshit. Over the two years it took for me case to come to court I couldn't even talk 'bout it properly to them. To this day I still haven't had that conversation with me ma. I was just hopin' that her knowledge of me as a person would tell her that it wasn't true. I knew deep down that she would've known it wasn't true, d'ya know what I mean? But I wanted her to have somethin' in black an' white, like a printed apology from the newspaper, that she could show the neighbours – not that she'd physically go round an' knock at her neighbour's doors to show them

– just somethin' appearin' in the press that belied all this bullshit that'd been printed about me. Above all else, that's all I wanted.

Before the solicitors would take me case they'd insisted on hirin' these private investigators to check out me story. They didn't want to go into court an' find out that the allegations about me were true an' lose the case. I remember they'd these private detectives go out into the heroin underworld, around Dublin, to make sure there was no truth in *The Star's* story. I'd to pay for these guys to go shiftin' through me background to see was I this big-time heroin dealer. It might seem that it was lack of faith on their part but I didn't have a problem with it 'cause I knew they could never find any evidence 'cause there was no evidence.

But it upped the stakes. They were on a retainer so they were bein' paid the whole time it took the case to come to court. An' they weren't the only ones. By the time the case came up I'd a barrister, junior counsel, senior counsel, solicitors. . . . There was about six or seven people with me an' I remember walkin' into the courtroom that day an' thinkin' everythin' was on the line. I'd had to put me house up as collateral. If I lost the case, if it went against me, we wouldn't even have a roof over our heads.

It was tough not only on me but also me family. Ya have to understand I'd already lost everythin' – the band, the record deal, all that stuff. I'd fucked up all over the place, right, an' I knew I was now jeopardisin' the little we had left an' here I was askin' Kathryn to trust me again.

She told me I was doin' the right thing but we both knew this was goin' to be one of the biggest fuckin' gambles of me life. Even me own legal people were warnin' me before we went into the courtroom, ya know? They were sayin' to me not to expect much off the case 'cause even if I won it hands down the jury would be lookin' at me as an ex-heroin addict an' thinkin' that there was no point givin' me money to spend on gear. They were warnin' me that if I lost I'd have to pay costs. So not only would I lose me house but I'd be in debt for the rest of me life. We'd never own anythin' again. But the way I saw it I had no choice – I had to risk everythin' to clear me name. *The Star* had said I'd blown heroin into the eyes of me child, ya know? That's what killed me. I had to walk into that court that mornin' or I'd never have been able to live with meself again.

We took our seats in the courtroom an' I reached over an' grabbed Kathryn's hand. When the judge sat down everyone went quiet. Then *The Star's* counsel stood up an' started talkin' in a loud voice, describin' this bloke to everyone in the room, sayin' somethin' like: 'Your honor, this man is a self-confessed heroin abuser. He has openly described his addiction to drugs an' admitted his involvement in the trade of extremely dangerous narcotics.' He was basically makin' me out to be a drug-pushin' scumbag – obviously not in those exact words but that was his vibe.

Initially I didn't even realise it was me he was talkin' about. I was sittin' there listenin' to this thinkin', 'if I was neutral in this courtroom today, I would say this bastard deserves to be strung up by the fuckin' throat an' hung, drawn an' quartered. He's a scumbag, who the fuck is this . . .' an' then I realised they were talkin' about me.

I kinda knew what I was takin' on when I walked into the courtroom but hearin' the savagery of the attack on me character, in a packed court like that, was worse in a lot of ways than when I read it in the paper. While this was goin' on I noticed the junior counsel, or whoever it was, runnin' back an' forward from one table to the other. In the middle of this fella's speech, makin' me out to be the biggest drug dealer on the planet, one of their counsel stood up an' said, 'Your honor, could we have a short recess?' The judge goes, 'You can have fifteen minutes.' An' we all went out into the hallway.

They were all standin' on one side of the circle outside the court while we were shufflin' round opposite them. Next minute one of the counsel runnin' round says to me, 'They're after offerin' five grand plus this, plus that.' I says, 'What about me apology? What about me retraction?' That wasn't on the table so I says, 'No way, I want a retraction; I want an apology.' As he walked back to the other side of the circle, over to their crowd, I shouted at him, 'An' I don't want it on the back page; I don't want it in little tiny print . . .'

The whole thing ended up with an offer of, I think, 25 grand plus costs, and, most importantly to me, a retraction. That was the main thing to me. I didn't give a fuck so much about the amounts of money they were arguin' about – I had cleared me name.

And that was that – suddenly two years of torment had come to an end an' I'd won. I just remember walkin' down by the quays that day with Kathryn an' both of us burstin' into tears that it was all over, ya know? The relief was kinda like gettin' a splinter outta yer eye, ya know that kinda feelin'?

I didn't even realise the pressure that it had put me under on a personal level. Ya have to understand, while all this fightin' the case was goin' on, I was also tryin' to rebuild me career. Me total qualification was bein' a singer. I had nothin' else to fall back on. But nobody was goin' to have much time for a fuckin' drug-dealer, shamed in court after a failed libel action, so I had to make the court case pay off – for me future.

The retraction appeared a week later in *The Star* an' it was like a little weather report on page two. I mean it was somethin' you woulda easily missed it was so small. Fuck them – I got what I wanted. Me name was cleared an' I was justified in all I'd been sayin' about me innocence. No matter how small or insignificant the apology was it was still an apology an' a retraction, which meant they were admittin' that they were wrong, ya know? That's all I gave a fuck about.

Before the court case I'd still been livin' in Valley Park in Finglas near to where I grew up. We'd been happy there when we first moved in but we couldn't live in the estate anymore 'cause I'd the memories of those journalists bangin' the fuckin' door down at three in the mornin'. I remembered havin' to climb over the back walls, through other people's gardens to get outta the house 'cause they were outside the front door all the time. So yeah, that house had bad associations for me. Me an' Kathryn agreed that the money I got from the case would go towards a new house.

There was a bit of justice at the end of the day but the ordeal I went through after that article came out was one of the hardest things I've ever had to deal with. It was bleedin' terrible. I'll never forget it. Kathryn still has this attitude now about journalists – she doesn't trust them – an' who can blame the woman? I mean as I said before I'd set meself up, right, an' reaped the rewards of bein' in the public eye but she didn't choose that lifestyle. Kathryn didn't choose for her family to be hung out to dry in public like that.

She was a mother who had to protect her daughter but she couldn't be there for her all the time. When the retraction was printed the story was back in all the papers. Kiera would've been five or six years of age at the time an' I remember her comin' in from school one day an' sayin', 'Da, can I have a five quid deal of skag?' I was paintin' away upstairs on the landin' when she said it. I thought that's what I heard her say but I obviously assumed that I wasn't hearin' right, ya know? So I said to her, 'What did ya say?' an' she repeated it. So I asked her 'Who told you to say that?' an' she says, 'The boy across the road told me to get a five spot of skag off me da.'

I dropped the paintbrush an' went out the door. There was a gang of kids across the road, 16 to 18 years of age, a few birds an' a few blokes, an' I says to Kiera 'Which one was it?' She points out the fella who said it. As I'm walkin' towards him he's kinda standin' there in front of his mates, ya know, pushin' his chest out, actin' the hard man.

I grabbed him by the throat an' started squeezin' an' fuckin' squeezin'. There was so much rage in me that all I could see was his face turnin' blue but I wasn't associatin' it with the fact that I was stranglin' him. His mates were all screamin' an' shoutin' an' I think maybe some of the girls were cryin' but I couldn't even hear them. I was only vaguely aware of this commotion around me while I stood there – holdin' this fucker off the ground by his neck. When I let go I remember he fell on the ground an' the imprints of me fingers were painted all over him where I had him by the throat. He started coughin' an' splutterin' an' cryin' but I just left him there an' went back to the house, took Kiera inside an' shut the door.

Kiera had to grow up with a lot of that shit, in school an' all, ya know? Other kids would be sayin', 'Yer da's a junkie,' all that sorta stuff. An' that really got to me. I think it's a very male instinct that ya have this ability to stick up for yourself an' fight yer own corner but when somethin' happens to your family, particularly your daughter, it goes deeper. As hard as it was for me to put up with this shit an' do nothin', I couldn't stand by an' let me family be abused like that. I think I'd have been able to justify it to meself if I'd murdered that fucker.

I'm from Ireland

With the court case behind me I was able to concentrate on me musical career again in the knowledge that, for some people anyway, I'd proved I wasn't a drug dealer. It wasn't like the retraction had a sudden an' obvious affect or anythin' when it appeared, like people weren't comin' to me in the street goin', 'Well done, Christy' or anythin' like that, but it was over. It was the end of that whole fucked up part of me life.

I was still playin' a few gigs here an' there – it wasn't so much a tour as we were randomly performin' where we could get gigs. We got on the bill of one of the first Féile concerts that was held down in Thurles but I kinda felt that I was just goin' through the motions. I'd allowed meself to be brow-beaten into playin' with a band that was made up of almost every musician who'd ever played in Dublin an' I just wasn't happy with it. But it's weird the way things turn out. Ya never know what's round the next corner an' the predicament I found meself in was solved as a result of a tragic accident.

I was back on the road with Conor Goff an' in between the gigs we decided to take a holiday. I remember I gave all the band 500 quid holiday money, which was somethin' that I didn't have to do 'cause they were just gettin' paid for each gig. While I was away an old friend of mine from the Finglas days was killed on a motorbike. Gerry Galvin was one of the most popular kids on our road growin' up. His family was the only one that had a TV an' Gerry was me mate who used to open the curtains so we could all look in. He was a big fan of Aslan an' he used to come to all our gigs. I remember once we were playin' the Olympia Theatre there on Dame Street an' Gerry was in the front row. He was wavin' to get me attention durin' the gig, tryin' to get me to let him up on the stage.

Now, *West Side Story* was on in the Olympia the next night so all the instruments for the orchestra were in a pit in front of the stage, under this big black curtain. I'd a big white line to show me where the stage ended an' where this curtain began so I wouldn't walk out on top of it but I forgot to tell Gerry. He was dancin' away an' he's lookin' at me goin': 'Can I get up? Can I get up?' Finally I looked down at him an' waved me arms at him to c'mon up. So he jumped onto the railin' an' started runnin' across this big black curtain. I was laughin' me bollix off in the middle of the song, lookin' at Gerry tryin' to get onto the stage. It was like a cartoon, ya know, where the character's legs are whirlin' round really fast? I could see the bewilderment on his face, as if he was sayin' to himself, 'Why the fuck am I not gettin' anywhere?' Next minute he just went down on top of all the drums an' cymbals in a big crash.

It was really sad when he died, ya know? He was just a young lad. On the night he was killed he was droppin' a friend home after a Don Baker gig in town. He borrowed his mate's bike to come back to Finglas an' he came off it. He was killed instantly.

I knew his wife well 'cause she'd be at all the gigs with Gerry so I told her I'd do a charity gig to help her get some money together, ya know? I asked the band to do this gig an' explained it would be a freebie. But they were like, 'No way, we've to get paid. We've got bills to pay . . .' an' so on. So I said, 'Hold on, I gave yis fuckin' 500 quid each the other week that yis weren't even due, as a goodwill gesture, an' all I'm askin' yis to do is this one fuckin' gig . . .' but they refused do it. I'd already promised Gerry's wife I'd do this for her. There was no way I could let her down so me an' Conor performed as an acoustic duo for the first time.

It came together really well that night, the whole acoustic thing. Conor just played a few songs on the guitar an' I sang along to them. The crowd loved it an' after the gig we talked about takin' it on the road. I knew that this was a new direction we should explore. I was pissed off with the band for refusin' to do the gig as well so when we realised that we didn't need them I just said, 'The band can go fuck themselves!' an' they were all sacked.

Meself an' Conor tried out the acoustic vibe in rehearsal an' we both liked it. We were writin' new material to develop into a set that we could play on our own. Now that I was kinda the sole lyric writer, a lot of personal stuff started creepin' into the music, more than it had with Aslan. I once read somewhere that Ray Charles said he could only sing about things that he'd personally experienced. I could totally relate to that. I mean I couldn't write a song about hijackin' a plane. I can only write songs 'bout stuff that has happened to me. In Aslan we were all contributin' to the songs an' it was all about stuff that we had in common – growin' up in deprived areas an' all the rest of it. Like, pretty much all the songs we'd written for *Feel No Shame* were 'bout where we were from an' who we were, ya know? That's all I ever felt qualified to write about 'cause that's all I knew. Conor was brought up in a totally different, I would say, more privileged background. I had less in common with him than I did with Aslan an' so the lyrics I was writin' took on this really personal slant.

One thing about writin' all me own stuff was that I had a bit more room to manoeuvre. I got the chance to sing about other things that mattered very much to me. One of the first songs I wrote when I was with Conor was called *Feel it in my heart*, which was about Kathryn. I'd always wanted to write a song for her, ya know?

There was another song I wrote around the same time called *Martin* that was about me. *Martin* is about fallin' victim to drugs an' that. It's about livin' that life, ya know, livin' the way I was – fightin' addiction, breakin' promises, tryin' to get back on me feet but fallin' over an' over again. The first verse goes somethin' like: *Left his home/ Didn't know where he was going/ Gone alone with nothing but the shirt on his back/ Got on a bus headed for the city* . . . I was basically describin' a day in me life – sittin' at home goin', 'I'm not gonna score today.' The line about nothin' but the shirt on his back is about how when yer gonna score gear everythin' else comes second. Ya don't bother gettin' done up when yer goin' into town to score. Ya just pull on the old clothes – ones that ya wore the day before an' the day before that, an' ya just go on yer way. Ya have one priority an' that's to score. Once ya did that then ya could relax an' get 'round to all the other stuff.

I'd be sittin' at home on hundreds of occasions sayin' to meself, 'I don't care how bad this gets, I'm not gettin' gear today,' but eventually the drug takes over. It'd get to the stage where I'd be thinkin', 'what's the point?'. I'd be sittin' there from 9 in the mornin' fightin' the need to rush out an' get gear an' I knew that sooner or later I was gonna go out an' get it anyway. In the end I'd go out first thing in the mornin' 'cause I couldn't be bothered about fightin' for those coupla hours. So that's what *Martin* is about. I couldn't have called it *Christy* – it would have been a bit obvious.

I don't think the records I did with Conor were ever really taken seriously, ya know? Listenin' to them now I think there's a lot of good stuff on there but we weren't really given a chance. I'd had a bit of success with record sales when I was on me own but the Dignam and Goff stuff wasn't given much airplay. They were only mildly successful. I could already tell that it didn't matter whether I was frontin' a band or playin' with Conor – the quality of a lot of the material wasn't up to scratch compared to the Aslan stuff. I was dependin' a lot on the old Aslan songs to fill out the set – which I didn't feel in any way uncomfortable about playin' 'cause I was there when we wrote them. I'd every right to play them. But the thing was they just reminded me that no matter how good I was with The Christy Dignam Band or with Conor Goff, I still couldn't get that same spark on stage that was happenin' when Aslan were together, ya know, that somethin' special. As good as all the other musical efforts were, I didn't feel they were gettin' anywhere close to that same vibe. It made me even more aware of this sense that, for me anyway, there was some unfinished business left with Aslan.

After a year or so playin' the acoustic set around Ireland Conor suggested that we try our luck in the States. He'd been livin' over there a few years before, workin' an' that. He thought we might have a chance at makin' some good money so I agreed to give it a shot. I remember Conor went over first with one phone number for this bar called the Red Lion in Greenwich Village. When he got to New York he mooched round his old contacts an' got a coupla other numbers for Irish bars round Queens, the Bronx, Brooklyn, all that area, Yonkers, an' so on.

I went over after him an' we did a little two-week tour of all these bars an' clubs, playin' our two-man acoustic set. We were gettin' a good reaction an' the gigs were goin' down well with the Irish crowd over there, ya know?

It created enough of a vibe with the bar owners that we were invited back to do a few more gigs. We came back to Ireland but as soon as we'd saved up enough money we were off back to the States, this time to do a month long tour.

When we arrived back in New York this fella that owned one of the bars we played in offered us the use of this empty apartment he had over his bar. We'd a deal that we could stay in this apartment an' in return we'd play once a week in his bar instead of payin' rent.

That kinda became our routine then for the next few months, goin' backwards an' forwards to New York, playin' gigs on both sides of the Atlantic. It was great over there. It really was. New York is a fantastic city. But the fact that I was away from the heroin scene in Dublin didn't mean that I was suddenly cured of addiction or anythin' like that. An ocean of water between you an' yer habit doesn't mean anythin' when it comes to heroin. When we first started to go over to New York I was tryin' to knock it on the head but sooner or later it was gonna come lookin' for me or, more likely, I was gonna go lookin' for it. I was actually off the gear when I met this bloke who was into it an' he brought me down to Alphabet City an' showed me where I could score.

Alphabet City was like the projects area of Manhattan an' I was goin' down there an' buyin' little dime bags they call them, ten dollar bags of heroin off this black bloke. I was gettin' a coupla these bags every day, goin' back up to get another one when I ran out. An' this bloke I was scorin' off said to me, 'Buy a gram, man, it'd be cheaper.' I asked him if he'd get me a coupla grams an' he said he would, no problem. I went down to him the next day an' he told me to wait while he went off an' got the gear. I was after givin' him a coupla hundred dollars an' when he came back an' handed me the bag I dipped me finger in it to make sure it was all right. I don't know what it bleedin' was but it wasn't fuckin' heroin so I ran up after yer man, shoutin', 'Oy c'mere'. Now, he's this big huge black guy but he looks back over his shoulder an' he sees me comin' after him so he legs it back into the projects. These would be like the Ballymun say of New York an' as I'm chasin' him through these really dodgy flats I realise I'm the only white fucker in the place. He musta copped it at the same instant 'cause he stopped an' turned around, just as I stopped runnin'. He musta said to himself, 'Hold on, what am I runnin' from this skinny little white prick for?' as I was goin', 'hold on, what am I gonna do if I catch up on this fucker?' Then it was like a comedy routine, he stopped, I stopped an' then he started runnin' after me. I seen him comin' an' I just turned an' started leggin' it back out of the projects with all these fuckers shoutin' for yer man to catch me. I got outta there as fast as I could an' I didn't look back over me shoulder till I was back out onto the main streets of Manhattan again.

I was way outta me depth when it came to scorin' in a city that I wasn't familiar with. I remember another time I was down around Alphabet City early in the mornin' lookin' for somebody else to score from, ya know? This guy came up to me an' he had this blanket wrapped around him. He looked a bit like Mike Tyson, ya know, a little stocky black guy. He starts sayin' to me, 'Aw man, have ya got anythin', I'm hurtin', I'm hurtin',' ya know? He was obviously in withdrawals. I felt sorry for him 'cause he was in bits. I was after doin' a gig the night before so I'd a loada money on me an' I took it out to give yer man a coupla dollars. I'd a big roll of about 500 dollars in me hand an' I was lookin' for a tenner to give to him. As I'm lookin' for a ten spot yer man whips out a fuckin' knife the size of me arm an' says, 'Give me all the fuckin' money.' I just pulled the first two notes outta the bunch in me hand an' sorta threw them at him. It only distracted him for a split second but it was enough for me to be gone by the time he knew what was goin' on.

It was stupid shit, ya know, puttin' meself in situations that were just ridiculous. I wasn't only dodgin' the dealers but the cops as well. I'd scored near these basketball courts one day an' as I handed yer man the money I saw this cop walkin' across the road, lookin' at me. The deal was in a little wrapped envelope that was sealed at the top an' I put it in me mouth immediately. But this copper stops me an' asks me for ID. I didn't have any ID on me so I tried to tell him I was from Ireland. But it came out like 'Imfolorland'. He says, 'What? I said where are you from boy?' An' I says 'Imfolorland'. His face turned a bit red an' then he goes, 'I don't care if yer from New Orleans, I asked for yer fuckin' ID, pal'. I patted down me pockets to show him I'd no ID an' he's starin' at me face, like he was memorisin' it. Then he says, 'Yer lucky I'm just clockin' out boy. I don't want to spend the next two hours doin' all the paper work on scum like you.' I didn't need to ask him if that meant I was free to go. I was round the corner before he changed his mind. I was poxed – that was a very close shave.

I was livin' the same kinda double life I'd been leadin' at home, takin' all these risks but still tryin' to keep me habit to meself. I didn't want to fuck up over there, ya know? We were startin' to make a bit of money. We also had this deadly apartment an' I didn't want yer man who owned it findin' out about the smack habit.

He was a cool bloke, the guy who owned the apartment. He ran a rugby team an' all his staff were made up of the players. He used to bring them all to a place in Upstate New York called Montauk, where that film *Jaws* was made. He'd bring everyone out fishin', the whole staff, us an' all, on these boats that went after tuna fish. Now, I didn't realise what tuna fish were like. I'd think of tuna fish as like those little yokes that come in a can, ya know, like sardines or somethin'. But they're not – they're these fuckin' huge fish that are like the size of a dolphin. An' over there they're worth a fuckin' fortune to restaurants, you're talkin' a good coupla grand. Yer man had a restaurant part to the bar an' what he'd do was he'd catch these tuna fish an' hack off enough to keep him in tuna steaks for the year. Then he'd sell the rest an' that would pay for the whole trip. It was like the staff holidays.

On one of these trips to Montauk meself an' Conor got a gig in a hotel. This guy, Eric Prager, was stayin' there. He approached us after the gig an' said his father was this big shot artist's manager. We didn't pay much attention to him 'cause ya get a lot of that at gigs over there, ya know? Ya get people comin' up to you an' sayin' they were this, that an' the other. But we found out that his father, a bloke called Bud Prager, was the manager of Foreigner, who were fuckin' huge in the States at the time. He managed Ben E King an' all these other artists as well so we realised that this guy was tellin' the truth. He introduced us to his aul fella an' he agreed to take us on. He really went for us in a big way – both of them were fuckin' fallin' over themselves for us. He said he could get us a six-album deal with Epic Records – a multi-million dollar fuckin' deal we're talkin' about. I'm sittin' back goin': 'Holy shit. One minute we're playin' these little Irish bars an' the next we're talkin' about signin' a deal for fuckin' millions of dollars.' It was almost too good to be true an' as always, when you start thinkin' things are too good to be true, they usually are.

I was still goin' home whenever I got a chance, just to see me family 'cause obviously I missed them a lot but this deal with Prager was lookin' like it might actually happen an' that would mean I'd have to base meself in America full-time. Conor was well up for that 'cause he didn't have so many ties at home, ya know, but I knew I was gonna have to make a decision soon about what I was gonna do. I was due to go home for a coupla weeks before comin' back to do a two month tour with Conor so I put off makin' a definite decision till then. As it turned out somethin' happened which made me doubt that I'd any future in America anyway.

One day me, Conor an' this other bloke were bootin' round in a car, actin' the bollix, pullin' hand-brakers in the snow. Now, Conor was shittin' himself in the back of the car, ya know? I thought it was just 'cause he was a bit of a bleedin' nervous aul wan an' wasn't used to that kinda thing. He shouts at us to stop the car an' then he splurts out this story about an accident he was involved in when he used to live in Florida years before.

He was workin' as a painter an' decorator at the time, right, an' he was after gettin' paid for a big job. He'd seen an ad in the paper for a Harley Davidson motorbike that was for sale. So he rang the number an' said he was interested in buyin' the bike. The guy who owned the bike drove it over to show him. Conor gave yer man the money to hold onto an' got on the bike with his bird for a test drive.

He booted about a 100 metres up the road an' hit a stop sign. His eye blew out of his head an' he was left lyin' at the side of the road in bits. His girlfriend broke her hip off the sign an' was unconscious. So Conor had this legal shit goin' on which meant that he was sittin' there in the car not wantin' the cops pullin' us over.

Now, all the work we were doin' up to then we were gettin' paid into the hand – like we were never officially in the country. We didn't have any workin' visa or anthin' like that but I started thinkin' that I'd no hope of ever startin' a career in America with Conor if he was havin' to sort out some legal hassle. I didn't say anythin' about it at the time but the incident lodged in the back of me mind.

* * *

All this was goin' on in America while, at home, moves were bein' made that would change me life round once again. While I was still in Aslan we used to do this gig called the South Band Show that was held in the car park of the Janelle Shopping Centre in Finglas every June. It was a free gig we did for the people in the area as a kinda thank you for the support an' that, ya know? Every time it came round to puttin' on the show the organisers would ring me an' Aslan askin' would we get back together to just do this one gig for them. 'Cause there was still a lot of bad vibes between me an' the rest of the band we'd never agree to do it. Maybe some years I said, 'Fuck it, yeah I'll do it,' but the band wouldn't want to. An' then other years they'd agree to do it but I'd say no, ya know? But in 1993, Robbie Foy rang me while I was in America an' said they were losin' their sponsorship an' he needed a big publicity buzz to kinda keep the whole show goin'. So he asked me, as a special favour, would I come back an' play the gig with Aslan. I told him to ring the other lads an' get back to me.

At this time Aslan had changed their name to The Precious Stones an' I was after kinda bumpin' into a couple of them a few times here an' there, after gigs an' that, ya know? We were kinda mendin' some bridges 'cause there'd been loads of bad-mouthin' each other in the press. For the first coupla years after the split it was all very bitter an' nasty from both sides. I can't remember any particular shit but what would happen was I'd hear that they'd said somethin' about me an' I'd get angry an' then they'd hear me sayin' somethin' an' get pissed off. Then I'd be like, 'What are youse bein' annoyed about that for? What about wha' youse said?' – an' it just went back an' forward like that. There's no doubt that a lot of it was fuelled by other people 'cause it made good press. But it got to the stage that I used to ring the Baggot Inn or wherever if I wanted to go to a gig to check was any of them in the audience. If they were I couldn't go 'cause we'd slaughter each other. That's the way it was for years. We never encountered one another in all that time 'cause we made sure we stayed out of each other's way. I'm tellin' ya, we would've kilt each other – that's how bad it was – it was really, really bitter, ya know?

But that all started to change after Billy an' Tony sneaked into the Baggot Inn to see me playin' with Conor Goff one night. This woulda been before we sacked the band an' went on as a duo. Tony an' Billy were standin' in the corner, keepin' to themselves an' checkin' it out. Now discreetly walkin' into the Baggot like that wasn't somethin' ya could do 'cause all the fans would've been well aware of the situation between us. Somebody recognised them an' it was like fuckin' wildfire goin' through the place. The crowd started booin' them an' givin' them a hard time. So I started into *This is* an' I asked Tony an' Billy would they get up an' do it with us as a way of sayin' no hard feelin's. An' they did. I don't think they'd much choice – the crowd wanted to kill them so I think it was probably safer for them in the long run! They came up to the stage an' the crowd fuckin' went apeshit ya know? It was the first time I'd stood on stage with any of Aslan for nearly three years. That was a big icebreaker, ya know? After that if we met in town or wherever we could kinda talk to each other while before it was all very eh, acrimonious, to say the least.

Over the next few months after that I'd meet up with a coupla the lads an' we'd kinda re-established a bit of contact. I remember meself an' Kathryn were out in Leopardstown at Club 92 one night when I was back from the States. I can't remember if they were playin' or if it was one of my gigs, but we met up with them. We all sat down an' we had a good yap, ya know? Everythin' was cool. Now, there was no talk of us gettin' back together as a band or anythin' like that but we'd re-established that we could at least stand in the same room together an' not cut each other's throats. That was enough at that time. Things had thawed.

I'd just gone back over to America to start another tour with Conor when I got another phone call from Robbie Foy to tell me that the rest of the lads were sayin' they'd play the South Band Show gig if I would. Now, it just so happened that I'd a gap of a week or two in the middle of the tour that coincided with the South Band Show. So I says to Robbie, 'Lookit, I'll fly back to Dublin an' do the gig before goin' back for the second month of me American tour.' That's all it was supposed to be – there was an unspoken agreement that we were doin' this as a favour for old friends. It was to be a once-off gig – that was it.

Lookin' back on it now I suppose maybe I was hopin' it would develop into somethin' else but I wasn't holdin' me hopes up an' I wasn't goin' in there beggin' either. I wasn't goin' to fuckin' accommodate the thought that anythin' would happen 'cause I didn't want to be disappointed. I didn't want to reveal me hand either. I can sit here an' say that both sides had determined that it would be a once-off gig absolutely, end of story, but what happened wouldn't have been possible if nobody had hoped it would be more than that – I don't give a fuck what anybody says.

I came home from America an' we went into the studios in The Factory on Portobello Street to rehearse the set for the gig. I remember goin' in an' pickin' up the mike while the lads were tunin' their guitars an' settin' up the drums an' all that. We were all very nice to each other an' we were gettin' on grand. There was no talk about all the shit that had happened before – we were just concentratin' on doin' the session. We launched into all these songs off the *Feel No Shame* album that we'd last played together five years ago but it was just like the split had never happened. We fit back together, just like a hand into a glove. It was amazin'. It was like finishin' work on a Friday an' comin' back in on the Monday mornin'.

I'd expected that the emotional baggage of the last five years would weigh us down but it wasn't like that at all. It was very cool – it was just like old times. It was fuckin' brilliant in fact. An' all of us felt it. It wasn't somethin' that we tried to make happen – it was just natural. Even before the end of that very first day there was a buzz. I think everybody was taken aback at how easy it all was – how it all fell back into place so quickly. I don't think anybody expected that, ya know? We'd given ourselves two weeks to rehearse but within a couple of days we'd all the songs down that we were goin' to do for the show. So we says, 'Why don't we try an' write somethin' new for the crack to play at the gig?' an' that's where a song called *Crazy World* came from.

If ya like *Crazy World* would become the *This is* of the next phase of Aslan. I think Tony had the idea for the genesis of *Crazy World* when they were The Precious Stones but it wasn't finished – it was just the guts of a song. There were some lyrics to it an' the framework for the melody was there but we'd to do a lot of work with it. I remember goin' down to Billy's granny's house with him an' tryin' to flesh it out a bit. We nailed it in about three days, just in time for the gig. I didn't think *Crazy World* was that great when it was finished, I thought it was a bit feeble. I wasn't a 100 percent sold on the song at all. It's weird. It wasn't like when we did *This is*, ya know? With *This is* I knew we had somethin' special but there was no tingle in the spine with this new song. I dunno, it could've been 'cause of all the emotion that was involved in the gig. Maybe I was afraid to get too excited about it. I don't really know why but I remember not being really convinced of it, thinkin' that it was an okay song but that it wasn't goin' to be the next *This is*, by any stretch of the imagination.

We walked onto the stage in our hometown on July 11, 1993 – five years an' one day after I'd last played with Aslan. There was a huge crowd there 'cause of the curiosity factor about us playin' together for the first time but then – I'll never forget it – it started pissin' outta the fuckin' heavens. The rain got rid of all the curiosity seekers pretty sharpish an' that just left all the old Aslan fans, people who'd been followin' us for years. For people in Finglas, who don't suffer fools gladly, to actually stand in the pissin's of rain like that is a testament to how dedicated they are. I remember bein' taken aback by the fact that they stood there for the whole time we played.

I brought Kiera up onto the stage an' held her in me arms while I introduced *Crazy World*. I started singin' the chorus, *'How can I protect you in this Crazy world? It's all right . . . yeah, it's all right'*. It was like, 'Here we are after leavin' all the years of bullshit an' crap behind us.'

When we came off the stage a guy from BMG Records, Joe Stewart was his name, came up to us an' immediately offered us a singles deal for *Crazy World.* We told him we'd think about it an' we went off to celebrate a good day. Kathryn was there at the gig an' I remember goin' over to hug her. Kathryn's a big Aslan fan but I think even she was afraid to get too excited – we all were – none of us knew what would happen next.

I Have Fallen . . .

I woke up on the mornin' after the South Band Show with one of the most difficult decisions I've ever had to make hangin' over me head. I was in a dilemma – there was this offer on the table from BMG Records to release *Crazy World* as a single in Ireland but I was still in the middle of the American tour with Conor Goff. I knew I'd to go back to fulfil me obligation to him. Not only that – I hadn't even decided whether I should get back together with Aslan. There was a lot of plusses an' minuses to both options, ya know? I was mullin' it over in me head an' askin' Kathryn an' me close friends what they thought I should do here. An', of course, people were pretty evenly split on what option I should go for. It was obviously vitally important that I made the right decision. The outcome either way was guaranteed to change me life – for better or for worse.

I wasn't privy to how the other members of Aslan felt about gettin' me back into the band. To put it in perspective though I think it was fair to say that they hadn't done well over the previous five years. They'd been dropped by the record company not long after I got sacked; their gigs were half empty an' each of them was gettin' a pain in their bollix with it. Well, I know Alan was anyway. I heard this story years later that Alan was rehearsin' with The Precious Stones one day an' the rest of them were waitin' for him to come in. But Alan pulls up with no drums an' walks up to the rehearsal studios in Capel Street an' his stance was, 'Look, if youse don't get Christy back I'm not botherin' me bollix with this Precious Stones business –

either we get back with Christy an' we get Aslan back together or forget about it.' They had a huge row an' Alan left them after that. They got in a different drummer to keep playin' gigs but they got Alan back in a coupla months later. They'd also lost Danny at this stage as well. He'd told them he was finished in the Irish music business an' he'd taken off to try his luck in America. He's still livin' there, in San Francisco, as far as I know.

So it was true they were strugglin' an' had probably been on the verge of breakin' up for good but that didn't make it an easier decision to make.

At the same time I'd me own doubts about me future with Conor in America. I just wasn't sure about goin' back an' tryin' to make a success outta the partnership. I'm thinkin' about it, thinkin' about it an' I'm mullin' it over. I just couldn't decide what to do.

Eventually I'd to sit down an' think it through an' what I figured out was, 'well hold on this is about music, it's about art'. I don't want to get into that whole art mode but, ya know, at the time I'd to identify what option offered me the best potential to create quality music – bein' with Aslan or with Conor Goff – an' Aslan won hands down.

Now, I knew, obviously, that I was sayin' goodbye to one of the top fuckin' managers in America. I was throwin' away a lot by goin' back to Aslan an' maybe a once-off Irish single. It was Mickey Mouse stuff in comparison. I mean it's alright now lookin' back an' seein' it all in hindsight but we'd no idea, nobody knew at the time, that *Crazy World* was goin' to be so successful – the bottom line was I would be choosin' a one single deal here in Ireland over a chance at a six album deal in America.

Sometimes you gotta go with your instincts. It just felt like there was an unfulfilled destiny for me an' Aslan. We were at the peak of our success when we fell apart. It seemed like we'd left it all hangin' in the air for five years an' now, here was an opportunity, a second chance, to have another pop at the cherry. Also, despite all that'd happened, these were still me mates. It was cool to think we might be back together – it felt right. I just knew that if I didn't do this there was every chance that I would fuckin' regret it for the rest of me life. They were the best musicians I'd ever worked with it an' I'd realised a long time ago that it'd never be the same without them.

A few days before I was due to go back to America, I got together with the rest of the lads an' we all sat down as adults to talk about what we were gonna do. I think they were as nervous of gettin' back with me as I was of gettin' back with them, ya know? There was a lot of trepidation on both sides. Water had passed under the bridge but it'd been five years since we'd all last played together full-time, so we were all holdin' our cards close to our chests, d'ya know what I mean?

I told them I was willin' to give it another go but I explained that I couldn't kinda commit meself there an' then 'cause I'd to sort out what I was goin' to do about the whole Conor Goff thing. I'd told them about it an' the lads knew the situation I was in. They didn't have anybody else to answer to so it was easier for them to come to a decision to give Aslan another go. We agreed that I'd go back to the States an' finish up me tour with Conor before comin' home to work out how to get Aslan back to the top. We all shook hands, each of us hopin' we'd made the right move.

I couldn't tell Conor about me new plan when I first met up with him. I knew it would've made the rest of the tour very awkward so it was only towards the end that I told him I was goin' back to Ireland to try me luck with Aslan. Now,

I'd always kinda known that Conor had the idea of settlin' in America for good, ya know? He'd no commitments in Ireland so I says to him: 'If you want to live in America we'll go back to Ireland first an' get whatever money you need to set you up. We'll work for another coupla weeks or months, however long it takes to get ya a few bob.'

I thought he took it pretty well when I told him. He was cool about it an' we finished off the month's tour. Then we both came back to Ireland an' we played a few gigs here for about a month while I was gettin' ready to be the frontman of Aslan again.

The whole time Conor seemed fine about the fact we'd be goin' our separate ways but he wasn't. It turned out that he was bitter about it, ya know? Around the time I came back I started gettin' these letters from an Irish bank sayin' I owed them money but I just ignored them 'cause I didn't remember ever havin' any dealins' with them. I just thought they'd made a mistake or somethin'. But the letters kept comin' an' they started gettin' more serious. Eventually I responded to one of the letters an' the buzz was that they were chasin' me for money to do with Dignam and Goff stuff. It got even more serious. I was gettin' letters from the Sheriff of Dublin an' the bank got a fuckin' judgement put on me house. They were goin' to take me gaff an' all off me. Conor'd just gotten married over in America an' I finally got in touch with him an' explained the situation. We got it sorted – the bank stopped callin' me – an' I never heard from Conor again.

I found out recently that there's still a Judgement Order on me house an' I've to get a solicitor to have it taken off – so the repercussions from all that shit are still goin' on.

* * *

When I came back to Ireland I hooked up with the band in The Factory, which we used as a base in the city centre. We all had our say about how we should avoid anythin' like what had happened before from happenin' again. We were all a bit older an' wiser now, ya know? We were a lot more tolerant of everyone's idiosyncrasies but there was still a couple of things that we needed to straighten out. I told them that the last time we'd let fuckin' managers an' accountants an' all sorts of people get between us. We'd started off as a unit of five people an' that's the way it should've stayed. I said, 'From now on, if we have a problem, it's the five of us against the world. It's not four of us an' the manager against another member.' I said that could never happen again. That was the one condition I had before I went back in the band an' it's somethin' that we still have today. They were cool about it.

It took a while for us to settle back into it. As far as the music was concerned that all just clicked back into place, like when we got back together to do the Finglas gig. But on a personal level we were all really kinda watchin' each other's Ps an' Qs, d'ya know what I mean? Sorta tiptoein' around each other. Havin' said that, it didn't take long for us to fall back into place with each other as people.

The drugs thing that had broke the band up in the first place was never fully discussed. It was never put to me that I was bein' allowed back in on condition that I didn't touch heroin again. I think I was off the gear at the time an' I probably did tell them that I was finished with it. That coulda been the truth but I was always kinda slippin' in an' out of it, ya know? The thing with heroin is that when ya do give it up you're givin' it up for good. You're never touchin' it again an' ya mean that absolutely, with every fuckin' cell in your body, ya know? But then shit happens an' ya fall back into it. The thing is though when you're sayin' to somebody that you'll never do it again, ya mean it. Any time I've given it up I've tried with all me strength to stay away from it an' ya tell yerself, as well as others, that. I would've really meant it when I was tellin' the band that I was finished with it.

A lot of people felt that I let them down when I got back with Aslan. When we'd split up some people came on my side an' told me, 'Fuck them – they're all cunts.' An' now here I was back with them again, d'ya know what I mean? They considered it a betrayal but what could I do? I knew Aslan were a great band an' I knew that we'd interrupted a great thing. It was only right then, when we got back together that the greatness we had before would re-emerge, d'ya know what I mean? That's the way I seen it. I know that sounds really fuckin' big-headed but that's the way I felt about it.

We were kinda negotiatin' with BMG ourselves, ya know? We didn't have a manager at that time. Nobody had approached us an' to be honest we weren't really lookin' for one anyway. Our whole buzz was it was a failure of management that had allowed us to fuckin' deteriorate to the point where we split up, so for the moment we were happier to go it alone.

We were back in the OFI studios in town recordin' *Crazy World* an' the spark I'd always had with Aslan just ignited again, ya know? I mean one of the main motivators for gettin' back together in the first place was that when we did start workin' together, the whole thing just happened with such ease. An' that continued on into the studio.

The result was the song *Crazy World* which went straight into the Top 5 in Ireland within a coupla weeks of its release in September 1993. It's one of those things that ya don't sit an' analyse too much at the time. I can see now why it was such a successful song but it took a while for it to sink in. Probably 'cause there was so much goin' on. For me the song wasn't allowed to stand alone as a song in its own entity. It was associated with all the baggage an' bullshit an' the possible repercussions that gettin' back together with Aslan could hold. It was only when I listened to it years later, in isolation, that I could see it for what it actually is – a crackin' song.

Emotions were runnin' high after we released *Crazy World*. We'd a big reunion gig at the Olympia Theatre in Dublin to announce we were back together an' we played the first full version of *Crazy World*. Everyone knew the words 'cause it'd been on the radio so much an' they nearly fuckin' deafened me when they sang along to the chorus. The creative juices were flowin' ya could say an' we recorded another single soon after called *Where's the Sun?*.

Aslan was on a roll for the second time in our lives. *Crazy World* stayed in the charts for somethin' like three months in 1993 an' then it won the Single of Year in the *Hot Press* Awards. We even won the 'Best Irish Band' in a competition that was decided by the readers an' the critics. Finally it seemed like we were gettin' the right attention from the music press that had slated us for so long. I mean here's what *Hot Press* said 'bout our reunion gig in the Olympia:

> *'Expectations an' emotions were high and the big question on everyone's mind was the obvious one. Could Aslan, after a five year break, still have the old, old magic? The answer is resoundingly in the affirmative. In a show that lasted 90 minutes they gave it their all and proved that rough edges notwithstanding, class wins out every time.'*

Ya see what I mean. An' when they reviewed *Crazy World* they said:

> *'The chorus will hook from listen one and when Christy Dignam signs the opening line* I have fallen down so many times *you know that he didn't stick those words together because they happened to look nice on paper.'*

They thought it was *'a sleek, luxuriant, anthemic nugget'*. It was the recognition that I'd always felt we deserved.

Ya know the way I'd said earlier that I'd lost all interest in reviews an' that after *The Star* story came out but now it seemed like we'd turned a corner as far as the press was concerned. Suddenly they were on our side. Everybody loves the underdog, don't they, an' journalists are no exception. It seemed like we were well on the road back to success. But then the music industry stepped in again an' fucked it all up for us.

We never saw it comin' 'cause everythin' was goin' so well. We'd cracked it in Ireland for the second time with another huge hit. That'd led to an international deal with BMG Records in Ireland to make another album. Now when you sign an international agreement the album still has to impress the record company people in the other countries where it's goin' to be released. We just assumed that 'cause *Crazy World* was such a good song an' had proved to be so successful in Ireland, that it'd naturally take off in Britain. We thought we were sorted.

We sent over the demos for the new album, which we called *Goodbye Charlie Moonhead* to BMG. I was really excited about the album. I thought it was great. While we were still writin' it *Crazy World* was already on its way to becomin' a hit an' I remember thinkin', 'well, if you like that wait till you hear '*Where's The Sun?*' an' '*Rain Man*' an' all these other crackin' songs that are goin' on the album'. I thought, 'man, they're gonna fuckin' love this shit'.

We called it *Goodbye Charlie Moonhead* as a farewell to that fuckin' begrudgin' attitude that'd followed us around for years. It was called after this bloke who used to take the piss outta us in Ballymun 'cause we wanted to be in a band. He was a symbol of some of that knockin' we'd had to put up with. Some people say it's a reference to givin' up drugs – ya know sayin' goodbye to cocaine an' all that – but it wasn't. It was all about not lettin' anybody else interfere with the music. It was about what mattered to us, the five of us, d'ya know what I mean? We didn't get any reaction from BMG but they'd scheduled a release date for *Crazy World* in England on, I think, June 29, 1994, so we thought everythin' was cool.

But, as we got nearer the end of June an' the 29th was comin' up, I started to suspect that somethin' was wrong. We weren't gettin' any feedback from the British company at all. There was no contact from them – even though we kept ringin' them an' ringin' them.

Finally we got through an' they just told us out straight, 'Well, we've had a meeting an' we don't think there are any hits on the album.' We were like: 'What? What the fuck do you mean there are no hits on the album? *Crazy World* has been a fuckin' huge hit over here an' there's all these other great songs.' I was goin', 'How can you say there's no hits on this fuckin' record – it's got more hooks than a fisherman's hat.' But there was nothin' we could do. They refused to launch the album in Britain an' the whole thing just stopped dead in its tracks.

We couldn't understand it. To this day I still don't know what happened. If I was to guess I'd say it might've been the fact that EMI had spent thousands on the band the first time round an', just when we'd been ready to hit the big time, we'd fallen apart. Then BMG in Britain had come along six years later but they'd got cold feet at the critical moment 'cause they'd seen how we'd dropped the ball before when it got to this level. They just weren't prepared to take the chance an' spend that sort of money on us in case we fucked up again.

It was a blow to the band but not a fatal one – ya could say it was a flesh wound. We just put our heads together an' said, 'Fuck it.' We'd had enough of fuckin' record companies – from now on we'd go out there an' do it ourselves. The first two singles we'd released were doin' so well in Ireland that we decided to have our own launch for the album. We also thought we'd use the occasion to have a bit of a laugh on some of the people in the press who'd had a go at us over the years.

We sent out invites to all the main journalists on all the papers in Dublin, all the music press heads, ya know? We told them we were pickin' them up at Lillies Bordello an' that they all had to bring their passports with them. They met us in town an' we put them on a double-decker bus an' started headin' out towards the airport. Now, they'd no idea where we were goin' but some of them were lookin' out the windows as we were drivin' in the direction of the airport an' they were probably thinkin' they were on a free trip to Paris or somethin'. But we pulled off the main road an' stopped at the fuckin' Towers in Ballymun an' we had the launch of the album in the place where I played me first gig with Electron. Ya shoulda seen the faces. I swear some of them had never been over to the Northside before, ya know? I enjoyed meself but I think some of the journalists were disgusted. It was a bit of a risk 'cause they coulda fuckin' slaughtered us for takin' the piss outta them like that an' lashed the album outta it, ya know? But they didn't. In fairness, they were all very supportive an' we put on another launch for them later in Lillies Bordello which was probably more suited to their tastes.

I really liked the *Goodbye Charlie Moonhead* record. We were gettin' back to our roots with that album. We'd kinda lost the plot I felt, when the success an' the fame first came to us all those years ago. We'd lost our way with Aslan a little bit an' the album was a way of reconnectin' with the things that made us get the band together in the first place. It was 'goodbye' to all the bullshit that's involved with bein' in a successful band an' all that crap. Most of the songs on the album have that thread runnin' through them. They're all about not lettin' it affect you, believe in yourself an' keep goin'. Ironically, when BMG decided there was no hits on it an' wouldn't release it in Britain that was just a verification of what we'd already written about on the album – that these fuckers hadn't changed. The lack of interest BMG showed was livin' proof that there was still the same old bullshit in the music industry. It persuaded us that we were makin' the right decision to go it alone from now on.

The release of the album was our comeback after the disappointment of of bein' let down by BMG but we'd left the next six months to a year free, expectin' that we would be tourin' *Goodbye Charlie Moonhead* all over the UK an' Europe. So we were kinda left sittin' on our arses with no work scheduled in when we found out that there would be no tour.

It looked like it was gonna be a waste of an important year an' even worse, we were hardly rollin' in cash. Gigs are expensive to put on, ya know? There's so many costs associated with puttin' a band on the road that sometimes it's hardly worth it. Of course, we were in the band for better reasons than just wantin' to make a bit of cash but the fact that we were up against the wall financially meant that we were restricted in where we could bring our music.

We stopped an' had a good, hard look at what we were doin'. A band that can't afford to go out an' gig is dead so we needed a change in tactics if we were gonna survive. That's when I started runnin' the idea around in me head of tryin' the acoustic set up with Aslan. It'd worked very well when I was playin' with Conor Goff an' there was a lot less costs with puttin' on an acoustic show – like ya need less equipment, less road crew, less transport an' all the rest of it.

A lot of the larger venues that we would've been playin' in at the time cost a lot of money. Ya can't just do them on a whim, ya know, ya have to prepare for them. Ya expect a big audience to show up so ya have to invest a lot of financial input into the show to pull it off. But from my time with Dignam and Goff I already knew that there was all these smaller venues around Ireland, good bread an' butter gigs, that we could play if we scaled the whole show down a bit. I suggested developin' an unplugged set so that if a venue owner came to us an' he only had a bar or a club that could hold 300 or 400 people we'd be able to strip our set right down an' play acoustic.

We went back into rehearsin' an' started scalin' down the Aslan sound. We'd always had electric guitars an' keyboards an' amps an' all that carry on, so with the unplugged thing we stripped all that away. There's no keyboards at all, just acoustic guitars, an' there's no amplifiers or anythin' on the stage.

We'd to change the arrangements of some of the songs to make them fit 'cause obviously if there's a lead guitar riff in or a keyboard part you're gonna have to replace them. There was a transition period of course, ya know? It took us a while to get the songs to work. Some of the numbers would be big electric kinda anthems so there was a bit of goin' back to basics to get it all down to an acoustic level but we worked all that out. An' that's what bein' in a band is all about – that's the whole gig. We were musicians an' we just created a new vehicle to deliver our music. Sometimes ya have to kinda cut your cloth to suit yer needs.

Most of our songs were written so that they could stand on their own anyway, ya know? We always had this thing about the songs, that ya could sing them with just an acoustic guitar. That was a sign that it was workin'. If you needed all this flowery arrangements an' embellishment then somethin' was wrong.

After months of fine-tunin' our new look we took it out on the road to all these places around the country that maybe only the locals would be familiar with. Durin' the summer of 1995 we played shows to 400 people in Tramore, 600 in Wexford an' to a coupla hundred in pubs all over the place.

Of course, a few of the other cool bands around Dublin said we'd turned into a cabaret act. We got a bit of shit 'cause we'd chosen to play in these smaller venues. But so what? I mean, the type of music ya play is defined by chords, melodies an' lyrics – not by the bricks an' mortar where the music is performed. It's a notion that still exists in the Irish music scene that there are these cool venues ya play if you're a cool act. If you're cool you don't play The Bottom of the Hill in Finglas an' you don't play the Ballymun Towers, an' you don't play the Royal Oak pub but we never really cared what people thought was cool anyway, ya know? I wasn't gonna let some bloke just out of journalism school tell me what was right an' what was wrong about the way we played rock'n'roll 'cause I'd spent me life playin' rock'n'roll.

The gigs became quite lucrative an' they paid a wage so we could pay the rent. Then all these bands that had taken the piss out of us started comin' to us an' askin' us for the phone numbers of all these venues. Up to then everybody was playin' the tried an' tested circuits. They were playin' the gigs that everybody had already played. So they seen that we were afta settin' up a whole new circuit of gigs, an' they wanted to try it for themselves.

But the most important thing was I was gettin' back into doin' what I'd always wanted to do. For me, music is at its most pure in those intimate settins', ya know, all sittin' down 'around the campfire' kinda thing. The further ya get from that ideal the more insincere, the more unreal, it becomes. The pressure to be a success mounts up an' then it's all about the money.

An' at these gigs I was reconnectin' with the audience. I could see the whites of their eyes. I remember the first time we played Slane I felt this uncomfortable distance between me an' the front row. Like, while it's great for the aul ego to be able to play these big shows, I've always felt that there's a much better vibe at smaller gigs.

All the pressures to succeed an' play all the right places an' make tons of cash dissolved. For the first time in a long time we were enjoyin' ourselves.

The Hit

When it comes to talkin' 'bout Aslan a lot of people pick up on the fact that I did drugs. I've always been honest about it, ya know? I don't kinda pull punches with what I want to say, particularly about me addiction to heroin. I've never held back when it came to discussin' me past but it does get frustratin' at times. My attitude is that it was a part of me life an' I accept that it holds a fascination for some people but I believe it should have the same significance in interviews as it had in me life. Like, I've spent over 20 years bein' a musician an' in that 20 years I spent a few years involved in drugs but sometimes that's all people want to talk about, ya know?

Like, I was on *The Late Late Show* when I got back on the music scene an' Gay Byrne was talkin' to me about me addiction to heroin. I talked about it at length with him. He was askin' me what it was like when I was on heroin, what it was like comin' off, was it hard stayin' off it, an' all that carry on. Then a few weeks later, I was playin' a place called The Boxing Club in Drogheda an' the owner of the club came up to me an' says like, 'I swore I'd never let ya play in me club again after I heard about ya an' read about ya in the paper. It's only that Gay said you're off the drugs that I'm lettin' you come back in me club.' When that happened I started thinkin', 'how many other jobs have I lost or not even been offered 'cause people had that mentality or that stance on the whole drugs thing?'. Now whether they were justified in judgin' me or not, I still thought it was a measure of the harm I'd suffered 'cause of articles like that in *The Star*. To this day I can't fully estimate the damage 'cause I don't know if there's still people out there who will never work with me again 'cause they think I used to deal drugs. There are times that I go into places today an' I get that fuckin' headline thrown back at me, ya know? I might be at a gig or maybe if I just walk into a pub an' I get called a heroin-dealin' scumbag.

I mean at the time that interview with Gay Byrne was me first real opportunity to talk about me musical ambitions to a lot of people 'cause *The Late Late Show* was at its zenith then. But Gay went for the whole drugs thing an' we ended up talkin' 'bout that for most of the time I was on the show. Now I didn't have a problem with that but when you're talkin' about drugs, particularly on a personal level, it tends to catch people's attention an' unfortunately, as I found out a good bit later, that interview caught the attention of the wrong people.

I was headin' over to the US to see me aul pal Bud Prager. The last time I'd seen Prager was to tell him that Dignam and Goff was over an' that I was goin' home. I remember he was absolutely astonished. He said I was throwin' it all away, ya know? But, he'd to accept that I knew where me musical future lay better than he did.

I'd stayed in touch with him an' he said he was interested to hear Aslan now that I was playin' with them again. He invited us over to play a showcase for him an' all these other big music heads over there. I suspected that he was more interested in seein' if there was a chance of me an' Conor gettin' back together. We decided to go over anyway an' play a few of the songs we were developin' for our acoustic set at the showcase an' travel around a bit while we were there.

We flew down to Shannon where we disembarked to go through immigration before gettin' back on the plane. I remember there was five counters ya went through with five immigration officers standin' at them. I'd been in an' out of America so many times I had what was known as a 'multiple indefinite visa' which meant I didn't have to apply for a visa each time I travelled over there. So I got through no problem an' I stopped on the other side to wait for Tony. While I'm standin' there I notice one of the immigration officers lookin' over at me. Suddenly I got that old junkie feelin' from years before when I'd have drugs in me pocket an' I just knew I was gonna be pulled. I dunno what it was but I knew somethin' was up.

We walked down the corridor an' we were sittin' down in the lounge, just about to re-embark, when I seen this fucker in the uniform that'd been lookin' at me walkin' over towards me with this other guy in a suit. There was a lot of other people in the corridor, like a coupla hundred passengers millin' about, but I just knew they were comin' straight for me. I'm thinkin', 'bollix, this is definitely trouble', ya know? They came down an' yer man in the suit says, 'Dignam?' an' I said 'Yeah.' He says, 'Could you come back into the office with us for a second?' I'm thinkin', 'here we go'.

I went into the office an' yer man in the suit is flickin' through me passport. Then he says to me, 'My colleague here says he seen you on a TV chat show one time.' I says, 'Yeah', an' he says, 'Ya mentioned a medical problem that ya had on that show.' I says, 'That's right, why?' An' then he says, 'Did ya mention this particular medical issue on your visa application?'

I'm kinda thinkin', 'bollix, what am I gonna say here,' 'cause I knew exactly what he was talkin' about. I'd written 'no' on the multiple visa application form where it asks have ya ever been involved with or addicted to drugs an' all that. I'm tryin' to think fast, on me feet, like, so I says, 'I didn't think it was relevant 'cause it was years ago that I'd that problem, ya know?' I was kinda just tryin' to bluff me way through it. He says, 'Wait here a minute please, sir,' an' he takes me passport an' stuff an' goes off to photocopy everythin'. He's left me on me own in this room with the officer who'd pointed me out. An' this fucker turns around to me an' says, 'D'ya remember that song you did on the *Late Late Show* that time? I think that's a brilliant song.' He was an American, ya know? 'Aw I'm a big fan of the band,' he says. 'I think yis are brilliant. Aw you're a great singer an' that song yis done is great, what's the name of it again? Oh yeah, I remember it, *Where's The Sun?* – great tune.' I'm lookin' at him thinkin', 'fuckin' nice one – you're our best fan, ya liked our song but you're after grassin' me up to your boss an' ruinin' me career'.

Next thing, yer man came back with all me documents an' hands them to me. 'Thank you very much sir,' he says, an' that was it. They let us get back on the plane. I was thinkin', 'that was close'. But when we got to America, this fuckin' really weird thing happened. Before we went to New York to meet Prager we stopped off for a few days in Boston, I think it was, an' we were on a beach somewhere playin' beach volleyball, right. These American heads came over an' started talkin' to us, ya know? They were really friendly an' we went to a bar with them afterwards. Then they met us that night outside our hotel an' kinda insisted on showin' us round the city. The other lads were goin' this is great, we're gettin' a free tour an' bein' brought to all the top clubs an' all that.

For the next few days we were in Boston these Americans kinda latched onto us an' started hangin' around with us all the time. I was gettin' really suspicious that somethin' wasn't right here, ya know, but I said nothin' for the moment. Then, when we were headin' off to New York to do the showcase for Prager they said, 'We've a few mates down there who'll show yis the town. Yis should hook up with them.' They gave us a few phone numbers an' we said we'd give them a ring or some shit.

We didn't get a chance to even do that. As soon as we got to New York all these other heads came to our hotel an' started hangin' out with us again, bringin' us to all the top places, showin' us a good time, ya know? This was startin' to freak me out so I got Joe into the hotel room one day an' I says: 'Listen Joe, does it not occur to ya that I'm after bein' questioned comin' over here about me drug takin' an' since we've been here there's been these guys followin' us around every fuckin' day? Does that not strike you as a bit of a coincidence?'

He says, 'Ah me bollix, yer bein' paranoid. Yer smokin' too much grass.' An'I says, 'I'm fuckin' tellin' ya now. I might be smokin' too much grass but I'm not bein' paranoid. This is gettin' too weird.'

The followin' night we played the showcase for Prager an' his buddies in Tramps in New York but it didn't pan out at all. We did an acoustic set an' a full live set but he just wasn't into Aslan. He was goin' on about me an' Conor, sayin' we were great, we nearly had it made, all this stuff. His attitude was that he'd given me a chance an' that I'd blown it. I thought he was a bit childish about it all. I got the vibe off him that I owed him a big favour for lettin' him down. I remember the band had gone over to his offices to meet up for lunch with him before we headed home but I didn't go 'cause I was sick. Prager talked about signin' a management contract with them but the lads wanted a few bail out clauses that musta fucked Prager off. As the band were leavin' they ordered some soup to bring back to me an' Prager told them that he'd be puttin' it on their lunch bill. Sure enough, when we got back home there was a bill for lunch waitin' in Joe's gaff, I think. An' there was the soup added on at the end. Joe just rang him up an' told him to fuck off.

I was rootin' through me pockets a coupla days later when I found this phone number that one of the guys in Boston had given me for when we arrived in New York. I'd forgotten all about it. Outta curiosity more than anythin' else I rang the number an' asked for Ross or whatever his name was, but the person at the other end says, 'There's no Ross here. This is Avis Rentacar . . .' or whatever the fuck it was. I knew it then. I knew those guys in the States were bogus. I'm convinced that the guy who questioned me in Shannon had tipped off the authorities that we were on our way over an' told them to keep an eye on us. I don't give a fuck to this day what anybody else thinks. I don't care. There's no way it could all have been a coincidence.

I'd always thought of America as a very liberal, cool country but it was only when I got back that time that I realised that it was very intolerant of anybody that stepped off the line of what they considered normal. Within a few days a letter came for me at home from the American Embassy, tellin' me to go up an' see their envoy there in Ballsbridge.

I went in on the day an' this woman brought me into her office. She pulled out me multiple visa application form an' starts sayin' to me, 'Did you realise you were lyin' when ya filled out this application form sir?' I says to her, 'Well, I didn't think I was lyin'. I thought it wasn't relevant 'cause I don't have those medical problems anymore.' I tried to skirt the issue but she kept askin' me the question in different ways, 'Did you realise that you were not bein' truthful when you filled out the form sir?'

This was goin' on for about twenty minutes, half an hour, until finally I says, 'Look, maybe technically I lied.' I was just about to explain how maybe ya could see it that way an' to qualify me remark when she just whips me passport off the desk. She stamps 'REVOKED' on the page with me multiple visa on it an' hands it back to me – end of conversation. That was it – end of fuckin' story.

To this day, if I want go to America, I'm refused every time I go for a visa. I have to apply for a special waiver an' they send me to a doctor of their choosin' an' he goes through everythin' with a fine toothcomb to make sure I'm not on drugs. I have to do a urine test, AIDS test, everythin' – even if I just wanna go on a holiday for a week that happens.

I remember actually the first time I did an AIDS test was when I'd to go over to the States. I remember goin' into the doctor's office in Drumcondra to get the results to bring them to the Embassy. The woman behind the counter handed them to me in a sealed envelope. I wasn't allowed to see what was in the envelope, ya know? It was marked confidential an' for the attention of the Embassy people. I'm standin' there sweatin' bullets 'cause although I was always careful throughout me history with drugs an' needles an' that, there was obviously some fuckin' lapses. I could never be always 100 percent sure. So I'm shittin' meself thinkin', 'bollix this could be the end of me life written in this envelope'. The receptionist must have seen the worry on me face 'cause she whispers to me, 'Look, don't tell anyone I told ya – everythin' came back clear. You're ok.' I'll never forget that.

* * *

When we came back from the States we continued on doin' the unplugged set around the country. We spent most of 1995 giggin' around this comfortable circuit of places we'd built up.

It was durin' this time that we were really comin' into our own as a band. We'd found our niche I suppose ya could call it. We'd always had a strategy 'bout how we presented our music on stage, ya know, an' now we were applyin' that to the smaller, unplugged venues. There's a natural order ya play the songs in to achieve that communication with the audience. Ya don't just go out an' play a load of songs willy nilly. Ya'd start off fairly slowish an' ya build it up over the course of the gig. Ya get to a crescendo, say *Crazy World* would be that crescendo, an' then you kind of take it back down again. But it's all done over the course of the show. Ya don't just drop it immediately. Ya just kinda take it down slowly. It's like a wave. It must be gentle – ya can't go from a hugely bombastic song into a love song, one after the other, 'cause it'd be too much. Instead, near the end of the gig for example we'd play *Angie*, then *Wish You Were Here*, before buildin' it back up. Then ya kinda end with *This is* to really get the crowd goin'.

It's part of the craft that we'd worked out over hours in rehearsals an' at hundreds of gigs. If, at a certain point in the night, everybody gets up to buy a pint an' have a piss, ya know, there's somethin' wrong with that part of the set. Ya have to adjust it. We were constantly changin' the order of the songs, swappin' them round so that we'd have a different show every night. Aslan had built up a loyal followin' by this stage an' we were gettin' a lot of people comin' to our shows night afta night. We were aware of this an' we didn't want them to see the same thing over an' over again.

It's a natural progression for a band to see when they've reached their peak with the material. Then ya know it's time to go back to the studio an' create new songs. We were comin' close to that stage by the end of 1995. In between gigs we'd be sittin' down writin' songs for another album or tryin' out new riffs or bass lines or whatever an' we were talkin' about goin' back into the studio.

Things were goin' to be a bit different this time though 'cause we didn't have a big record company backin' us up. We'd have to finance a lot of the production costs ourselves. We kept giggin' hard to make up the money right through into the spring of 1996.

Denis Desmond of MCD then stepped in an' offered to cover part of the costs. We'd had a few dealins' with Denis over the years an' we were on good terms with him. He'd given us free rehearsal space in town an' that in the past when we needed it. So with his help by April we were ready to go back into the studio. We decided to use the same studio in Ringsend where we were recordin' the last album when the band broke up. The last time I'd been there was the day I got sacked.

We got in a producer called Declan Sinnott who was makin' a name for himself in the Irish music industry at the time. Declan was very professional in the studio. But he was also about 'the vibe' ya know? If he didn't like somethin' he'd just tell ya an' that would be that. It didn't matter even if you thought ya were well up for it. If Declan didn't feel the vibe was right, it just wasn't gonna happen.

We were in the studio for six months workin' on that album. When we were finished we christened it *Here Comes Lucy Jones* an' released it in October 1997.

I thought it was a great album. I still do. At that time I think we were a little bit influenced by what was goin' on in the music scene around us, ya know? Like, nobody lives in a vacuum – you're goin' to absorb a little of what's goin' on around ya at any particular time. I suppose if ya want to play it smart ya have to be aware of what music is popular. You've to try an' capture that an' put yer own slant on it.

There was kinda all that Brit pop stuff happenin', ya know? There was Blur an' all those bands an' we put our own spin on that with *Lucy Jones*. I didn't sit down consciously an' think, 'right I'm gonna copy this'. It was just that sound was popular then an' I think it shows on the album.

In the first week it was released it got up to Number 14 in the Irish charts. The press went for it big time. It was such a turn around for us to be gettin' this acknowledgement an' it was even more gratifyin' than before 'cause on this one it was just us. They gave it the same level of positive feedback that the *Charlie Moonhead* album got. They were sayin' it was our finest work to date. I can see the great things on that album but I can also see the flaws. I think it's a fine record but I believe the financial limitations imposed on us did have an effect on the final product. I don't believe that ya need millions an' millions of quid to make a great album – more money doesn't necessarily mean better music – but there is a minimum amount of money that ya need to make a competent album. Unless of course you're a complete fuckin' computer whizz kid who can make records in your bedroom but we're not computer whizz kids – we rely on the old traditional recordin' methods. Ya need a certain level of investment to make an album an' I felt that we were only barely above that level an' I think it tells.

* * *

While Aslan was back in the spotlight with the new album, in me private life I was havin' to deal with a very serious problem from me past.

Pascal Boland was the name of yer man who'd been in the house on Clonliffe Road the day it got raided. He owned the heroin in the house an' he'd been arrested an' sent to prison. He was doin' an 8-year sentence for that bust an' a couple of other charges that were all kinda rolled into one.

After he got sent down I started hearin' that he was goin' round sayin' that he'd taken the rap for me that day an' that I owed him. In fairness now, he coulda said nothin' an' we'd have all been charged so credit where credit was due, but while he was in prison he was tellin' people that I was in his debt an' that he wanted to see me.

He was sendin' out messages with people who were visitin' him that he wanted me to look after him while he was inside. I couldn't go near him 'cause it was 'round the time I'd the court case comin' up. I mean I couldn't afford to be seen visitin' a convicted heroin dealer while I was denyin' I was involved in dealin' drugs so I'd to stay away from him.

When the court case was sorted out I did go up to see him. I remember bringin' a tracksuit an' runners an' stuff like that but he wasn't interested in a change of clothes. He mentioned that he'd heard I got a loada money from *The Star* an' made out like I would have to share me new wealth. 'Ahh now, Christy,' he was sayin', 'Ya better look after me when I get outta prison.' I was goin', 'Yeah, whatever Pascal, I'll see ya again when you get out.' That was pretty much that as far as I was concerned.

The next thing I heard was he wanted 50 grand off me when he got out of jail or he was goin' to ruin me career the way I ruined his life. When he was asked what he was talkin' about he started tellin' people that I'd set him up that day – that I'd ratted on him to the police. Now, he knew I didn't set him up, right, but he was usin' this bullshit as justification to the other scumbags in there as to why he wanted 50 grand off me. But in reality he just saw me as a fuckin' easy touch.

He thought I was worth millions so when he came outta jail years later he started puttin' the word out on the streets that he was gonna catch up with me an' sort me out, ya know? I heard that he was goin' round sayin' he was gonna do this, he was gonna do that – he was gonna slash me face, he was gonna kill me – all this shit.

I was watchin' me back. Pascal Boland was a hard bloke an' he was well-connected with some serious fuckin' gangsters in Dublin. He was friends with this one well-known criminal in particular, who we'll call 'Peter', who put a price on me head over this shit. I'd heard that this bloke 'Peter' had suffered some form of abuse from a Christian Brother or a priest or somethin' like that when he was younger an' that Pascal had done somethin' vicious to the abuser which indebted this criminal to him. So 'Peter' decides to repay Pascal by puttin' a £30,000 contract out on me.

I didn't know 'bout the hit 'til years later. The first I heard anythin' 'bout this guy was when I came home one day an' Kathryn handed me a card with a name on it. She said a guy called 'Peter' had left it an' a mobile number to ring him on.

I thought it was about a gig or somethin' like that. I picked up the phone an' rang the number. This voice answers an' I says, '"Peter", this is Christy Dignam, Kathryn says you were round an'. . .' but this voice at the other end of the line cuts me off an' says, 'Yeah, I wanna fuckin' see you.' I says, 'What's this about?' an' he says, 'I'll tell ya when I fuckin' see ya.' So I ask him, 'In regard to what?' an' then he screams down the phone, 'I'll fuckin tell ya when I see ya.' So I says, 'See you – ya came to my fuckin' home lookin' for me. If ya can't tell me what this is about you can go fuck yourself.' An' I hung up on him, right.

The next day Kathryn says to me, 'Eh listen that fella 'Peter' came lookin' for ya again.' He had called askin' where I was. When he was leavin' Kathryn looked out the window an' saw he was drivin' a little silver Honda Civic. She recognised Pascal Boland sittin' beside him from photographs in the paper an' she described this 'Peter' fella to me. So I went up to Finglas an' started askin' who's this red-headed, stocky fella that Pascal knows, drives a silver civic? An' I was told, 'That's 'Peter'. . . such an' such . . .' – I knew who he was straight away. He was after bein' all over the *Sunday World* every other week with his eyes blacked out. He was in it 'cause when one of his lieutenants disappeared they never found his body. They just found his teeth an' his fuckin' nails.

I realised that this 'Peter' was the same bloke that I was after givin' a bollickin' to down the bleedin' phone, tellin' him he's to go fuck himself. Obviously I didn't know who I'd been talkin' to when I was givin' him all this verbal. It was only when I went to Finglas an' sussed out the name of this fucker that I realised it was the same bloke that I'd lifted out of it.

I nearly fuckin' vomited with fear. This was round a time when people like that were runnin' free in Dublin. Gangland was absolutely out of control an' he was on the front page of the papers – one of the main men. I didn't know what to do. This is not the sort of thing that ya can go to the police about is it? I mean what could they do? I was fuckin' terrified in case they tried anythin' on me family. Now I knew who Pascal was hangin' round with I knew he was capable of anythin'.

From then on – this is honest to God – I'd get to where you turn off the Navan Road to me house an' I used to say an *Our Father* every time. I was just waitin' for the night that I opened me front door an' boom, boom – a shotgun in the back of the fuckin' head.

As it turned out 'Peter' wasn't around for much longer. He was killed in Finglas in December 1996. But Pascal was still around.

Now an' again I'd hear that Pascal was gonna sort me out. Then I wouldn't hear anythin' for a while but he was always there, in the back of me mind, ya know? I knew h'd never let this go 'cause he was crazy.

A year or so passed an' then the next thing I heard he was gonna kidnap Kiera. He was sayin' to people this is how he was gonna get the money off me. I was sayin' earlier 'bout the lengths you'd go to protect your family – this was enough for me. I went up to this bloke in Finglas an' I says, 'Get me a number for Pascal Boland, I'm gonna sort this out for once an' for all.' I kinda made out that maybe I was runnin' scared an' that I was just gonna hand over the money that Boland was sayin' I owed him.

So I got a number for Pascal an' I arranged to meet him in a pub in Finglas. He turned up in the pub with this bird, his girlfriend at the time, an' we were sittin' there talkin' away like we're old mates. We're all yappin' away 'bout bullshit but I was just waitin' for a chance to get to the point. Next minute, his bird walks out to the jacks an' he leans over an' says, 'Right, I've got a business proposition an' I want a lend of money off you to finance it.'

'Pascal, I haven't got any money,' I says to him. 'Ya done the time but I lost just as much as you did in that raid on Clonliffe Road. I lost Aslan; I lost me record deal; I lost everythin'.' Yer man Pascal's just lookin' at me. 'So,' I says 'I don't have any fuckin' money. I'm tryin' to support a family an' I have a fuckin' drug habit. I don't have a pot to piss in.' But I could just see he wasn't gonna go for it.

I tried to explain that we didn't have big record company deals or anythin' like that but I was wastin' me breath. 'What about yer court case? Ya musta made a bit outta that,' he says. He still assumed I'd got millions outta *The Star* even after I'd gone an' told him all about it that day in prison. He'd been readin' about some celebrity suin' *The Sun* after they called him a queer. They'd called me a drug dealer so in Pascal's head I must've got a 100 million. This was the way he was goin' on anyway.

I couldn't get it through to him that I didn't get fuck all outta the case. He wasn't listenin' to me. He just leaned in towards me again an' stared me in the face an' says, really quietly, 'Go to a bank Christy an' take out the money or I'm gonna take out yer fuckin' daughter.'

I just snapped – I couldn't take it anymore. When he threatened Kiera it just hit a different fuckin' nerve. He went to a different level. I'd already put me family through enough – there was no way I was gettin' them dragged into this as well. I just went: 'Alright Pascal, this is the bottom line. I've been livin' in fear for me life expectin' at any moment to get blown away over this. I said me prayers every single night comin' home an' now you're threatenin' to take me daughter off the street? Well I'm tellin' ya now Pascal, ya touch me daughter or me wife or anybody in me family an' I swear to God Pascal, I'm not a hard man an' I'm not a gangster an' I've no back-up at all, but if ya touch them ya better make sure I'm dead 'cause I'll kill you, stone fuckin' dead. I just don't give a fuck any more.' An' I walked out of the pub.

I think he was a bit shocked 'cause he knew how fearful I was of him but he must've seen that I'd had enough. The next thing I start hearin' on the street was that Pascal had got 15 grand outta me but I didn't give a fuck – if that's what he wanted to do to save face, to tell people that that's what happened, then so be it. I didn't give a shit. I said to meself, 'I'll let sleepin' dogs lie.' I let it go an' that was that.

Pascal ended up gettin' shot dead a coupla months later. I have to admit that I wasn't fuckin' cryin' over it. After he was killed I found out the full story about the hit that was put on me head.

Me front window downstairs had been broken one night at the start of all the shit with Pascal, when he'd first got outta prison. I never knew how it got broken but I found out years later. After I'd screamed down the phone at this guy 'Peter', he was seriously fuckin' pissed off about it an' himself an' Pascal decided to sort me out once an' for all. So they pulled up outside me gaff one night with this third bloke in the back seat – a hired hit man.

Now, I actually got to know someone close to this hit man bloke a couple of months ago an' they told me the whole story. Yer man the hit man was sittin' in this car with Pascal an' 'Peter' outside me house. They'd a brand new Magnum .38 gun, fully-loaded. The hit man was to come in an' shoot me, right, but he felt hinky about the job. Now, I'd heard this fella had done things, so I don't think it was bullshit when I was told he didn't have a problem killin' people 'cause he'd done it before. But the hit man used to say he always done it on a principle – he couldn't kill people just for the money. I hadn't done anythin' on him so he was gettin' a bit uncomfortable 'bout the job.

When the hit man arrived down outside me door that night, he started gettin' second thoughts. He broke the window an' told Pascal to get in an' go round an' open the front door. But Pascal hesitated an' said he didn't want to go in.

At that moment both the hitman an' the other bloke 'Peter' realised Pascal was lyin'. They knew that if Pascal was tellin' the truth – that I'd been responsible for him goin' to prison an' had done all the things he'd said I'd done – then Pascal would've had absolutely no fuckin' problem walkin' into me house there an' then an' shootin' me in the head himself. The other two looked at each other an' nodded. It was acknowledged that Pascal was bullshittin' them. They knew that none of what Pascal had told them had ever happened. That's why the job was called off, I was told.

Pascal's gangster mate 'Peter' was always livin' on borrowed time. When he was killed, I hate to admit this, but I breathed easier, even though Pascal was still in the background. It's the first time that anybody's death had a positive effect on me. A few years later an' Pascal was gone too. I'd nothin' to fear from either one of them but the guy 'Peter' was so dangerous that even now, after all this time, I still wouldn't mention his name.

Unfortunately, what happens is when you're involved with drugs ya have to go into that environment an' deal with dangerous scumbags. It was a frightenin' lesson to see how it could affect not only my life but the lives of me family so directly. The way I was thinkin' was that none of me family had ever taken drugs so they should never have had to suffer the consequences of the drug life. But, of course, the people ya get mixed up with when you're livin' that life don't give a fuck what you think.

The Madness Ends

In 1993, I walked out onto a stage in Finglas, where I grew up, with four of me best mates. It was five years after we'd last played together as a band. What was supposed to be only a once-off gig changed me life – for the better. As soon as I started playin' again with Aslan I knew we'd made the right decision to get back together an' within four years we'd proved it.

In 1997, we were nominated for seven categories of the *Hot Press* Readers Poll an' we were up for Best Band in the IRMAs' the same year. We released a new re-mixed version of *This is* in 1998. Our debut song that we'd first recorded for £400 in 1983 went back into the charts at Number 7. We put the new version of *This is* together with most of our hits from the last three albums an' released them on a 'best of' album called *Shame About Lucy Moonhead* in July 1998. The first week it was out it was Number 1. Musically an' professionally it seemed we'd come full circle.

Around this time we even found a new music venue that would become what the Danceline was for us in the 1980s. It was called Vicar Street an' it was owned by a guy called Jim Aitken. Jim had always been good to the band an' treated us like rock stars, even when we were on our arses. I have to give him credit for that – he's a gentleman. To this day he's brilliant to work with, ya know? We did a deal with Jim that we'd play a series or four or five gigs in Vicar Street in March 1999. All of them sold out. One of the gigs was for charity an' all the proceeds went to Temple Street Children's Hospital. But the money that we made outta the rest of the gigs we invested back into the band. We could have split it up an' all bought a nice new car an' shit like that, but we didn't. That's somethin' that we've always done, ya know? Most of the money we ever made out of Aslan we put back in – to make it better an' to keep the thing goin'.

People were always sayin' to us that we produced these great studio albums but that we'd never captured on record what we were like on stage. Before we started the series of shows in Vicar Street we'd all sat down an' talked about that idea. In the end we decided to use the money on doin' a visual an' audio recordin' of the gigs an' usin' them to make a documentary album an' video of the band.

Denis Desmond had the option on our next album but we felt he didn't have the distribution network to do it justice an' get it into all the places where it needed to go. So we went to Denis an' we asked him could we take the material to EMI an' he kinda grudgingly agreed. But the problem was EMI weren't trippin' over themselves to produce it either. It was gonna cost somethin' like 70 grand to make an' I remember them sayin' that it just wasn't financially viable for them to invest that amount of money. So we settled on a small Irish production company which did a fuckin' great job in producin' what we called *Made In Dublin*.

Made In Dublin is basically a recordin' of us live in Vicar Street, cut up with interviews with me an' the rest of the band. It was a great laugh to make. We spent a few weeks doin' the interviews for it an' in September we had a big launch. We even got the Taoiseach, Bertie Ahern, to come down an' do the honours for us. We were obviously hopin' it would do well an' make a bit of cash but we'd no idea how successful it was goin' to be. We thought it would only appeal to the grassroots followin'. We were convinced that only the staunch fans that every band had would buy it. It took us completely by surprise when it became the most successful album we've ever done. Both the album an' the video went to Number 1 in the same week an' within three weeks they turned platinum. It still flies outta shops – only last Christmas we released it on DVD an' it was snapped up.

We're a powerful band when we're live on stage an' I think we managed to capture that on the video. The album an' video did show some of the things we were doin' live at that time. Like, we'd brought in stringed instruments that added, I think, to the sorta intimate vibe of the place. Personally, I think our records are as good as our live shows. A live show after all is only a performance of our records. I still think we make great records but I can see why people consider we're stronger in the live settin', without a doubt.

I can't really say what it is about our gigs that attract the same people to them time an' time again though – 'cause we do get a very loyal followin'. I don't know. That's somethin' that you'd have to ask the fans, d'ya know what I mean? But for a lot of them I'd say they come away from our gigs satisfied 'cause first of all, we all know how to perform. We've had a lot of experience in playin' live an' we love it. Also, I've always tried to be totally sincere in how I express meself an' how I sing the songs an' I think that sincerity endears ya to people. I think all those things come across. They can see that an' the feedback lends ya a certain dynamic.

I remember lookin' at *Made in Dublin* for the first time an' bein' surprised at how I acted when I was on stage. Obviously I've seen photographs an' videos of meself at gigs over the years but they don't illustrate a performance as well as a whole hour an' a half recordin'. When I watched the video I thought it was interestin' how me stage persona had developed. I'd come a long way from that first night in the Towers in Ballymun when I'd stood in one spot, grabbin' the microphone in fear.

I think me stagecraft developed through a sense of frustration bout tryin' to connect with the audience against the restrictions that technology imposes. It's probably from doin' gigs for years where the sound wasn't up to scratch or I couldn't see the audience properly or whatever. I'll try to portray the intensity of what I'm singin' in a visual way as much as lyrically. I'll use me body to illustrate a line in a song that I feel is important. I mean there are certain lyrics that are absolutely essential. Sometimes they almost encapsulate the whole song. I want there to be no ambiguity about what they mean but sometimes the words on their own can't get across the importance of what I'm singin' about an' I have to act them out.

There's a song called *Rain Man* an' there's a line in it that goes *'If I should crawl beside . . . smash my face against a wall'* right, an' I'll fall on the floor an' start bangin' the monitor. I'd hit it so many times I'd nearly break me hand off it. I'd get off the stage later an' have little rips on me head an' bruises from throwin' meself round the place. I'd have hurt meself on stage a good few times. Like I've often cut meself – me head an' me hands – doin' certain songs 'cause I've put so much into them.

I absolutely don't feel a thing in the height of the performance but when I get off the stage later I'm in a fuckin' jocker. I'm gettin' on a bit an' it's really startin' to take it out of me. I'll do four nights in Vicar Street, go to bed on Sunday night after the last gig an' I won't get up 'til 8 o'clock on Monday evenin'. It really fucks ya up for days 'cause performin' is not just physically demandin', it's emotionally drainin' as well. It's just the way I was trained – to put everythin' into every note. I don't know, maybe I'll drop dead at forty fuckin' eight years of age 'cause of the years of strain but even if I knew that was goin' to happen I don't think I'd be able to change what I do. Anyway I don't think I'd want to.

Not long after *Made in Dublin* went triple platinum we were playin' on the *Late Late Show* an' we asked Pat Kenny would he do a special presentation of the discs to us after the song. One of the researchers or whatever said there wouldn't be time to do it so we said fair enough but we were disappointed. We just wanted him to say somethin' like, 'Thank you, thank you – that was Aslan an' ladies an' gentlemen we'd just like to present the lads with a. . . .' It'd have took him 30 seconds to do that. I mean I remember on the same show Pat did a thing on llamas. They'd built a pen in the middle of the RTÉ studios an' he went an' spoke to this aul wan about her two fuckin' llamas for five minutes. I remember lookin' at the llamas thinkin' 'they aren't even nice lookin' animals' – sure they're not, are they?

* * *

There are certain advantages an' disadvantages to bein' a band outside the control of a big record company. Like they've the resources and the cash to put ya up there an' to make everybody in the world know yer there with distribution networks an' that but the disadvantages are you're obligated to the company an' your artistic freedom can be quashed. Bein' independent we've a lot of freedom to do what we want when we want, ya know? Like in the summer of 2000 we decided to travel over to Australia to promote *Shame About Lucy Moonhead*. It was so successful it even put *Feel No Shame* back in the charts. Here was an album we'd recorded 12 years ago an' it was back in the charts at Number 14. It was a great note to leave on for our first tour Down Under.

It cost us about £30,000 to do a small Australian tour but it was worth every penny. When we got there we realised that all the gigs had been sold out months in advance. The first place we played was called the Metro in Sydney. It was kinda like the Olympia Theatre in Dublin an' it could hold about 2,000 people. We got an ecstatic reaction. This was without the big corporate back-up of a major record company behind us. I mean without all the big promotion that a record company throws for ya we sometimes found it hard to get into the newspapers or to get interviews, yet all the gigs were sold out.

What happens is Irish kids who are into bands at home bring the music with them when they travel. They go off an' work in bars an' that, playin' the albums an' passin' them onto other people they work with. I suppose a sorta word of mouth springs up. I woulda thought that only really applied to the cities where there's loads of Irish, like in Sydney. But in Melbourne we got a really mental reception an' they were mostly an Australian audience so that was a nice fuckin' surprise, ya know?

An' this is somethin' that's kinda since developed outside Ireland for us where we get round by word of mouth. We ended up playin' gigs in Italy and Holland an' that – places where we wouldn't have broken the market – an' we still play to full houses.

Sometimes over in Australia I'd think back to when me an' Kathryn had been there, almost exactly 20 years before. It was weird to think we'd loved it so much an' I'd promised her that if it didn't work out with the band we'd come back an' live there. Obviously events overtook our plans but a little bit of me always wondered what it would've been like if we'd jacked it all in an' gone to Australia instead.

It's pointless thinkin' that it might've been better or worse – it would've just been a different life. From where I was standin', despite all that had happened, I think I could say that I'd made the right decision.

We arrived back in Ireland an' found out *Shame About Lucy Moonhead* had sold about 30,000 copies in 12 months. We were on a roll. We'd played our first sold out gig in the Point Depot the previous Christmas an' in December 2000 we took to the stage again. Over 9,000 people woulda been there that night, out celebratin', just after Christmas. It was some buzz to walk out in front of that crowd. Everybody was in flyin' form, the band were havin' a laugh, the audience were goin' mad – it was fuckin' brilliant. I was on a real high playin' a gig that size again.

* * *

Not long after we got back from Australia I faced me final battle with heroin addiction. By this stage I'd been usin' heroin on an' off for nearly 20 years. I was still usin' on a regular basis an', physically, the years of abuse were about to catch up on me.

When I started off as rock singer I used to think I was cool doin' drugs, ya know? To me it was all part of the life. I'd look round at people like Keith Richards from The Rolling Stones an' I wanted that look, ya know, the gaunt face, the sunken-in cheeks an' all the rest of it. To me, he was a rock star. I used to do all this stupid shit that rock stars did. Like in 1988 I think it was, we'd dinner in the Mansion House with Ben Briscoe who was Lord Mayor then. I remember smokin' heroin in the toilets just so I'd able to say, 'I smoked gear in the Mansion House jacks.' I thought it was very cool an' clever when it was actually crazy shit. I was justifyin' this behaviour by sayin' it was 'cause I was in a rock'n'roll band, ya know? But after a coupla years of injectin' heroin into me veins I didn't think it was such a glamorous thing to do. It got to the stage where I couldn't even find a vein in me arms anymore 'cause they'd all collapsed, so I was injectin' into me neck.

I remember back when I was just gettin' me musical career together I'd to go all the way out to Bray one day on the DART to get the gear 'cause there was none in Ballymun. By the time I got out there I was in bits. As soon I scored off the guy I went down to the nearest place I could find to shoot up. There was this run-down amusement arcade on the seafront where I went into the jacks. The light in the fellas was broken so I had to go into the ladies.

I couldn't find a vein in me arm. I'd injected there so many times that I couldn't get one to come up, no matter how many times I furiously tapped on me arm with me hand. I decided to go for me jugular. I was lookin' in the mirror an' I'm tryin' to get the point of the needle into the vein. I'm lookin' at me reflection so I'm doin' everythin' in reverse. I'm tryin' to stick the needle in this way but I'm seein' it comin' that way. It was hard tryin' to work all this out in me head, ya know? I mean a couple of millimetres either way an' I was gonna miss. The whole time I was afraid that somebody's gonna walk in the door, any fuckin' second, ya know?

Finally I get it into me jugular an' I pull back on the plunger so there's kinda blood an' heroin mixed in the syringe but then it slips out an' blood squirts from the vein onto the mirror. The sweat is pumpin' outta me at this stage right, blood is dribblin' down me neck an' this fuckin' syringe is hangin' outta me, full of blood an' stuff, when these two old ladies open the door behind me. They just looked at me with abject horror. I'm lookin' back at them in the mirror thinkin', 'd'ya not think yis are over-reactin' a bit now? C'mon, fuck off. I'm not that bleedin' bad? Have ye never seen a junkie before?' It was probably the most horrific thing they'd ever seen in their lives, yet I actually, genuinely believed that they were makin' a big deal outta a minor fuckin' incident. I thought, 'yeah it's not the nicest thing to see but c'mon . . . it's like . . . it's like a woman breast-feeding a baby in public'. I didn't realise how much a shock they musta got. It was only later when I remembered that incident that I thought, 'holy shit, was I really so bad'. But at the time all I was interested in was gettin' that heroin into me – to kill the withdrawals. So I turned back to the mirror, cursin'. I don't remember what the aul wans did. I didn't care.

I still don't have any visible veins left on me arms. Now, there are other veins that run deeper under yer skin that are still workin'. Otherwise the blood wouldn't be able to get round. But you can't get at them with a needle.

What happens then is 'cause yer veins are so fucked from usin' needles all the time that ya have to start what's called 'skin-popping'. It basically means ya inject a needle straight into the muscles to get any sort of hit. But the residue from the heroin doesn't circulate so freely as it would if it was injected straight into the bloodstream, so it remains there, under yer skin, for years.

I'd been bangin' away for ages into the same place on me shoulder– just bashin' the needle in, just stickin' it in there like that. A few years later, like I woulda been back with Aslan an' all by this stage, I got an abscess on that spot.

Now, I'd had abscesses before but this one was different. Normally I would've just waited 'til an abscess ran its course an' came to a head. Then I'd lance it. But this one wasn't fuckin' doin' that. It just stayed under the surface an' it got bigger an' more painful. It got so bad that I remember drivin' to a gig in Longford an' I couldn't even change gear in the car. At this stage me arm had swollen to the size of a bleedin' orange an' I went to see a doctor.

I've always been reluctant to go an' get medical help 'til things got really bad. You're treated differently when they find out you're a junkie, ya know? I remember I'd to have a kidney stone out only a coupla years ago so I went up to Blanchardstown Hospital. The nurses were all comin' up to me, goin', 'Aah it's yer man outta Aslan,' an' askin' me for me autograph, ya know? I was brought into one of the wards an' the nurse was tryin' to get an IV into me. She says, 'Eh, did you spend a lot of time in hospital as a child?' an' I says 'No why?' An' she says, 'Yer veins are very weak.' 'That's 'cause I'm a heroin addict,' I says. The second I said it she was gone. She came back about 10 minutes later with aprons, safety glasses an' gloves on. None of the other nurses came near me after that.

Another time I was gettin' me teeth done an' the dentist says, 'I haven't seen ya for a while, Christy.' So I says, 'Aw, I got into the whole heroin thing an' I kinda let meself go a bit.' I was just gettin' into the chair but he took his gloves off an' fucked me out of the surgery.

Now, this doctor who saw me for the abscess was used to treatin' addicts an' he'd seen it all before. But even he fainted while he was tryin' to lance it, that'll tell you how bad it was. He'd to get another doctor in to finish the job for him.

The next day I was goin' down to get it dressed an' he came in to see me. He says, 'Lookit, Christy, you're not 18 an' I'm not sayin' this to frighten ya away from drugs. I know at the end of the day you're gonna do what you wanna do, you're an adult,' he says. 'But if you hadn't a come in here to get that lanced ya woulda died. It was about to burst inside ya an' if it had, it'd poison your system. Ya don't have enough fat on you to sustain a sickness an' you'd have been dead within two to three days.'

I'd been warned about drugs all me life – 'If ya smoke hash you'll become a junkie' or 'If you take heroin you're goin' to die' – but ya think that they're bein' dramatic to frighten you. It was different bein' told, 'Had ya not come in here you'd be dead.' As I said, normally I woulda just taken care of it meself, but this time somebody actually forced me to go to the doctor. Had I not done so I was dead.

* * *

I'd slipped in an' out of heroin so many times I'd lost count. Nothing was workin'. By this stage me body had started to rebel against all the fuckin' toxins I'd poured into me system. I started to break out in all these terrible abscesses all over me body which I still get to this day. The pain from them is just impossible for me to describe. They're almost as bad as goin' through withdrawal sickness. Ya get them everywhere – under yer arms, in yer crotch, on yer neck – huge boils full of the poison that you've injected into yer body for years.

I remember goin' over to Lanzarote with Kathryn a coupla years ago just to get away from the heroin scene an' give me body a break. But when I got there two of these abscesses came up – one at the top of each leg – where me arse meets me leg. One of them had burst an' when they burst ya kinda get some relief from the pain 'cause a bit of the poison comes out an' it's not so intense. But the other one hadn't come to a head. It was just formin' up under the skin an' I was in fuckin' agony. It was the worst one I'd experienced for a long time. I couldn't walk; I couldn't sit down; I couldn't bend me leg. It was gettin' too much.

So I went down to a chemist an' I bought a packet of blades an' I went back up to the bathroom. I remember I'd the mirror behind me, ya know, an' I was turned round, tryin' to lance it. I'd kinda slice at it with the blade but I couldn't do it.

Three days in a row I went into the jacks to try an' do it. Each time I could make meself cut it enough to make it bleed but I couldn't get the courage up to kinda go right into an' at it.

But on the mornin' of the fourth day I just couldn't take another minute of it. I couldn't sleep; I couldn't lie down; I couldn't eat. So I took a hit of gear, went into the bathroom, locked the door an' braced meself against the wall. I gritted me teeth an' dug in with the blade, cuttin' the fuck into me leg. I looked back at the mirror an' I just seen meself standin' there, cacks down round me ankles, blood pissin' down me legs, a big abscess on me arse an' a blade in me hand. I looked at me reflection in the mirror an' I'll never forget the look on me face – I looked like a vampire, me eyes were so pinned from the heroin. I just got this moment of clarity I think you'd call it, an' I just thought, 'fuck me, yer mother didn't raise ya to do this shit. What are ya fuckin doin' to yourself?'

Somethin' shifted in me that day. I couldn't define it but I felt sad for what I'd done to meself an' everyone round me. I didn't know it at the time but I was startin' to bottom out – I'd hit me rock bottom, as the alcoholics would describe it.

When I came back from Lanzarote I managed to stay away from the gear for a few weeks. I'd nearly kicked it for good – it was the longest I'd gone without heroin for years but while somethin' might have changed in me mind I was still physically addicted to it. The withdrawals got so severe that I just snapped.

I went down to a bloke's gaff, down on Hanlon's Corner to score. I knocked on the door an' while I was waitin' for him to answer I seen a silver car parked across the road with a bird sittin' in it. As soon as I caught her eye she kinda ducked down an' hid behind the pillars of the car doors, ya know? But she was still lookin' over at me an' I instantly knew she was the police. I got that old 'hinkie' feelin' that junkies get when cops are around an' I thought, 'bollix, they're watchin' me now'. But I couldn't just walk away. It was more important to me that I score the gear. Normally I'd get the fuck outta there, but not this time – me priorities had changed.

So I says to meself, 'If I get in here an' get the gear, I'll work out then how I'm gonna get it past them.' Somebody answered the hall door an' I walked in. I knocked on the door of yer man's flat but he wasn't there. I was thinkin', 'fuck, fuck,' knowin' the police were outside. As I opened the front door to go back out it was just like – Whack! I was punched straight in the face an' I fell back. About five coppers jumped on top of me an' dragged me across the floor an' back into the gaff. They'd been sittin' outside waitin' to raid this place an' they decided to do it just as I came along. I hadn't got anythin' on me an' there was nothin' there so they let me go. This had happened at a time when I'd nearly beaten the addiction an' it was like a final warnin', 'Listen, don't get back into this world,' kinda thin'. But I ignored me instincts one last time.

I started ringin' round everyone I knew to get some gear. There was this bloke I used to score off ages before but I didn't know if he was still dealin' or what the story was. I found his number an' rang him in desperation. He answered the phone an' I just blurted it out. I was like, 'Jaysus, John, I'm in a bleedin' jocker an' I need to get somethin' off ya, please.' An' this voice says, 'Who is this?' I said, 'It's Christy.' An' he says, 'Christy who?' 'Christy Dignam for fuck's sake,' I says. An' he goes, 'This is John . . . ' an' it wasn't the John I was lookin' for – it was another John I knew who was in Narcotics Anonymous.

I just broke down. 'Lookit John,' I says, 'I'm in bits, I need fuckin' help.' So he came up to the house an' sat down with me. He kinda just latched onto me. He steadied me for a coupla days. He brought me to a NA meetin' an' all that, ya know?

An' all I can say about that is that it was a turnin' point.

* * *

All durin' the recordin' of our last two studio albums I'd been flirtin' in an' out with drugs. If I wasn't on heroin at the time I was still doin' the odd bit of cocaine here an' there. I was discreet about it. I didn't go round in bits like I had been before but by April 2001, when we went into rehearsal for the next album, I hadn't done any drugs for a good few months.

The Waiting For The Madness To End sessions were a big departure for Aslan music-wise but for me it was an even bigger move away from me past. Things were back to the way they'd been at the beginnin' with the rest of the band as well. We were all kinda on the same page.

We'd worked our bollix off to generate the money to go in an' record this album. It was gonna cost serious money so we'd to work for a long time to raise the cash. The thing is even when ya release an album ya don't know if it's goin' to have any fuckin' success. If past records were anythin' to go by, there wasn't even goin' to be any huge financial reward for makin' the album, but we're in a band, that's what bands do – they make records. We'd taken a break from the tourin' to get ready for the studio an' we all kinda knuckled down to come up with songs for the next album. We rented a place in Ashtown, a little rehearsal room, an' we just went up there every mornin' at 10 o'clock an' stayed 'til 5 o'clock every day. We were back to just doin' what we did in the pigsty all those years ago – rehearsin' an' writin', rehearsin' an' writin'.

We wanted to do somethin' different. We wanted to depart musically from where Aslan had always been goin', simply for the reason that we wanted to avoid the mistake that bands like Oasis had made with *Standing on the Shoulders of Giants* in that they were accused of just repeatin' their back catalogue. We didn't want to be makin' the same record over an' over again. After all, what's the fuckin' point in that? We were prepared to take the risk of doin' somethin' different even though we knew that we were gonna lose some of our grassroots followin'. There's a weird irony happens with bands that have such loyal support. The fans want ya to do somethin' new, fresh an' different, yet if it's too new, fresh an' different you're gettin' into stuff that they're not into. On the other hand, if ya did just recreate the same album again they'd be givin' out 'bout that as well. Ya have to stay loyal to yourself as an artist an' try to ignore the voices of the maddenin' crowd. I didn't go into this new album with the idea of pleasin' other people. I did it for meself 'cause ultimately, at the end of the day, that's all you're left with. I don't know how many people that follow Aslan today were there from day one. I mean people come an' go but I'm there all the time.

There'll be a day when everybody'll be gone an' it's just me left – then I'll have to know that I'm proud of what I've done.

We stayed in our little studio room right through the winter of 2000 an' then went back into the Westland Studios in April 2001. It was the same place where we'd recorded *Feel No Shame* all those years ago. We were different people walkin' back through those doors. The last time we were there we believed we were about to set the world on fire. We'd no idea when we wrapped up those last sessions what lay ahead of us – we assumed that this could go on forever. Now we were back 13 years later an' we'd changed as people – an' as musicians. We were older an' wiser. We also realised we were gettin' on a bit. We were like, 'God knows when this thing could end . . . let's get in there an' make a fuckin' really good album.'

We've always relied on the fact that people have been so loyal to us an' that has convinced us that we're doin' the right thing by goin' on. I honestly hope to God that never changes but maybe the day will come when we won't have a say in the matter anyway. Like the fans could decide to move on tomorrow an' start likin' whoever else has come along an' we'd be finished regardless of what we wanted. All those people that are big into the band now might get new friends or get married an' the next generation that were there as kids mightn't like it as teenagers. Ya just don't fuckin' know.

When I said that the album could be our last one I didn't say it out of any sense of doom – it was more that we were startin' to see the reality of this business. From our own experiences we'd learned that every record could potentially be our last. We knew that the only reason Aslan was still goin' was 'cause of the sheer determination to keep it goin'. A lot of people had said to us over the years, 'Yis would've been well justified havin' thrown in the towel at this point.' I think most people would've forgiven us if we'd said, 'Ah look we've had enough of this bullshit, ya know, we're jackin' it in,' but we didn't – we kept goin'. We kept strivin' forward. It was vital to us to get it right 'cause, as I've said, a record is just that – a record of where we are as a band. That's why *This is* was so important – 'cause it was our first record. This album was equally as important 'cause it could be our last, ya know?

I'm very happy with the way *Waiting For The Madness To End* turned out. We'd Ian Grimble in to produce it. Ian had worked with The Manic Street Preachers an' Travis an' we just felt that he could give our sound that bit of an edge. It's a really beautiful album – I have to say. If this was to be our swansong then it was a good one to go out on. I know some day I'll be able to sit down with me grandkids an' show them all our albums. I think I'll be able to stand over every one of them but I'll be especially proud of *Waiting For The Madness To End*. I think we did some really good tracks on it.

I like how the duet numbers with Sinead O'Connor worked. I'd met her at a charity gig just before we sat down to do the album. We got talkin' an' I realised we had a few things in common. She'd gone to the same singin' teacher as me an' she was sayin' she'd love to do somethin' with us so I asked her to do a duet with me on *Open Arms*. She's fuckin' brilliant. It worked out better than I thought an' I asked her to sing on *She's so Beautiful* as well. She's a genius. I think she's a great singer an' she added her star quality to those songs. I remember some people sayin' to me that I should be honoured to have her sing with me. I did feel honoured but I think she would've felt just as honoured to be workin' with us.

One of me favourite songs off that album is the last one. It's called *Hang On* an' it's an anti-drugs song. It was my farewell to the drugs that'd had a grip on me for so long. The image is there again of drugs as this beautiful woman lurin' ya to her before ya find out she's this old hag.

Took the apple from the tree/
Then she told me/
This would set me free/
Like a fool I took her hand/
Said she'd take me to the promised land/
But I found when we got there/
There was nothin' at all/
The promises she made meant nothing at all/
© Aslan

End of Story

We were flyin' to Sligo in a little Fokker 50, kinda propeller plane, to do a gig in November 2002 I think it was. It was a real blustery day an' as we were comin' in to land at Strandhill Airport when we hit really bad turbulence. The plane start hoppin' all over the sky. Billy was actin' the bollix, imitatin' the bloke from *Star Trek* goin', 'I cannae hold it taegether captain, she's breakin' up.' We came through the clouds, an' ya know the way normally the runway's way down there, well we came through the clouds an' the runway was right there, d'ya know what I mean? We were right on top of it – as if the clouds were two feet off the bleedin' ground – an' we were whorin' along, way too fast.

Where I'm sittin' is right over the wing an' I'm lookin' out the window, right, an' as the plane hit the ground the wheels just flattened out an' then – BADUM – exploded. The tyre wrapped round the rim of the wheel an' at that moment I realised we were in serious shit. I turned to Billy an' I said, 'I don't believe it, the fuckin' wheels are afta burstin'.' Alan's sittin' on the other side of the plane an' he shouts over that the wheels on that side have burst as well. I remember the whole plane just went silent. I was thinkin', 'I hope to fuck the pilot knows the wheels have burst, 'cause if he doesn't, he'll try to take off an' when he gets up there he'll realise we've no poxy tyres an' then we're fucked altogether'.

We skidded across the tarmac for a few seconds before the plane went right off the runway an' into the grass, right. All this muck started gettin' sprayed up onto the windows. I looked ahead an' there's about 20 feet of grass left an' then the ocean. I'm watchin' the sea rushin' at us an' I just knew by the speed we were travellin' at that there was no way this plane was gonna stop – it was goin' over the cliff.

I thought we were gonna die, ya know? I thought that was it – it was all over. Then it struck me how calm everybody was. Ya know the way ya see in movies when the plane's gonna crash they're all goin' Aghhhh – there was none of that. From me perspective everybody seemed to be on the same kinda wavelength. Ya looked an' seen what was happenin', thought you were gonna die in seconds an' accepted it, d'ya know what I mean? It was like everyone knew there was no point in fuckin' screamin'.

The plane crashed to a stop an' tipped forward over the cliff. There was a few seconds delay while everybody looked round to see had it burst into flames an' then they all jumped out of their seats. The aul wan in front of Billy turned around an' tore the head off him 'cause he'd been takin' the piss earlier on. Billy had shut up fairly fuckin' sharpish when he sussed that it was gonna crash. He was tryin' to get the door open to leggit when the air hostess came runnin' up the plane to stop him 'cause the propeller was still flyin' round.

Man, that was somethin' else. Everyone was shakin' when we got off. Nobody was injured an' we were still able to go off an' do the gig that night in Kelly's pub, just down the road. But I'll never forget it. It got me thinkin' 'bout how lucky we were that we weren't dead.

A few years before the plane crash the papers already had me dead. We were doin' another gig out in Charlies in Howth. When I got there I went into the dressin' room an' Tony was on the phone to Kathryn. He'd this funny look on his face as he handed me the phone. Kathryn was on the other end goin', 'Oh thank God, I knew you weren't dead.' I was like, 'What?' She told me a friend of mine had called to the house in his slippers an' knocked on the door sayin', 'Jaysus Kathryn. I'm so sorry. I just heard Christy's dead.' I was sayin' to her, 'Listen, relax I'm obviously not dead, I'm on the phone.'

But after the gig I was talkin' to a few heads, an' they were sayin', 'Great gig for a dead man Christy. We weren't even gonna come down tonight.' By now I was seriously wonderin' what the fuck's goin' on.

The followin' day Gerry Ryan was playin' *Crazy World* on the radio an' he stopped it half-way through the song an' said, 'I've just heard some dreadful news, we're waitin' to get confirmation that Christy Dignam has been killed.'

I was thinkin' somebody was takin' the piss, ya know, an' now the whole place thinks I'm dead. The vibe was there was a guy who lived round the corner from me called Christopher Duignam – a busman. He was in his fifties an' he'd died suddenly of a heart attack. The rumours went on for days that Christy Dignam the singer was dead. There were still people comin' up to me afta gigs an' that sayin', 'Jaysus we thought it was strange that Aslan would go on considerin' you were only just dead . . .' an' I'd to say, 'Well, ya can see I'm fuckin' not.'

It's things like that over the last few years that has made me realise that life has taken me to some strange places. When I was a teenager growin' up in Finglas, I'd sit in me bedroom, listenin' to David Bowie an' Dylan, wonderin' what would it be like to be a singer in a cool band. I thought it'd be great to get to wear deadly clothes an' be on *Top of the Pops*. Maybe buy a nice car an' give me aul lad some money so he could stop workin'. It was all the obvious, positive aspects of music I was thinkin' 'bout. I didn't realise in that journey that all this other shit could happen. I didn't think that one day I'd be starin' at two aul wans in a dirty mirror with a needle hangin' out of me neck. I didn't think I was gonna be sittin' in an office in the American Embassy with the envoy shinin' a light in me face. I didn't think I was gonna be lyin' in me bed one night with a hit man outside me door goin' to blow me poxy brains out, ya know?

I think I've led a charmed life in a lot of ways. I consider meself a lucky person when I think of the shit I've done in me life. I mean all the chances I took. The first time I smoked a joint I thought I was takin' me life in me hands. I started off naively thinkin' I was riskin' me life by smokin' hash to a point when I'd do just a gee-hair of heroin below overdose level so I'd get the best effect an' ultimate buzz without killin' meself.

It still baffles me how I fell into that whole mess. I know I'm not an idiot, so what the fuck, as an intelligent person, was I doin' watchin' meself slip into addiction. That's a huge mystery for me. I was ignorant 'bout heroin at the very start but I'd plenty of time to find out about it. I knew enough to know that heroin cuts across all levels of intellectual ability – all race, all creeds an' all sexes. There are no barriers because everyone takes it for their own particular reason an' there are so many different reasons. But I was still convinced that I was smarter than everyone else – I thought I could keep it under control.

I was even more convinced that nobody else knew. I found it easy to live the lie of bein' a junkie. I think I was well-versed in how to live with secrets. For me, bein' on heroin was like havin' the same dirty secret I'd carried round after I was abused as a child. Like I said, I'd always felt that it was me own fault that I'd been abused – that I kinda had a hand in it somehow – so I didn't tell anyone. When that happened to me I felt I was on me own an' I kinda insulated meself from that moment on. An' with the heroin ya almost have to adopt the same personality manipulations to sustain the secrecy. I'd say the rock'n'roll lifestyle I led woulda lent itself to me bein' an addict but I can't blame everythin' on it.

I think I've been very lucky to have escaped death considerin' I was addicted to drugs for so long. But in January 2003 I got pneumonia an' was hospitalised for weeks. I really was at death's door.

Years of snortin' cocaine had weakened me. I got an infection an' it spread into the chamber that surrounds me lungs. One of them collapsed an' I was rushed to the Blanchardstown Hospital. I'd to tell them that I was a recoverin' heroin addict an' that I couldn't be given anythin' with opiates in it, ya know, anythin' with opium. So they couldn't give me any painkillers. When they were treatin' me it all had to be done with me wide-awake. The doctor put me sittin' backwards in a chair with me arms draped over the back of it an' he got a scalpel an' just cut a slit between me ribs. Then he got his finger, opened a hole in me side an' pushed a tube into me lung to drain all the fluid off it.

The tube was connected to this little glass bell jar on the floor an' all this bloody water started flowin' into it. There was little measurements on the side so they'd know how much was comin' out. Every mornin' they'd give me an X-ray to see what fluid was left. They'd shift the tube round me lung to drain off all the rest of it but there was one part higher up in me body that wouldn't shift. The doctors couldn't understand it, so eventually they just stuck a needle into it an' drew it back, an' a load of shit came out of it. That's when they realised it was an abscess growin' on me lung. Now I was in trouble. The doctor says to me, 'If ya don't get this thing sorted now it's gonna burst inside you an' you'll die instantly.'

I was in Blanchardstown two or three weeks at this stage an' there was nothin' more they could do for me. Basically they didn't have the facilities there to treat me further so they said I'd have to go to the Mater Hospital. I rang the Mater from me hospital bed but they said they didn't have any beds free. They said it would take about two to three weeks before they could admit me. I was like, 'Hold on, the doctors here are tellin' me if this bursts I'm fucked – I'm dead. I don't have two to three weeks.' She says, 'Well I'm sorry, there's nothin' we can do unless you go private.'

I'd to go to the band. We'd money put away to go tourin' in England an' I'd to get 20 grand off them to get the thing done, right? I got an ambulance from Blanchardstown to the Mater, carryin' this jar full of fuckin' filthy, bloody water with a tube comin' outta me. When I got to the hospital they brought me up to the private ward but as I was takin' off me tracksuit bottoms the nurse stopped me – I'd to give her 10 grand before she'd let me get into the bed. I swear to God. Had I not been able to put me hand on that money I wouldn't be sittin' here. I'd have been dead – end of fuckin' story. It's as simple as that.

Every day is a battle to stay off the gear but every day that I do is a success story as far as I'm concerned. Heroin is not somethin' that you're ever totally finished with – ya never really escape. Even if you've been clean for years ya never think, 'yeah, that's it, I'm not takin' another drug again'. Ya can only hope that ya never do but ya never know what's round the next corner. I've been there before.

I've been clean so many times, for loads of different periods of time, an' then somethin' happens an' it sets me right back. I hope, I really hope, it never happens again but then, ya know, never say never – that's the nature of addiction.

The other consolation is I didn't lose me family over it, like what's happened to loadsa other people. I still have me family who believed in me through all the shit – me parents an' me wife Kathryn an' daughter Kiera, who now has her own baby, Cián.

An' I still have me music. Gettin' back together with Aslan was probably one of the better things I did in me life. I'm glad we're still doin' what we're doin', ya know? There's nobody else I'd rather be doin' it with than them. In the end we survived. When you're in a band like Aslan, it's a full-on experience. Like sometimes I see a lot more of them than I do of me family. We've all learned to tolerate each other. Once you learn that, ya can relax 'cause ya know you're with the right people.

As long as we're able to keep makin' music then I'm happy to do that. We know we'll never be the coolest band on Earth but then again, we never were. We were never really admitted to that whole 'cool' Irish music scene. But I'm happier playin' in a good workin' band. I don't buy into all the other bullshit any more.

I look at so many other bands – good bands that didn't even achieve what we achieved – an' I think we can keep on achievin'. I'm still writin' new songs an' a lotta the time the finished product still doesn't resembles what's in me head. It's a pale reflection. I listen to an Aslan record an' I can hear the mistakes. It's those imperfections that drive me on to do it again. I'm thinkin', 'the next time I write a song I'm gonna make sure I don't fuck it up – I'm gonna get it bang on'.

I hope that our next album will be produced with the same determination an' viewed with the same freshness that the '*Madness*' album was. I'd love for it to be successful in commercial terms – I'd be a fuckin' fool if I didn't admit that – so I could keep that promise I made to Kathryn an' she could give up workin'. I still believe that album could be in there, ya know? I believe that there are more crackin' songs, but it's not down to me. Its future success is not determined by the quality of me output – it's determined by who believes in the quality of me output.

As a band I'd like to think, lookin' at what we've achieved, that we always kinda gave it our all. An' we were always honest in what we did. That's the one thing 'bout the music we do, there was no airy-fairy approach to it. We sang about the reality round us, as we saw it. But I'd also like for us to be remembered as a band that never forgot where we came from.

I think we've already done enough creatively to consider that we've been a success. We've created a higher standard of music than many other artists I know that are hugely successful on the world stage. We can book ourselves into Vicar Street for four nights on the trot an' sell out every night. We could put on more shows an' the touts would still be sellin' tickets outside for €200. Ya could count on one hand the amount of Irish bands that could do that. Then we can go an' play a place like The Point Depot an' sell that out as well. We did that for a coupla years in a row.

But how do you measure success anyway? I do a job that I absolutely love doin' an' I live quite comfortably from what I do – that to me is a measure of success. The fact that we're not more commercially successful seems to bother other people more than it bothers me.

If the next album is not a big money-maker then I'll just have to live with that. As long as I can be proud of it then that's what matters to me. I don't equate artistic greatness with commercial success at all.

We don't have the big record companies behind us but that's freed us up to do what we want to do an' in our own way. We're not restricted to any structures or procedures. We can take off an' do gigs when an' where we want. Without all the pressure to make money that a big recordin' artist is under we can go out an' do gigs for free if we want.

We do gigs to help out charity. It's somethin' that we try to do – to kinda give somethin' back, I suppose. We get requests to do charity gigs all the time. At least four people ring us every week but we obviously can't do them all. So we pick out a few at the beginnin' of the year an' that's what we do for that year. An' I love encouragin' new artists. We reaped the benefits of the music business so it's only fair that we give somethin' back. I'd be the same as yer man Chris De Burgh if I didn't. How could I criticise anybody like that if I'm gonna be behavin' the same way. Like, see George Murphy, the young fella outta *You're A Star*, the TV show? We invited him to play with us in Vicar Street on Paddy's Night 2004 'cause he got fucked outta the show. I thought he was great. He's a good young fella, very talented an' so we gave him a support slot to try an' cheer him up. I think it's the best thing that ever happened to him anyway. I mean fuckin' hell it's the Eurovision.

Some of the gigs we do are brilliant; they're like an adventure. In February 2004, the Irish army brought us over to play for the troops based in Kosovo. The soldiers had a poll to see which band they'd like to come over an' play for them an' we won. This guy, a Corporal Buggy is his name, from Coolock, approached us an' asked would we do it. We immediately said yeah. We'd never done anythin' like that before. I felt like Marilyn Monroe goin' over there!

We played three gigs over the week to hundreds of soldiers. An' they weren't all Irish. A loada them were from Finland an' that. I don't think they knew who we were but it looked like they were havin' a good time.

The only thing about the place was the poverty, ya know? We were bein' driven' round in these massive Irish Army' personnel carriers, through this beautiful countryside. Ya really wouldn't know there'd been a war only a few years before. We were brought to this shootin' range that the army used for target practise an' while we were there we could see all these kids hangin' round. We were askin' one of the captains what the story was with the kids an' he said they were waitin' for us to finish so they could run round an' collect all the empty shells to sell. This was in the middle of fuckin' freezin' weather, minus centigrade or somethin', an' they were sittin' there, no coats or anythin'. That was tough to see.

* * *

Since I was a kid I've always felt the indignation at what I feel are the injustices in life. Ya have to understand there is a lot of shit an' a lot of discrimination that workin'-class people in Ireland have to put up with. I remember I was drivin' along listenin' to the radio one time an' the DJ was goin', 'Everybody get their Ronnies an' their Ben Sherman's out, Aslan are playin' in Vicar Street tonight,' ya know? Like that can be kinda funny an' all but at the same time, it's still a prejudice.

We've fought through all that, all those obstacles, an' we've kinda come good. We've written songs that speak for workin'-class people. I feel that when we're on stage we're actually representin' them. I think there's a lot of kids out there who'll continue to fight against the injustices 'cause they seen that we've succeeded an' that makes it worthwhile for them to give it a shot. What I'm sayin' to ya here is bigger than music, d'ya know what I mean? I'm not talkin' 'bout that we inspire some other guitar player or some other singer. I'm sayin' we might inspire some potential scientist or chemist, or a fuckin' horse rider from the same kinda background as ourselves – it's beyond music. I feel that I've been bestowed an honour to be offered an opportunity to take part in that.

There are a lot of other people out there who've an attitude towards the band 'cause of that prejudice an' they've written us off without havin' ever seen us. They would've dismissed Aslan 'cause they've read about us in a magazine that's been influenced by an article written by some guy in *The Irish Times* or somethin'. The guy who wrote in *The Irish Times* had read somethin' in *Hot Press* an' *Hot Press* decide what band is cool, ya know? It's all self-perpetuating – one feeds off the other. So they read this an' they won't bother to listen to Aslan. Yet had they sat down honestly an' listened to us with the same objectivity that they listened to David Bowie or U2 or whoever, then they probably would've liked our music.

That kinda epitomises to me how we view bands an' music, right? There used to be this band out years ago called Then Jericho. The singer used to wear a cricket jumper round his neck on stage. I immediately dismissed them because to me he looked like a rugger-playin', dickhead, wanker, d'ya know what I mean? I didn't even care how good they might have been 'cause of that one thing. When ya go to see a band that you haven't seen before, I think if you're honest, ya don't go hopin' you'll enjoy them – ya go hopin' you can dismiss them so that ya don't have to bother with them anymore. Think about it. It's very important. If ya like that band then there's a responsibility invested in that decision. You're goin' to have to go out an' buy their records an' all the other things that likin' that band entails. If ya go to see a band an' they're crap, ya can just dismiss them an' never think about them again. Ya can get on with your own comfortable little world. I'm the same. Like, I found a reason to dismiss Then Jericho, over the jumper. I'm only human like everybody else – I'm not sayin' everyone else is wrong. I'm sayin' I'm just as wrong as everyone else. I've done the same thing an' ya know how I know? It's 'cause I'm also a music fan.

Some of the shit that ya hear about Aslan doesn't necessary mean ya think we're knackers from Finglas but it does give ya a reason to think, 'that's nothing to do with me life'. I think if you were an honest rock fan an' you came to see us ya might not like us but I don't think that you could dismiss us as a crap band.

Once somebody comes to one of our gigs I think in the majority of cases we have them. There are very few people who come to an Aslan gig an' walk away an' never come to another one or, at least, if they don't come to another gig they might think, 'well, I don't like their music but they're good at what they do'. I don't doubt that 'cause I know we're shit hot at what we do.

People enjoy our gigs 'cause they know we're sincere. I put me life an' soul into each an' every performance. Obviously if I'm a bit down I'll try maybe to portray meself in better fuckin' form than I am but I try an' not bullshit people – that's very dodgy territory. People aren't stupid; they can sense if you're bullshittin' them. I don't want to seem like I'm patronisin' people. I hate sayin' things like, 'Youse are a great audience an' it's fuckin' great to be here.' I mean it sounds like that scene from *Spinal Tap* when the singer goes up to the mike an' says, 'Thank you, it's great to be here in . . .' an' he looks down at a bit of paper, '. . . Hamburg'. I don't think we come across as anythin' less than totally fuckin' honest. That's how Aslan has been sustained for such a long time.

I think I can communicate with people regardless of where they come from. I can touch people across the board. As good as some of the new singers are out there today, can you imagine them playin' at the Ballymun Towers tonight an' sittin' there in front of a load of workin'-class people an' dishin' it out? Aslan can go into any pub in the country, whether it's full of the artistic élite or whether it's a place for the socially underprivileged an' come out with the same results.

To me, Aslan's musical appeal is in the fact that it's upliftin' – it's a celebration of music, d'ya know what I mean? I don't need to go to a gig an' pay money to be brought down. If I want to be brought down I only have to look at some of the shit that's happened in me life an' I'll be brought right down. Music should be an escape from life. Life has the ability to deliver all the depression an' negative bullshit that ya can take. Ya don't need to pay for somebody to give that to you.

The reason that we've been able to continue doin' what we're doin' is 'cause we do have substance. Now, whether people think that substance is common or shit or whatever, I don't give a fuck – it's substance.

If ya haven't got any integrity or quality or substance in what you're doin' you'll be found out anyway – absolutely you'll be found out. They all are eventually. Ya can fool some of the people some of the time but ya can't fool them all, all of the time – simple as that.

* * *

I would hate to become an embarrassment, ya know? That's me greatest fear. I'd hate to be out there floggin' a dead horse an' for people to be goin, 'Jesus, give it up man, for fuck's sake', d'ya know what I mean? That'd kill me. I hope that I could step in if Aslan started to slide an' stop it before it got too bad. I want us to quit with our self-respect intact an' with some modicum of success. I don't want to be seen as havin' stopped 'cause I'd no option but to stop. I want to finish while we're still a little bit ahead. Every time we've a series of shows lined up in Vicar Street we book three an' then have to add another one 'cause the others are sold out. I know that there's still a passion out there for the band while that happens. When we put on four Vicar Street shows an' we have to cancel two of them, we'll know we're on the slide. When we're doin' two an' we have to cancel one of them? Then that'll be the end.

I still don't take it for granted that we sell out a whole series of shows. I think that's probably what keeps ya on your toes as an artist. Ya can't ever take it for granted 'cause the day you start takin' it for granted is the day that you're fucked.

I'd look round when we play places like The Point Depot an' they're all there to see Aslan – from the age of 8 right up to 50 – an' they're all reactin' with the same fervour. I feel honoured that that exists. I can't get me head round how all these kids are comin' to see us. I mean they've to overcome all that pap that they see on TV. How many other bands that have been around for as long as us have to put on matinée shows in Vicar Street so the under-18 fans can go an' see them? That to me is fuckin' enormous, ya know? It's brilliant. That's what Aslan's music is all about. For me that's what makes it all worthwhile. It makes all the other bullshit tolerable. It's worth it for those few moments onstage 'cause then it doesn't matter that ya can't be the coolest band on Earth; it doesn't matter that you don't have a record in the British charts; it doesn't matter that you're not on the cover of *NME*. You're playin' a gig to yer people in the country that ya grew up in. We play gigs all over the country an' the people who come to them aren't doin' it 'cause we're from Dublin or 'cause I did heroin or 'cause I wear cool clothes. No, they're there 'cause we're a good band – end of fuckin' story.

It's only now, when I put it all into words, that I realise how I feel 'bout Aslan an' the music an' what an eventful life I've had. All these things happened over the course of a whole lifetime so it never seemed to me that it was that unusual at the time. I knew that it wasn't your average 40-year-old life but it wasn't 'til I sat down to actually put it all together that I thought, 'well fuck me, that's been a bit of a fuckin' journey'.